THE J.D. DIPALMA COLLECTION

JD DIPALMA

Red Penguin
BOOKS

The J.D. DiPalma Collection

Copyright © 2021 by JD DiPalma

All rights reserved

Published by Red Penguin Books

Bellerose Village, New York

Library of Congress Control Number: 2021923792

ISBN

Print 978-1-63777-185-3 / 978-1-63777-186-0

Digital 978-1-63777-187-7

To Don
Always and Forever, your little brother

Contents

How To Be Mediocre

Curveball

Shots With Mom And Dad

Part I

Part II

Intermission!

Part III

How To Be Mediocre

Meet Doug, The Loser

So I head down to the basement as I've done God knows how many times before. I duck under the low hanging part of the ceiling, the one disadvantage to being six-foot-two. I flick the amp on and wait for it to warm up. I walk over to the guitar rack, consisting of five guitars I overpaid for and treat like crap. I've got three electrics and two acoustics. An Epiphone Les Paul, a Mexican Fender Strat, an Ibanez hollow body, a Martin DRS1, and a Guild acoustic from '75 that was a gift from an ex-fiancee's mom; the deal was I keep the guitar, she keeps the big T.V. I know the Epiphone needs to be re-strung so I break out a pack of Ernie Ball 12-gauge electric strings. I love a full sound over a thin one. Typical punk rock. I imagine this is how hunters feel cleaning their guns as they need to every so often, just getting in the mindset of what to expect when they get out there. I start taking the old strings off and putting the new ones on. I tighten the top three strings, turning the pegs away from me, and tighten the bottom three towards me. The tuner's battery is low so I go over to the piano to tune. The only bummer is I have to run upstairs and turn the lights on. The only way to turn the piano on is to flip the switch; God only knows how many other people have those kinds of outlets in their place. I hit E2, A2, D3, G3, B4 and E4 all to the sounds of the dehumidifier in the background. I plug in and de-tune the top E string to drop D.

My pad and paper are right where I left it the day before, and the ideas start flowing. Time to write a hit song that most likely will go nowhere, and I will be the only one who hears it. I'm good—but not quite up to par with what's marketable. I'm not where I need to be with my social media presence so they're going another way—a feeling I know every average-joe musician can relate to. I just want one good show, one good EP, and one good swoop of recognition for something I've worked hard for and won't see the recognition.

This process has gone on every other day from the time I was 11 until now at 26 years old. I know I have to grow up—and I have, to a certain extent. The fiancee' and I didn't work for many reasons. I was always trying to be creative and she just couldn't see why I try so hard for something that'll never love me back. She gave me all the love I could want, but it wasn't the love I wanted. I wanted attention and I see that now. I don't regret ending things with her, God knows she spent all her time and effort on material things, too. Hers were shoes, booze, and dudes with washboard stomachs; apparently, dad bods are only cool if you're a dad.

I have a full-time job at a school for disabled children as a teaching assistant, and I'm almost done with my degree in early childhood education. So I'm well aware that being a rockstar is well in the past, but fuck, it would be so cool. The girls, the house, the money—who knows what I could have been if I had gotten lucky and played that show that one time, or met with that agent who was a little skeevy. All the things you hear about having to sacrifice everything about yourself and your morals for the entertainment business seem to be all too true. There doesn't seem like a whole lot of room for real art unless you're a trendsetter, and I know damn skippy I'm not one.

I love every type of music you can throw at me. Punk, Rock, Alternative, Jazz, Hip-Hop, Country, R&B, Soul, Blues, on and on it goes. There's no genre I dislike, but certain artists I can do without; no shit-talking here. Every song is someone's art and a pure expression of what they may be going through or what they need to say, even if it is about drugs, ass or their pickup truck. I'm no different. I've written about girls, anti-government protest, medical conditions, all while silently ripping off the Beatles like everyone else.

I finish the "session," if you can call it that, and walk upstairs to be greeted by a wet-nosed creature by the name of Bruce, the family dog. He's a standard poodle who thinks the world of me and my crumbs. He follows me into the kitchen where Mom has made dinner. Living with your parents at this age really isn't that bad, but you can't help but feel a tiny bit of shame when all your buddies went away to school and you're still asking her the same question for fifteen years: "How'd that sound, Mom?"

"Sounded good, hon!" She's always been the support system I need. She lets me do what I love while making sure I don't fall behind and end up a loser. I've come pretty close a few times, but she knows when I go too far. Spending a month's paycheck on a new amplifier is all well and fun while living under Mom's roof, but she made it clear each time with her usual jingle: "Doug, you know you can't be spending money like that when you're on your own." There are days when I think Freud would tie me to a couch and make me ramble until I'm blue in the mouth.

She plops down the usual Wednesday dinner: spaghetti bolognese with garlic bread. We chat about our respective days while Bruce damn near plops his head in my lap. Say what you want about the little scrounger, but his sense of timing is better than most rhythm guitar players. As I finish rattling on about the latest Blink 182 record, because Matt Skiba is a legend (piss off if you think otherwise) Dad pops in from a long day at work. You want to talk about honor and conviction, talk to him for ten minutes and be prepared to be humbled. Dad was a drummer in a wedding band back in the day and has always been my coach and critic. The words "that riff sucks more than a taj massage parlor," will echo in my brain forever. Nobody gets anywhere without responding to criticism. Say what you will about music critics or people on any social media, but to me, the best work comes from the knee jerk reaction of "fuck you, I'll prove you wrong."

Dad always seems to know what I'm up to musically. He knows all my really great days through to my taj massage days. I feel like artists can sense when you lie through your teeth about how things are going. Being full of shit is a given when dealing with people like me. You have to play the game of "I'm the next best thing," and after a while, it's incredibly tiresome. I've quite had it, to be honest, hence why I'm shutting down operations on being the next KISS, Ramones, Toby Keith, Zach de LaRocha, or whatever phase I'm into that week. Putting on a happy face while internally screaming takes a toll on you.

"Sorry, hon, it was all hands today. Four hours overtime, though, so progress." The fact that the man can work four hours overtime doing engineering at a hospital and I can't even man up to going in on a holiday to help when grading falls behind says volumes about the differences in our work ethics. Maybe it's because he has a wife, house and a kid at home to feed, and had it all by the time he was my age, but it's things like this that snap me back to reality. There is no real substitution for hard work and it took me a while to learn that.

Mom gives him a big hug while he gives her a pinch on her backside, as I throw up in my mouth a little and die on the inside. I ignore it and ask him about his day. "Had to fix the AC in the ER and co-ordinate where the cement truck will go tomorrow to fix the sidewalk, so a pretty standard day. How about you, big man?" he asks, almost as though I'm still seven years old to him. Then again my mentality isn't that far off. "Just went to work, came home and played a little while," I reply, rotating my fork full of spaghetti into a spoon like I saw my grandfather do once.

"How'd work go? Anything on an open position?"

"Dad I still got a semester left to go. I sort of have to be certified to be a teacher to get a job as one."

"You have to market yourself now while you're a possibility. What's the point in putting in all that effort if you're not going to make them recognize it when the time comes?" I truly hate it when he's right, which is often.

I finish up dinner, do some studying and then lie down in bed. I start jotting down some lyric ideas on the notes app on my phone when Dad pops in.

"Hey, you awake, bud?"

"Yeah, what's up?"

He turns my light on and sits on the edge of my bed. All that's missing is a glass of chocolate milk and footy-pajamas and we've got my "birds and bees" talk all over again. Spoiler alert, both experiences have an equal amount of tears.

"So I was thinking about when you get a job and everything. I know this is going to sound harsh but I'd like you to move out when you save enough for rent on an apartment and make it on your own."

I couldn't help but drop my jaw. "You're kicking me out?" He looks at me as though I wasn't listening at all.

"You heard what I said. When you get a job and start making real money."

"Dad what about all my equipment? I can't take all that to an apartment."

He takes a deep breath and states the words I was hoping would never come. "Well you can keep a lot of it here still but maybe you can sell some of it and—" I don't even hear the rest because it's not an option. I say without thinking about it, "What the fuck? No way—I use all of that stuff."

"Tell me one time in the past three years when you used that sound system at a live show Tell me when you used that recording software, or even when the last live show you played even was."

I know the answer of course; five years ago at a block party that went down like a Led Zeppelin. Spoiler alert, that's how they (Led Zepplin) got their name. Inspired by Keith Moon, no less.

"Why are you doing this to me?" He says as calmly as he can while clenching a frustrated fist.

"It's time to grow up. You have tried this for long enough. Obviously, music is as important to you as it is to me. I'm not saying get rid of the guitars or pianos, but the stuff you don't use can go on to someone else who could get more use out of them since you're not. I wouldn't be doing my job as a father if I let you continue this same delusion of fame that I had. You're a dreamer, but someone has to keep you tethered."

The lump in my throat grows until my larynx peels. I am so upset.

"Think about it. Please. I'm sorry to do this but it's time."

I know it's time, but it's not even on my terms. It's not even terms I agree with. I know in my heart of hearts that he is right, but as I said; sometimes you get that drive of "Fuck you, I'll show you I can do it." And my motivation changes from "Alright, it's time" to "Here we go again."

2

A Day in the Life

So I wake up the next day feeling fresh as an open bag of manure. I'm pretty sure being hit with a shovel is far more pleasing than your support system giving up on you. But this is how it is. Even if I had made it, sometimes a record label will not have faith in the work you do. Sometimes you have to crack your fingers, look yourself in the mirror and say, "It's go time." I'm pretty sure if all those action heroes can do it, I can too. When I get home, I'm going to figure out a kick-ass song and prove to everyone I'm not a loser. But until then, I've got work and then attend the school my parents have paid for like a blessing: who am I kidding here? It's not going to happen.

That, quite literally, is how most of my mornings are. A hot cup of optimism to be spiked with a shot of steaming reality. Look at it sitting there like vegetable oil on top of water high-lighting differences in density. Speaking of which, that's what my preceptor is showing my class today. I take a shower and sift through the checklist in my head on what I have for today. I don't know why I think about it in the shower since it feels like two different types of drowning. And of course, Bruce is there licking my leg to try and get some water. I get out and fill the bowl for the silly creature. Man, some days I wish I had it as easy as he does. All he has to remember is where to poop and which couch not to jump on after Mom cleans it. All greeted with a nice belly rub and treat. Lucky little twerp.

I get dressed in my usual sweater vest and khakis. The kids usually get upset if I don't wear my vest. It's become my thing, although, I did try the whole Angus Young getup with an inflatable SG to walk around with for Halloween. It was all fun and games until I bent to get a pencil and ripped a hole exposing my butt crack. I almost was seen, but I walked horizontally to the bathroom with a pin to close the back end of the shorts. I could have been forced to stay at least 500 feet away from the school if I had been caught.

My car isn't too much a dumpster pile, but a 2004 Jeep Wrangler sure knows how to fall apart if it knows how to do anything at all. Girls sure do love a lift kit with the doors off in the summer, though. The commute to school is only about 20 minutes but I make it about 30, waiting in line for coffee. Molding America's youth is tiring work, especially with the shit pay that TA's get. I can't wait for that pay bump when I graduate.

Cut to my dumb ass spilling coffee all over me while putting a bit of sugar in. So now I look like I used to look in third grade with a water fountain, or if you want to get to the pathetic part, last summer at the Honolulu beach party for the staff. Although to be fair, in third grade it wasn't either my fault or real.

I run into the bathroom to try and dry it off for a split second but it never seems to really help. Guess I'll be walking around all day with my jacket in the front and tied around my waist like a kid on 90s Nickelodeon, huh?

It's scenarios like this that make me come back to Earth and send my delusion of fame and fortune down with it. I can't even keep coffee together so how am I supposed to play the Garden with a stain on my pants? I ought to stamp "Loser" on a couple of different angles of my head so that I'm covered 360 degrees. But then I get in the car and a killer song comes on the radio and I fly full speed to work with all green lights and get a good parking spot so I feel all ten kinds of awesome. If you think the sudden ups and downs are a little concerning, I've noticed them as well. The truth is, the feeling of trying to make it in this world comes and goes this often. To be able to stay positive, and know that I have made a positive impact with music is all I want. Any observer of my situation can point out that I already make a contribution and impact by helping kids, and they're right. I do. But the impact with music is something I just want a little notoriety for. If not the world, just a little respect on my scene. I live on Long Island in New York. It has God knows how many bars, but the venues you want to play are well known: The Last Exit Club, Point Ollie's Bar and Grill, and even some of the coffee houses like Milk and Sugar. Those are the spots most bands play. The crowds are either really vocal or talk shit behind your back. So if you suck, you'll know it, but in the worst ways. The kicker here is, I've been told I'm really good and should keep going. But the agonizing disappointment is just becoming too much to handle. I love writing music and I don't know if writing is something I can stop doing. Give me a little time and I can figure out where you want the song to go and how to make it appealing. But lately every time I get up on stage I realize, "Fuck, I'm going to be here a while." Doing things for me is really not how making it works. To really "make it," you have to love performing and singing things to which you had little-to-no contribution in their creation—unless you really are the best of the best with writing. I know I have talent, but I'm not good enough. It's like I want to perform, but have no interest in what a ghostwriter wants. It sure would be great if I could put as much knowledge and effort as I do with music and art into work, though.

There is nothing quite like that morning wake up and hearing your first class roar with morning hormones while you open the door. God, I hate middle schoolers, but the kid I sit with is pretty awesome. Bobby has autism but is far smarter than me or anyone my age. He just has a hard time with his behavior and staying focused. So I sit next to him and practically point my finger on his paper and say "focus."

After about six-and-a-half hours of paper tapping, I run home and shower before going out to school, although I can't help but notice something peculiar about my car. You see, I never drive a car with a tire that's flat. It's so bizarre. It's like I grabbed the wrong tire for my car today—just threw it on by accident while leaving the house.

Sarcasm has become the best coping mechanism for frustration. Beats throwing a fit and jumping up and down like a pissed-off student when we commandeer a vape pen. I have no fathomable understanding of why kids use these things. They don't have enough problems in life to know about smoking in order to de-stress. I used to be a pack-a-day smoker until it killed my singing voice—like I'll need it in the future, anyway.

I zip through traffic and hop in the shower to be greeted by a particular poodle. I lay low for a little while, then grab some food. I hate cooking for myself. It makes me feel self-sufficient. No, I'm not that totally useless, just lazy. I grab some food from the nearest fast food joint while dripping their special sauce down onto my beard and driving with one hand. Nobody can drive and eat quite like me. I've got it down to a science. I plop the fries and drink in the cup holder while . . . wait, why am I telling you? Piss off, it's my secret.

I whip into the parking lot then jolt into the building all the while crying on the inside at the stomach cramp I have from eating fried food too fast and then running. I'm quite the slob and dope, I'm well aware.

So now you've seen what my normal day consists of. Pretty bland, isn't it? Well, it was all pretty bland until this happens.

I turned a corner and out of nowhere I felt something nail me in the back of my head and I crash to the ground. "Oh my God, I'm so sorry!" a total babe yells as she jumps down the steps two at a time. "No worries. I'm okay," I say while pushing my sweatshirt to my head to stop the bleeding. She holds the sweatshirt for me while I rest on the wall and says "Did it hurt?"

Do any of you ever have an inner monologue? Of course not; you're normal people. My inner monologue is using the Carlin 7 dirty words in various sentences that could scare away anyone, but I have to play it cool, you know?

"A little bit, but it shouldn't be too bad. Are you okay?"

"Yeah, I was just . . . you're going to laugh at me," she says thinking twice about it.

"Try me."

"Well the new Slipknot just came out and I've been air drumming the blast beats all day. So it just slipped out of my hand and . . . "

Ladies and gentlemen if you think I stopped listening because of a severe head injury, you're only partly right. The fact that this woman listens to Slipknot, all the while knowing what a blast beat is, ordinarily makes my heart pump enough blood to keep all systems going. However, in this case, it's rushing to my forehead to clot the wound. I didn't even give a shit I was now late to a class that I'm only allowed two absences for. For a girl like this, whom destiny reaches out and chucks literature at you for, you stop and pay attention.

I look at her in sweet sincerity and utter, "To be fair, Weinberg does an outstanding job and nailed the last album." She looked at me as though I just uttered the secret phrase to her heart. This felt right. Keep in mind, I was engaged to be married, and I wasn't this optimistic in the entirety of our relationship. It's almost like that book to the head just dropped a shitty four-year relationship out and dropped in the most euphoric 70 seconds of my life.

"You like other types of music?" she inquires.

"Oh yeah," I reply in an understatement. "Primary thing I spend my income on. It's what I wake up in the morning for." She bites her lip in a way that makes her seem a bit turned on. Hell, I'm down. She then said, "I was supposed to go to this concert on Friday but my friend didn't buy me a ticket so I can't go now." Anyone else spy an opening to flirt? Oh, I do. I say with as much cool as I can muster, "So that means you're free on Friday for dinner then?" I've never seen anyone blush this hard. Nailed it.

3

The Rolodex of Girls

She finishes blushing, I get her number, and then run off to class. Turns out her name is Angela. And I can't remember anything about the class I was taking because all I can think about is how Angela made me feel like I had been seen for the first time in my life. Obviously, I've been noticed and observed my whole life, but she really made me feel seen. In the brief time we saw each other, we had an unspoken connection and both agreed that we're into each other.

I bail out of class, get to my car, pull out of the parking lot and drive home. I start to have the usual bout of anxiety I usually have at night time. The kind you usually have laying in bed thinking the world is about to crash down all because you did something stupid years ago. There's tea time in London, smoke breaks for health care workers, and anxiety time for me. Can't help it, it's in my family history and it'll only get passed on to the next in line.

I can't help but think, "What if this girl sees the real me? The real loser that lies just below the surface of the usual mediocrity I have?" I honestly think this is why I perform and write music. I can't feel my own happiness so I get on stage and act the fool to make people like me. Isn't that pathetic? I know I'm not alone, other performers feel similar, but there are times where I can't help but feel I'm alone; just this overwhelming feeling of the whole world shrinking down to the size of my silhouette and applying enough pressure to make me crack and spill. This girl and I exchanged maybe five sentences before I ran off to class, but what if in those five sentences she could see I'm full of shit? I'm a performer, therefore a liar. A lot of the things I say or do are just carbon copies and ideas I have seen before; I re-structured them and made them my own. Do you know how many times E—B—C#m—A chords have been used over with new words? Ask any musician, they'll tell you.

This cackle of nonsense is what goes on in my head at any given time. Something positive or negative can happen, I'll still be rambling. But in all seriousness, my collective dating history is not New Year's highlight reel of the progress I've made and great events that have taken place. It looks more like an in memoriam or old DVDs of hockey's best fights. And that doesn't just apply to women, but the riffs I've written, the script ideas I've jotted down, or the aspirational dreams that get anchored down by life and time. So let's see the "who's who" of Doug's greatest hits, including cameos from one night stands and fuck buddies, you never know who'll pop in—or out.

So let's start with the obvious, the ex-fiancee'. Catherine and I met online and if not for that we never would have met. She was working finishing up college and taking her final teaching exams, while here I was . . . not. For the lack of better wording, I was more or less a fish on an unlit barbecue; I was about to be burnt. I had all this stuff going with music deals I was so underprepared for. When we started going out I was about to sign a contract with a foreign record company. Her dad was a lawyer who said: "Bullshit, let me read it." Thank Christ he did because I was about to sign a 360 deal—a deal that takes money from every aspect of revenue including live shows and merchandise, which is ordinarily where musicians make most of their money. I bowed out and was swimming in familiar waters again. She really took care of my dumb ass while I couldn't have cared less about myself or what happened to me. I did tell her though I would be a stay-at-home husband if it came down to the idea of having children and forming a future. But the more she'd tell me about her school assignments, the more I became fascinated by it. I told her about writing music and said that if she ever needed help with an assignment, I'd help. Kind of like telling a lawyer that you've read Cat in the Hat and going "Yeah, I can read all good like!"

But the more I read up on her books and papers, the more I knew I should go into this myself. I got it so much easier than I got into music. It felt like it was written for me. I'm a firm believer that if something is coming naturally to you, you should dive deep with it. It could be the answer or droid you're looking for.

But I still had this pinging in the back of my mind about music. I wasn't ready to give it up yet. I would go to school part-time and be writing constantly. I believed in myself even if nobody else did. But I was still getting my school work done and passing everything with top marks, so nobody could say shit to me. The more classroom time I did the more I realized that this was my niche, but I realized this wasn't the atmosphere I wanted to come home to. I wanted to come home and be with a wife and enjoy "playtime." Yes hanky-panky, but I wanted to travel and act like a kid when I didn't have this looming sense of responsibility—to be selfish and not have to care about anyone else when I finished work. And when you have kids, you can't be so selfish. So I dropped that bomb on her and the next day there was an engagement ring on my bedside table. I thought that I'd have been crying like a baby, but I sat there, exhaled and went back to sleep.

I know it sounded shallow and hollow to not show more emotions, but what can you do when you know this is the right decision for two of you? You just have to accept that though you may love each other, it doesn't mean that you're right for each other. Heavy shit, right? Not all pussy and music jokes up in here.

Before Catherine and the two other lovely ladies you'll meet—that's right, two more—let's talk about Winnie. Winnie is a lovely young lady who I met while cheating on my high school girlfriend. What a catch I am, huh?

Winnie and I met in person, which is odd enough for this day and age. During my first attempt at college, at the time I went for nursing but dropped it because of catheters—well, yuck. That's the joke version. I left because I was atrocious at the topic and I didn't feel like wasting time on something I knew I couldn't do. I digress: I was on academic probation with Winnie and we hit it off with a reference I made from a movie she saw. We exchanged numbers since the counselor advised us to—therefore he's to blame. But when the flirting started I quickly advised her I had a girlfriend. However, that didn't seem to stop her (or me) from exchanging dirty texts. And although this behavior was beyond revolting, I have to say I was having quite fun with a girlfriend and a dirty secret. The girlfriend and I ended without speaking of Winnie but I'm sure she must have known. She was not a dumb girl and you can only say "I'm sleeping over at my classmate's house" so many times while explaining that Winnie is a guy's name, too.

Not even a week after that relationship ended, I set up a proper date with Winnie. And I have to say after the facade dropped and we were two single people, it was an absolute mismatch. There was a true sense that we should just be friends—naked friends at best. However, she couldn't see it. She really loved me and wanted to be my girlfriend. I realized I needed time to grow, to mature, and become a better person, but she was not having it. It got rather crazy the way she would retaliate against me. What started with pictures of her with other guys to make me jealous turned into trips to my job to see me.

You have to be careful with what you set onto the world through your emotions or your genitals. I wish I hadn't hurt her. I really do. I feel that in a way I could've loved her more than just as a friend, but the people we became when we were around each other was just not who we really were. I set out to get a jump on my attempt at a music career and she went into a five-year relationship and found the love of her life. A messy beginning turned out to be a great ending, for one of us, anyway.

It's like life takes one turn and—fucking hell! Did you see that? That squirrel popped out of nowhere, man. I swear to God they are the ballsiest animals to run across the street. It's like that scene in "Watership Down" when that bunny wasn't expecting anyone to pop out on the road and then . . . sorry! I have become distracted by the girls. Last time, I promise. Although, this is the one with the two girls. I have to tell this one in the car before I go in.

So I started working really hard when it came to honing my craft as a songwriter and performer. For five solid years, I was really killing it. Growing and maturing along the way. I stayed single for five years to make sure that when I met someone I was ready. And then there was this one show when I was knocking the crowd dead. I actually sold the place out. The first and last time it ever happened for me. No album or EP, either. All of it was word of mouth and the occasional fan posting my set on a social media platform. I was hanging backstage and someone actually asked me to sign a flyer. My first autograph! I couldn't believe it. She was a real stunner too, so I was sure someone had sent her back as a joke, but it was real. She even asked me to dinner in this nervous way, as though I was almost unobtainable. She said "Ummm, if it's not too much to ask, can I, like, I don't know, ask you to dinner sometime or like . . . no, it's so stupid. I'm sorry." I was stunned saying, "Can you? Please, this never happens to me."

Let me tell you all something. Artists are people, too. They have families they have hopes and dreams, but they aren't above anyone. We're all the same in the way of hierarchy. No matter what anyone says, we're all the same degree of scum, and I say that in the nicest and most sarcastic tone.

Anyway, we exchanged numbers and Grace took me out. It was nice, very romantic and very quaint. But even sitting down getting to know her I could tell I was not ready for commitment. We walked to the car and she asked me out again; I told her, "This is all very sweet and kind of you, but I have to tell you I'm not looking for anything serious. The best I can do right now is be casual with no expectations, but I doubt you're interested in that."

To my surprise, she said, "Actually, I was thinking the same thing." So we would hang out whenever we had the time for each other. She had her own place so it was always there where we'd have nights in, nights out, or nights in the bedroom. Those were becoming far more common than anything else, however. Those nights in the bedroom became lunches in bed, then those lunches became "I have 30 minutes before my next set. Want to get a quick one in?" We both agreed that even having a casual commitment to each other was a little more than we could handle so we agreed to be friends with benefits. And we were great friends with each other in the meantime. I'd drive her to doctors' appointments, she'd be there for me at shows when I was nervous, and we couldn't believe how great it was going. Then, a monkey wrench was thrown in.

A similar scenario happened with a girl named Alyssa. The difference was, she wanted something more serious with meaning. Though I was skeptical at first, we went out. And we fitted together like a puzzle. She was my other half for that time. She knew about Grace but was okay with it until we became monogamous. While on a date I mentioned to her, "You guys would probably get along well."

She chuckled and said, "We should probably get together without you and make you jealous."

I said in an entirely joking manner, "Threesomes are on the table then?"

And she didn't laugh but said in all seriousness, "I've always wanted to try it, so why not?" Without a second to lose, I texted Grace the pitch for one and somehow she agreed.

The number of times I said to myself "Holy shit, this is happening," can't be measured. I was bouncing off the walls for the date we had arranged. But alas, reality came crashing in. I don't know how open relationships or swingers do it because, in my experience, three-ways never end well. Someone just gets hurt.

The closer and closer the day came we'd all be texting each other in a group chat to define our limits and boundaries. The more they started chatting, the more they started to get to know and like each other as people. However, Alyssa couldn't help but notice I wasn't coming to my end of the bargain of committing to her. I wasn't changing my ways in the ways I had promised. And the inevitable question came up, "What does she give you that I don't?" And it's not that Grace did anything different or better, it's just I was set in my ways of being a free man and though I thought I could drop my fucking around, my actions were showing that I had no intentions of slowing down and being monogamous. So after she came into my car and saw Grace's sweatshirt in the back seat, it came crashing down on her that a future with me was not a possibility. In the next few days, Grace found a new man to whom she wanted to be faithful. I went from having the best possible arrangement there was, to having nothing.

The number of times I went to my basement to write while I was depressed couldn't be counted. And this was not something I'd want to vent to Mom about, so I kept it to myself. Bottle after bottle was being purchased, shows weren't being played when I was booked for them, they stopped booking me altogether, and I was left with nothing to show for my work. The last five years of building my act were now awash.

As I park my car and walk inside and down to the basement again I look at all the holes in the wall I've punched, dents in the ceiling I have made from lifting my guitar too high, markings on the wall from carrying amplifiers and cases in at 03:00 AM and I have come to a sobering thought. The choices I made are the ones I have to live with.

I made the choices to dedicate time and effort to these girls and gave less than what they deserved. I should have been all in for them because they were all in for me. Can I say they were regrets? Maybe, but it would be unfair to the life I live now. If I want things to work with this girl I met, I have to put my own selfish crap aside and realize it's not all about me anymore. Relationships are partnerships. If you can't commit, don't start one.

And as I sit here and play my acoustic, I have to say that— hold on . . . this sounds really good. What if I try it like . . . yeah! Holy shit! I love the way this sounds.

The above passage is what most musicians think when they find a riff they love or a melody that makes them stop a lesson they learned or a composed thought, and then focus on finishing what they deem a "masterpiece." Spoiler alert: most aren't, but this one, you can say, has potential.

4

First Date Doug

H oly shit, I think I've done it. I really think I've done it. I've written a hundred good riffs before and said to myself, "This is the single when it comes out," all the while never releasing anything I've recorded. But honestly, I have goosebumps. "Dad! Come down here quick!" My parents have had infinite fucking patience with me, and this is probably where they use it the most. I can hear to this day the sound of Dad exhaling, getting up slowly, muttering "Fucking kid never gives me a break." Then slowly comes down the stairs.

"What now?"

"Dad, I swear to God I got something good." I adjust my tuning and get my tempo back, and I start going to town. Even he looks at me with these wide eyes and is floored by it. He doesn't say anything though. He just gets behind the kit and starts playing. I know he likes it when he jumps behind the kit. He does this thing that sounds okay, but not great. "No, Dad, stick to the snare and go to the hi-hat on the pre-chorus."

"Want one or two pedals on the kick?"

"Just stick to the one. Keep it simple." We hammer it out and take our time. It's kind of weird how when two musicians know they have something good, they laugh. Dad was laughing like he had just watched "Life of Brian."

Oddly enough a lot of the big "hits" in music were written in only a couple minutes. Sometimes if an artist is taking a long time with something, it just isn't right. But if it flows out naturally, you know you have something great. Sammy Hagar wrote how "Rock Candy" was a last-minute song because Montrose needed one more good song. It was damn near written in only a couple of takes. "The Lumberjack Song" was written in only twenty minutes because Jones and Palin needed a "way out" of the homicidal barber sketch. Even McCartney said "Yesterday" came to him in a dream. He just didn't believe he had written it for about two weeks. Sometimes a song just comes to you. Inspiration doesn't have a schedule.

"Doug I don't know how you came up with this but I really like it. The first song I've really loved of yours in a good many years." That hit me like a truck, man. When the guy you admire most loves something you do, no amount of money or fame can come close to the amount of pride and contentment you feel.

"So what do I do with it? I know I'm out of the game but, man, this one is good." He sits on his drum throne pondering. He told me the other day it's time to grow up, and here we are right back in the thick of that bug we both can't seem to shake. Creative people can't shake it no matter what. Years can go by and one song can get you back into "edit mode." If the song is good, they'll say "Shit, I should have thought of that." If they don't like it, they'll go sift through every second going, "Who the fuck thought of this?

Dad stands up and says, "Call Tim and just get it on tape." Tim is my producer/engineer who handles everything musical I do. We must have recorded a good twenty-plus songs, but we released none of them because I'm so scared of the rejection.

"Did anything happen today that got you grooving or thinking?" I have a big shit-eating grin on and tell him about Angela.

"You guys been texting?"

I know I have forgotten to do something. "Not yet. It only happened a couple of hours ago." "Text her tomorrow. Don't seem so desperate."

"Yeah, that sounds good."

I think we all know I don't make good decisions, so of course, I text her when he leaves and goes upstairs. "Dad, I'm actually pretty nervous about texting her."

"Why?"

Like he doesn't already know. "I'm so lousy at giving my all to people and I want this to be right, so if she agrees to go out with me, what do I do, how do I do it, what do I say?"

He makes a "timeout" motion and says, "One step at a time. I've never seen you so nervous, so when I tell you this, try to follow through with it, please?"

I put the guitar down so he knows he has my full attention.

"Take a look at yourself and figure out what you as a person like to do when you're alone. Or what you do when you're in a bad mood to make yourself feel happy. After you work that out, ask her to do that with you as your first date. Because you'll know you've found the one when you can take them along and still enjoy yourself because their company makes you enjoy it more. Because if they can do that, you'll never want to be alone again."

And there I was thinking to myself, "Fuck, I should have thought of that." Sorry, it's the writer in me. So Dad runs upstairs and I do as I said I was going to do. I send her a text that keeps things light. Not too much pressure, yet sweet. "Hey! Great to meet you today. Can't wait to see you soon!" Then I wait a good fifteen minutes for a response. Fifteen minutes seems like an eternity to a millennial. She sends back "Heyy! Great bumping into you, too! Sorry about your head again! (It's my personal belief that if someone you're into gives you more than one "y," they're into you, too. Obviously, it's not a fact, just my experience.)

Though I'd love to chat back and forth with her all night, I have sleeping to do and I want to talk with her more in-depth when we go out. I text her back, "No worries! It's not every day you get hit in the head by a beautiful girl. I usually have to wait for a relationship for that and it's usually a frying pan."

"Oh my God, you must have brain damage because I am not beautiful, but thank you. And I have a few pans so I'll practice my aim."

By the way, she is a stunning woman. She looks like one of those girls who was an emo kid in junior high that's into flower power now that she's an adult, but would also look at home at an emo night. I send back "Oh lucky me. Btw when are you free?"

"I'm free Friday night if you are"

"I am, and that sounds good to me. What would you like to do?" What she sends next kind of breaks my heart. Because this is like the fifteenth time I've heard this in my time of dating. "Umm, I've never actually been on a date so I don't quite know what to do. Up to you really."

Now I'm all for feminism and breaking the glass ceiling, but some things shouldn't totally go away, in my opinion. Good men shouldn't be a dying breed. Netflix and chilling is fine when you're in a relationship, but have some substance, you low-aspiring fucks. Have an imagination. So I send her this, "That really breaks my heart in a way. What do you like to do as your hobbies?"

"I just listen to music, watch TV, hang with my friends and go to school really."

I'm about to shoot this date right in the five-hole. "How about I take you into town, go to the record store, book store, then grab some dinner? Keep it low pressure and just have fun?"

She steals my heart by saying "make it a comic book store and I'm ready to rage." God, she's one of the good ones.

Now it turns out we only have that one day together on campus so we can't even meet up for stuff before or after class, because she's a nursing major, so she's a busy girl. And I was hit in the head with a sociology book. I'm just grateful it wasn't anatomy and physiology. I don't know about anyone else, but when I have plans at the end of the week I'm looking to speed up time just so I can get going. My God, I hate waiting for a good thing when I know it's coming around the corner. Today was my average day minus meeting Angela. But my week has been more or less the same. Work, lounge around, school, then go and play music. The only other thing I could do was obsess over this song. I have all the music written but no lyrics at all. I'm sure that'll come in time slowly but surely. But until then, you have to move on with your life.

Friday comes and I'm at the record store an hour early. I actually shop before I'm supposed to shop along with her. I get the really good stuff and hide it in my car. As I shut the door she pulls up; success.

She comes out of her car and I'm already convinced that a ring is all I need. We have texted intermittently all week and she is as beautiful on the inside as she is out. She gives me a hug and the best date of my life starts.

She stops hugging me and says, "Let's go. I've been looking forward to this all week." We walk inside. "So where do you want to start? I know you like Slipknot but—Angela? Where'd you…"

"I'm over here!" She yells from behind the stacks. She's flipping through the stacks like I wasn't even there. "I've been on this punk kick so I'm probably going to be here a while." Starting at "A" she pulls out a record or two (Alkaline Trio and Anti Flag) and puts them on the side. Moving on down the line she grabs Circa Survive, Descendents, and I Am the Avalanche. All awesome bands I listen to often. She hops over to metal and picks up Avenged Sevenfold. Rap and hip-hop get a look through and I hear "already have a lot of these." I think I'm tearing up. Then I hit her with the question of all questions that don't involve dropping to one knee. If you had to pick three records that can sum up who you are, which would you pick and why? I get a thousand-yard stare. A look that almost says, "That's not possible."

"Hold these and I'll go look."

I'm sitting on these chairs at a listening station watching these records like they're a new diamond necklace. I'm contemplating my own three records because I know she's going to ask me for my choices. I know not many people in this day and age buy full-length albums or take the time to listen to them, but some can change an outlook on life in just one listen. I've always heard of a song changing someone's life, and it happens more than you think. One lyric or the way a progression is played has sometimes turned my world upside down. So I urge everyone to take a listen to a full album that one of your favorite songs is on. She comes back with her three picks. And man oh man are they good picks.

She whips out the "untitled album" from Blink 182. "I don't know anyone our age who didn't listen to 'I Miss You' and cry a little inside," she says. "This whole album, bottom to top, is outstanding. It just goes to show a change in direction in life is not a bad thing. It could be the best thing. You can be the same person and mature without losing your friends or fans." She puts that aside and puts up "Good Apollo. I'm Burning Star IV, Volume I: From Fear Through the Eyes of Madness" by Coheed and Cambria. "There's always going to be songs about relationships, drugs and alcohol, even politics. But hell I never knew you could write a song about the graphic novel series you have. You never know where inspiration can come from or the story behind it. Have you read the books he wrote? Goddamn, that guy is talented. Honestly one of the most influential artists on my life." Then finally she pulls out the red herring of the three, but holy crap it's a good pull. She pulls out "The Low End Theory" from A Tribe Called Quest. "I grew up with jazz around the house so this will always hold a place in my heart. It couldn't be more on point than in the opening song 'Excursions.' You can find the abstract listening to hip-hop. My pops used to say it reminded him of be-bop. You can take one kind of music and make it your own by adding, subtracting or flipping it entirely around. What you do with your art is up to you." Does anyone know if a minister is available? She sends me out to get my own stuff and I come back quickly.

"I was thinking of mine while you got yours." I spread them out like they're playing cards. "Pick one, any one!" She closes her eyes and pulls out the first. It is a single by an artist named Marcaux called "The Over Under."

"This one I don't know."

"He's an up and coming rapper. The whole song is about how he deals with his mental illness. Did you ever hear a lyric that knocks you on your ass? Well, in one verse he says 'I don't like to express who I am outside of music, I've got depression that's seeping into my spinal fluid, plus I lost the only woman who would guide me through it, and I been praying that she ain't doing what I've been doing.' Though I don't have depression, I have anxiety that sometimes can make me make the dumbest choices and steer me off in a direction I would never drive in. I never considered suicide, but man this song hit hard with letting me know there's someone else out there." She looks at me with that look of "I've been there too." God this woman's awesome.

Next, we have Fleetwood Mac's album "Fleetwood Mac."

"Though God knows how many timeless songs are on this, it goes to show you can establish a following and support system in one iteration, then start all over again with new people and sound and come back even bigger and better. Not just in music, but life, too." She nods accordingly and says "Do you try and scare your first dates like this all the time?"

"No, just the ones I really like."

She giggles and pulls out the last one. "Then lastly, Linkin Park's 'Meteora.'"

"Their first album everyone puts on their list of 100 albums to listen to before you die, but I so prefer this because they evolved so much in a short amount of time. Just goes to show if you do something once, you can do it again. And I prefer a lot of the songs on this like 'Breaking the Habit,' 'Faint' and 'Don't Stay.' Don't even get me started on 'Numb.'"

We go buy our selections then split to go to the comic book store. I realize she's consistent because she goes in and buys a hard copy of the collected works from The Amory Wars, the graphic novel series to the music of Coheed and Cambria written by Claudio Sanchez.

Then, we split towards dinner. I treat her like a gentleman and I hear this:

"Stop being nice. It makes me uncomfortable."

I make a stink face. "Why would it make you uncomfortable?"

"It makes me feel like you're expecting something at the end of the night."

"Angela, you know I'm not—"

"I know, I know but it makes me feel that way."

"So I'm damned if I do, damned if I don't."

"Now you're getting why I'm a single pringle."

"What if I am a gentleman, but drown it in sarcasm?"

She has a face of contemplation. "That could work." "So if I pull your chair out, for now on I'll say shit like "I know it's hard for you to do simple things on your own, hon," then peck you on the forehead?"

She laughs into her entrée "I love that."

I look at her fingers and notice she seems around a size 8. You don't let the one getaway guys. We finish our meals; I pay but let her leave a tip because I figured she'd kill me if I don't let her. I walk her to her car, give her a hug. For some reason, we don't let go. So I ask her, "Is someone expecting something at the end of the night?"

"Shut up. This is different."

I back up and say "I don't usually do that on a first date."

"Well, this is my first first date so let me make a mistake if I want to."

We have this kiss that makes planets melt. I don't know where she's been and I don't really care. I'm done with this dating and music life. It's all over and it'll never see my face again. Hey, that sounds like a hell of a lyric.

5

Recording a Song You'll Probably Never Hear

I wake up the next morning elated. I have just had the best first date of my life. Is this how Ross and Rachel felt kissing in the rain? It must be. Speaking of which I need a shower. In all honesty, I keep thinking about her in everything I do. I even think about her as Bruce knocks his head on the door to drink some of the shower water.

Usually, at this point I'm highly overthinking what I do and the things I say. Having this much anxiety over such simple tasks is really irritating. Sometimes it makes me dizzy and frustrated. When it gets that bad my old mental health counselor used to say, "Just find a place to stand or sit, close your eyes and realize that it'll pass. A viable solution will come, you just can't see it right now." Wait a second, that's not a bad lyric.

Just so you all know, I am one of those freaks who can't help but write something down when it comes to him. I open my notes section of my iPhone and jot down for quite possibly the hundredth time a new set of lyrics. "One step forward, ten steps back, overthinking the things I lack," yeah that's not bad.

It's All Over-

HAVE I Been Here for way too long
pondering how I missed it all
turning the lights off they flicker they fade,
pondering all the mistakes that I've made,
 and did I push myself too far?

IS IT OVER?
Am I done Here?
Have I lived through, this hole that I've dug, waiting for you

I'M DONE HERE It's all over
You'll Never see my face
You'll never see who I am
Or what I have become

ONE STEP FORWARD, and ten steps back
overthinking the things I lack
I constantly feel like I'm under attack
The whole world is spinning it all fades to black
And now I'm left alone, without you here to pull me out

.   .   .

IS IT OVER?

Am I done Here?

Have I lived through, this hole that I've dug, waiting for you

I'M DONE HERE It's all over

You'll Never see my face

You'll never see who I am

Or what I have become

Why don't you just come over, you've always seen through me, I'm not who you want me to be and you don't believe in me

I'M DONE HERE It's all over

You'll Never see my face

You'll never see who I am

Or what I have become

Why don't you just come over, you've always seen through me, I'm not who you want me to be and you don't believe in me

NOTHING HELPS inspiration more than a standard poodle moaning at you to take him for a walk or pay attention to him. "G'day, Bruce. We'll walk in a bit."

"I constantly feel like I'm under attack; while the whole world is spinning, it all fades to black." Being real with lyrics has almost become a form of journal writing. It gets the bad out to make room for more good. "And now I'm left alone, without you here to pull me out." Man, this song is hitting me like a flood.

I get out of the shower and call Tim to set up some studio time. Though we get along great, and in all honesty, he's probably my best friend, when he gets a call from me he knows that his work will probably go unnoticed since I've released absolutely nothing. Yes, I pay him his fee, but some take pride in their work. I'm getting there, but to some, they like to have something to show for their years of hard work. That's why I think when this is done I may try and at least get it copyrighted and maybe put it on YouTube at best. Give him something for his endeavor.

I get dressed and wait while chatting with Tim about what we'll need. I sit in Dad's chair; this big chair he uses for reading. The man inhales one good book per week so he needs his space for that. It's so comfortable, and he's kind enough to let anyone sit in it, but if he's got a book and a glass of milk, he'll just stare at you like, "You know the drill—up." Not even Bruce is sacred on that chair. He damn near comes with one of those brushes that umpires use to clean home plate: "Up, you stinking dog." I'm sitting and texting back and forth with Tim but I don't need to put his lamp on since I have the phone so it is a bit dark in the room. And here it comes again. Another bout of anxiety almost on cue. I suddenly have this feeling that I've been at this way too long and I've been missing the outside world and not progressing myself as a person. What am I saying? I know I have and that's the whole point of going back to school, but my anxiety is so strong that it makes me say this stupid shit that I know I don't mean. So, time to settle in.

I buckle down, put my head back to the edge of the chair and mutter to myself, "It will pass, it'll end, just hunker down until it ceases." Sure enough, it does. Obviously, it's my method, but whatever's legal and works for you, give it a shot.

I get out my notes and start jotting down the second verse. "Have I been here way too long, pondering how I missed it all? Turning the lights off, they flicker, they fade, pondering all the mistakes I've made, and did I push myself too far?"

This is how songwriting is, everyone. When inspiration hits, it hits. It takes time, elbow grease, and trial with a whole lot of error. It's not how everyone does it, but for me, this is it.

At around noon Tim opens up shop and gets everything warmed up. I pull up to the studio and in the meantime help him with his chores. By the way, the studio is in the basement of his parents' house. A lot of the glamour and show you see in Hollywood aren't exactly how most studios are. When you're starting out, often enough it's on a computer program in your bedroom or basement. I've even seen one in a greenhouse. There is nothing quite like getting drum sounds next to a bag of fertilizer. Talk about sounding like shit.

We bring everything down usually one or two items at a time. Today I brought the acoustic, one electric, an arrangement of five or so pedals, a bag of cords, and the amplifier, and that's a light load. From time to time I bring the keyboard, bass, or pedal steel, all with their own individual amplifiers. Luckily the basic recording I sent to Tim of the riff made him confident enough for him to use his own bass.

What most do is start with a drum track. They get the rhythm for the song and structure it before everyone else adds on their respective instruments or sound effect. Often, in my songs, it starts with the guitar or vocals. Maybe from time to time a bass starts out, and since Tim's usually my drummer and is hearing the song for the first time, I'll start with whatever, then when he feels confident enough, he goes in and lays it down while I play into an amplifier that only he hears with head-phones on.

What we do after all that depends on the individual song. This song is very bare-bones so we're using only the acoustic, the electric for one solo, and maybe the synthesizer on his computer for one or two notes on a keyboard with a certain sound effect that isn't available on mine.

Speaking of "bare bones," if you ever walk into a recording session and hear some of the musicians talk, you'd swear they were speaking another language of stupid similes and moronic metaphors—especially when using pedals and other things to alter the sound an instrument makes. Let's say I'm using fuzz, a sound effect used a lot in grunge or alternative music. I've heard people use it then say, "Man, that sounds like your guitar got dragged through mud then plugged in to make some music, right on." Can someone tell me why I'd do that? Hell, if I could do that I wouldn't have bought the stupid pedal. Or if I use some phaser and put a delay on, "Sounds like you're in outer space bro, righteous." If space had sound, people could probably hear you scream, so shut up and don't screw with good movie quotes. Let's say I was doing a heavy song that involved me using my voice to be more heavy-oriented, I swear to God you'd probably hear, "Your voice sounds like you're boiling screws and nails with lava from a volcano, dude." Need I say more? They mean well, but, holy shit, is it goofy.

We set up, hit "record" and each part is recorded individually. And I have to tell you, it came out great. Even he was impressed. This is the guy who has heard every song I've ever been willing to record. So of the songs I'm proud of, this is by far the proudest I've ever been.

To show someone a song you wrote, or any art for that matter, really takes a certain type of confidence. Art is the extension of your reality, so when someone hears a song you wrote and says, "Eh, I don't like it," it really kind of kills you. Obviously, there will be songs and other forms of art that don't speak to you and you yourself may even say, "This sucks." I've done it myself, even on the way over here. But just understand—if the time ever comes when someone shows you what they're working on, criticism is important, but be constructive. Tim may say that something sucks, but he says it in a way that's more palatable. He says "It's not for me," or "That doesn't speak to me the way you want it to." Even today, between the two verses of lyrics, he liked them but flipped the verses. He put the second verse first. Producing is one hell of a job that I want nothing to do with. God bless him.

I'm packing my stuff up when he comes in after being on the phone for quite some time. He looks me dead in the face and asks "how would you like to keep this going?"

"Dude, I'd love to, but I have a big day ahead of me."

"That's not what I mean," he says in a serious and optimistic voice. "You seem really on your game today, and if you can keep that up, I'll be happy to record and play on this for free. You don't have to pay me and we'll have an agreement to make it official."

I was flabbergasted. "Tim, you know I'd never let you do that for me. It's not right to do all this work for no money and I respect you too much for that crap."

"Doug, I think this is the best song you have and, in truth, you seem a lot different, in a good way. You seem more relaxed and with a greater perspective of who you are. I think the idea of never doing this again is making you take more chances and make better songs. I want to see where this goes. What do you say?"

You have to understand what all that means to me right now. This is his job, his trade and his profession. It's a very rare occasion when someone who does his job as well as he does offers to do it for free for the sheer reason of "I want to see it happen." It only happens so often. Good will like this is miraculously rare, and to not do your absolute best by that person would be a moral sinkhole. So though I promised myself not to get sucked back up into this business, not to subject myself to the inevitable let down of doing something creative for money, not to give my all to something that won't show me love back, I said: "let's do it, man."

6

Date Number Two: The Meaning of Ang

I know what you're all saying. "You just told yourself you'd never do it, you promised yourself, What the hell is wrong with you?" But that's the story of an artist. They think they have run out of ideas, but just like that, they get a good one and it's off to the races.

There's always the story of actors who talk about "Oh I did this play in high school, got the acting bug and I've been here ever since." And it's entirely true. The acting bug is basically the artist bug, it catches you and causes you to give everything you have, and to be left with nothing just for a few compliments. It's so strange and powerful. It's like chasing this high of "I can make it. I can see it and this time it will work." It's the power of an idea, good or bad. The only problem is, you can't see exactly how it's a good or bad idea until you bring it to fruition. You spend all this time and money to show someone your sense of self-expression, only to be left with this voice at the back of your mind saying, "Was it worth it?"

Sometimes it is, sometimes it's not. At one point I was in three different bands. Each had their own different idea of their self-expression. One was a straight-up rock band that performed all its own original music. My idea was that this is the one that's going to make it and be a "success." I'll play the Garden with this band and tour the world. I can see it, absolutely. But here's the problem, I had the dream that an uncountable number of people have. I was thinking that mine was more important than theirs. Everyone has their own voice, that doesn't mean yours will sell well. It all fell apart after we all got tired of each other and gave up. We'd start bickering about who was in charge, where the next show should be played, how much money is paid to each member, and after a while, it stopped being fun. We were playing together purely because we got each other's vibe. Some people can work with each other without liking each other, but I just can't do that.

The second band was exclusively a "cover" band. We'd play anything the crowd asked for or whatever the vibe of the venue was. Whether it was a pool party, dive bar, or sidewalk: they asked for it, we delivered. It was all for money and that's it. It was fun, but we didn't see it as much more than a job that pays for the drinks.

The last one was bizarre. It was this concept band that was like a bad Coheed and Cambria or IF2112. The singer had written this sci-fi short story that he thought was excellent and wouldn't let us read until all the songs were done. When we read it, it was full of the same sci-fi crap that everyone uses. It had no originality and was really awful. We should have realized he had written the whole thing chain-smoking joints while listening to new wave music. He made us incorporate all of these instruments that none of us knew how to play and be experimental. Don't get me wrong, some of these bands are cool as hell like Coheed, Rush, and even Frank Zappa, but there's nothing more cringe-worthy than a really bad experimental band.

For every good idea, there seem to be about a million bad or half-assed projects. I can think of five of my own offhand that are too awful to comprehend or share. But just know that if your idea didn't cut the mustard, you aren't alone. Hell, I had a bad idea about the music driving to Angela's house to pick her up. I thought it would be a good idea to play a show with all my old songs just to show off the new one. Show seven bad songs to get to one good one? I don't think so, bud.

But I shake it off, park it, and text her saying I'm outside. She comes out and I get her door.

"Nobody ever gets me the door, thanks!" There she goes again, a compliment that makes me feel like shit.

"So what's the plan?" I ask.

She says, "Well, I thought about what your Dad told you: do what you love the most, and I couldn't help but love that. So my favorite thing to do when I'm alone is to get coffee and go for a walk. How's that?"

"Sounds great to me! Where is your favorite place to grab some?"

She opens up her maps app and types it in. We're maybe down the block when I get so eager about the song I have to just tell her about it. "So I don't know if I told you, but in my spare time, I'm actually a singer/songwriter. Mind if I show you something I'm working on for research?"

To my surprise, she grits through her teeth and says. "Yeah, sure." I am a little taken aback, but I open the app Tim uses to send me things and start playing it for her. After a minute or so, her facial expression changes and she says, "This is great! Not at all what I was expecting." I can't help but ask, "Did you think I would suck?" She says, "I thought you were going to show me this rap you did on an app on your phone that sounded like crap. Like the really bad SoundCloud rappers."

And to be clear, this book is not anti SoundCloud rappers, but on the contrary, I like a lot of them. Some are talented beyond recognition, but oh my God, they make a bad name for themselves sometimes.

We arrive at the coffee place still laughing about it. We walk in and there's a bit of a line. We both chuckled at the little tip jar that says "It's bean a pleasure." Get it? Coffee beans? I'll shut up.

We pull up and park the car at this trail she told me she loves, and we go for a walk. While walking down the path we both point out similar things like signs, certain trees that are shaped weird, homeless tents, really showing how warped our senses of humor are. We even started holding hands while also making inappropriate hand gestures. We were two fucked up people falling madly for each other. We walked further along and stopped at this little lake to sit on a nearby bench.

"So I'm always talking about me, how about you tell me a little bit about you?" I ask, tucking my legs up on top of my knee as though I'm playing unplugged in a coffee house. All I need is a scarf, a beanie, reading glasses I say are prescription, and to hold my coffee with two hands and I'll be a hipster in Brooklyn.

She says plainly "There's not much to know about me, honestly. I'm into the arts as much as you are and I'm a nursing major."

"Woah slow down, Ang, you're too chatty," I say drooling with sarcasm.

She bumps my knee. "I'm not interested in talking about myself. If I had to tell you something I haven't told you yet, then maybe I'd like to travel more."

"Anywhere special?"

"All over the country, to be honest. I've never really left the state besides on a plane to visit my grandparents in Florida. My parents aren't big on leaving work."

"Well let me ask you, if you could travel to anywhere in the world, where would it be?" She puts her coffee to her lips and thinks it over. "I never really thought about where outside the country I'd go," she replies with coffee dripping down her chin. "To me, going out of the country was about the same as going to Mars, it's just not going to happen, you know?"

I am honestly really confused when she said this.

"To be honest, I'm okay with just leaving the state for a weekend just to check some stuff out. I get overwhelmed when it comes to new things, so only little bits of things at a time is all I can handle."

Now it kind of makes more sense.

"I've always wanted to perform in another country," I said taking a swig of my coffee. She perks up, "You totally should! Any chance you get to perform anywhere you should play. I read this one interview where this rock star said 'If you play anywhere and there's only one guy in there, you play your ass off for that sucker.'" I don't know if it's what she said or how she said it but I have to say, I'm pretty turned on.

Well, that's a good bit of advice; my producer talks about stuff like that all the time. "If they say play "Three Blind Mice", you play "Three Blind Mice" got it?" I say in a voice that sounds nothing like the guy, but it gets a laugh. Anything for a laugh, right?

"Does your producer always get on your case with stuff?"

"Not really, he's really cool and recently told me he actually believes in me for the first time. He wants to put more songs together and make something of them."

"That's awesome," she says in a higher pitch of excitement.

"Yeah it sounds fun, but I don't want to get my hopes up for the hundredth time. If we do anything, I want to do things differently. I know I say I want to perform in another country and all, but I haven't even tried to play out of state. We'd have to expand our market, not just play for the same five clubs in the area everyone knows me in. Maybe a music video or something we haven't done yet." She perks up and raises her hand saying "I volunteer to be merch girl."

I can't help but giggle. "You got it, babe" and I give her a big kiss. There will be plenty of times when I'll say, "Nothing is better than…" and say something. This will be no exception. There's nothing better than having someone be supportive of your ambitions. What's even cooler is someone who wants to volunteer their time to help you succeed and push you to be the greatest version of all you can be. Between her, Tim, and my parents, I have to say I'm one lucky son-of-a-bitch. There's always the part of me that will say 'Fuck you I'll show you!" to haters, but it has to be balanced with, "Thank you for being there for me." Gratitude has to be shown on stage at all times. Even in punk. Being too cool for the room gets old and people only seem to notice after the audience has already left. Always be humble towards those who put their money aside to be sure they can purchase a piece of your self-expression. You have truly nothing without them.

7

"No Pressure"

T hings could not be going better with Ang. We had the
same things in common, the same pet peeves, and we
started adopting each other's phrases and mannerisms. After a
couple more dates like that, we decided to be exclusive. I was
right about our instant connection and now I have proof. I
even liked who I was becoming around her. I was more
cheerful at work and wasn't an insufferable dick at home. The
honeymoon phase was going great and I couldn't have been
happier. But the honeymoon was about to come to a plane
crash of a halt.

So was finally the end of the fall semester and the Christmas
vacation at work. The principal of the school decided to have
a Christmas party for all staff members and one guest each.
Since Bruce was unavailable, I decided to take Ang. They
were throwing it at a hotel instead of the gym since the last
thing anyone wants to do is be caught sober. Obviously, you
don't need drugs or alcohol to have fun, but we all love to talk
shit about students and how we all hate our jobs, though it's
the only thing we would do for forty years and tolerate it.

Black tie was optional, but fun was mandatory. Jesus, even Bruce could write a better slogan than that. Ang doesn't drink so she volunteered to pick me up. Modern women are the best, aren't they? Although it's best if they give you an inch, not to take the whole football field. She pulled up in this stunning black dress and a smile; I walked out putting on my jacket with an undone tie, and a flask in my mouth with my head tilted back to take a swig. I'm such a charmer it's sickening.

Her smile quickly turned to a frown. It turned to outright disgust when I give her a peck on the cheek, reeking of bourbon.

"Are you seriously showing up at this party like this? In front of your future colleagues and your bosses? You smell like a bar." I took out my cigarette since I only smoke when I drink.

"No worries. I'll change it to a smokehouse." I got in the car and she slammed her door shut.

"We're getting you some coffee to sober up before you get there," she said like I had no say in the matter.

"Sounds good. How was your day?"

"I'm not talking to you until we get there. Jesus, I haven't been this angry at someone in a long time, Doug."

I exhale my cigarette and say with sarcasm. "At least I know you care," but it was lost entirely. She slammed on the brakes and said,

"Take it back or I'm turning around." Now shit was getting serious. "I was being sarcastic, babe, I know you care, otherwise you wouldn't be mad. I'm sorry I overdid it with the pregaming." She noticeably lightened up but squeezed in one more line.

"Grow up, Doug."

Best "I forgive you" ever.

We grabbed coffee and along the way I cracked a few jokes to get her giggling. Now I was not totally sober, but I was getting away with it. We parked the car, she gave me a stick of gum for my breath, and we started to walk in. As we walked in, my coworker Brenda spotted me and said "DOUG." We whipped around to see this woman with a champagne bottle in each hand, mascara running, and a dress hanging so low I could count stretch marks near her areola. "Are you ready to get fucked up?"

I couldn't help but laugh and say, "Yeah, we're just trying to figure out how to pull your dress up, bud." She looked down, dropped the bottles and shattered them to pick up her dress. She looked down and started to cry.

"They were so young!" and she walked off crying. I turned to Ang and inform her that Brenda is the health teacher who specializes in drugs and alcohol. This is as much irony as one can muster for a lifetime.

We walked in and it was packed to the wall with people. So I started hammering them down to match Brenda, not thinking about the woman I was with or the conversation we just had in the car. I wanted to have fun with my friends, all the while disregarding the woman I loved the most. Boyfriend material, I am not. I turned around and notice she wasn't there. She wasn't even on the premises. She drove home and left my dumbass there. At least this girl had a head on her shoulders.

Initiating sequence, turbines to speed, loading program, and here we are! Loser mode! The state of mind I reside in the most. I just shunned the girl who could have been the one all the way home. Let's see the fabulous prizes. Why, it's a bottle of lotion, my left hand, and the Internet, what else could I fuck up today? Oh but wait, there's more! I just threw up the appetizers all over my father's suit. That's right, I can't even afford my own suit. I love my shit life deci—the rest of that sentence had been cut off by the second coming of vomit.

It's no secret that rock stars and their wannabe counterparts enjoy drinking the island of Ireland down to the last few drops. They get so demolished on a frequent basis to deal with their absolute shit self-esteem. Obviously, there are those who have a head on their shoulders, but that's all two of them. Most people who go into entertainment have the self-image of a banana slug. We have already talked about how they perform and make a group of strangers like them, but when they get off stage, they all go home and they're left with nobody but themselves. The loneliness gets overbearing and they drink to "feel happy." The truth is, booze doesn't make you happy, it makes you feel nothing. To some, nothing is better than pain. But contentment and self-love are better than anything else. If this wasn't a wakeup call as to how I could lose her, I didn't know what was.

I went up to my reserved room and fell asleep while the rest of the party enjoyed dessert. I woke up the next morning and I'm so hungover that I could hear the carpet scrunching. I had never had a hangover as bad as this and I hope to God I would never get this way again. The only thing I could do now was assemble the clean clothes and put the dirty clothes in a laundry bag. So I put on my jacket with no shirt, pants with no underwear, and socks with no shoes. Looking like a big star right about now, huh?

I caught an Uber home and let myself in. Not even Bruce wanted to say "hi" because I smelled so putrid. I threw my clothes in the wash and hopped in the shower. No inspirational song now, just running water of the shower sounding like the blessed rain down in Africa.

I got out, grabbed three to four bottles of water and lay in bed, lifting my body only to drink whatever I could keep down. And I stayed there the whole day. I didn't get a text from Ang the whole day. That made the hangover feel like a halo by comparison. I called her about once an hour until eight in the morning the next day. I'm an overnight caller, that's how pathetic I am.

I felt well enough to get out of bed and drive, so I drove to get a greasy burger and damn near swallowed it whole. I just want to have something in my stomach to soak up the alcohol. I then zoomed over to Ang's to try and talk to her. I knocked and rang the doorbell for just shy of fifty-six minutes judging by how far the guitar neck had swung around my watch compared to the whammy-bar. Cool watch right? She finally came to the door.

She opened up and I started in on my bullshit. "Look I know what I did was fucked up and I shouldn't have been as bad as I was. You told me to cut it out and I ignored you and I shouldn't have—" and she looked past me the whole time. She did the coldest thing I ever saw. She picked her phone up and went, "Sorry, Mom, nobody's here. Nobody living to me, anyway."

Obviously, she was furious but there was a small part of me that thought "This is the end of it. The final nail in my coffin." I drove home. I had a stare that I never had before. The "my life is over" stare. Everyone has had it at some point in their lives. But this was the lowest I had ever felt in my life. My ended engagement seemed like Mount Olympus by the view from the bottom.

I got home and did the only thing that made sense. I went downstairs and tried to find the hit song I would never release. I don't know why, but this seemed like a good time to play acoustic. Maybe find the "I'm sorry" song I've re-written about a hundred times before.

I mentioned back at the studio about pedals that artists use to modify the sound or tone they play in, but let's take a tour of mine. In order of the proper layout, it goes filters, distortion, modulators, and time-based. I don't really play with any filters, but distortion and fuzz take up three pedals on my board of six. It can fit up to about twenty, but I'm not so high maintenance. Then I have one echo pedal, one reverb, and oddly enough, a loop pedal. A loop pedal is the master tool behind acts like Ed Sheeran, KT Tunstall, and Grace McLean. You step on it, play something, and step on it again in time when you want the loop closed. It will then play the loop over and over again. For some reason, I just felt drawn to it that day. I played around and found these two notes that I liked. I played them in a certain rhythm and then found some notes to harmonize with them. "Holy fuck, that sounds full," I said out loud to no one. I figure out the key and chord structure, and the words fell out of my mouth. "Roll me over, I'm not sober, I think I've had one too much. I've lost my brain, my life is in vain, and I've lost all self-control."

No Pressure:

Roll me over, I'm not sober

I think I've had one too much

I've lost my brain, my life is in vein

And I've lost all self control

You know I'm sorry for what I've said before

If you're not ready for me I'm out the back door

There is no pressure here, I want you to know

But these are the stories that I've been told

Wake me up, I'm fast asleep

You're my nightmare, you're nobodies dream

Tighten my grip, clench my teeth

You'll never see, what lis underneath

You know I'm sorry for what I've said before

If you're not ready for me I'm out the back door

There is no pressure here, I want you to know

But these are the stories that I've been told

You know I'm sorry for what I've said before

If you're not ready for me I'm out the back door

There is no pressure here, I want you to know

But these are the stories that I've been told

And if you could see me, for more than just a minute

You will finally realize why I'm never finished

There is no pressure here, just want you to know

These are the stories that I have been told

To me, if a song comes together so easily and almost on its own, you didn't write the song, it wrote itself, and came out through you.

I recorded it on my phone and send it to Tim. I received this text back, "Tomorrow at noon and we'll hammer it out. Don't show anyone else and we'll get the girl back with it." And we did just that. I ran over and we figured out I wanted to let Ang know there was no pressure to get back together with me. I know I fucked up royally and don't expect any forgiveness. Hell, I had coworkers text me stories of what happened. I got so wrecked. So once we figured out the last line in the chorus "there is no pressure here, just want you to know, these are the stories that I've been told," we named it "No Pressure" and Ang took me back on the condition that I seek help. So, I was on the gravy train of taking each day one at a time. It was already rolling, might as well blow the whistle.

8

Meeting Ang's Parents

I never had a huge drinking problem, but whenever I have gone out drinking, I have gotten absolutely obliterated. Just completely hammered. I could go months without drinking. But when I drank, I couldn't do it in moderation. After Ang gave me her ultimatum, I started getting help. I started eating right, going to the gym, I even started running. And I'm not a runner. It hurts my man boobs too much. But after I got the ball rolling, I started getting crushed by it. I started calling myself on my own bullshit. No matter what I do, I'll always want to be creative. I'm just wired that way. There's nothing wrong with it, just have to realize when it's an appropriate time. I learned through my meetings that I create a world making myself seem grander than I am. I don't want to have to get to know the world around me that doesn't get me. I'd much rather make my own world up with content that I can grasp. But you can't be so locked up in your own crap all the time that you forget you have responsibilities. There are people who rely on you and may need your assistance without a guitar in your hands. Yeah, the guitar is cool, but tough shit. You have to go to work, help Mom and Dad, and walk your silly poodle. You'll always have music and art, but responsibility comes barreling through the doors on occasion and you may have to give it up for a night to do something for someone else. Cue the next stage of my relationship.

So, Ang and I now have been dating for around three months: it's not a long time, but it is a noticeable amount of time to not have met the others' parents. I'm too chicken shit and she isn't sure if she's ready. Though I'd usually be upset or feel some type of shame, I'm in no shape right now to put myself on display like that for anyone. I'm doing too well, having too much fun in a new relationship, doing well in class and work, and experiencing the greatest revelation of creativity I ever had. Why screw it up? I'll tell you why. Standing still in life gets you nowhere, obviously. You have to keep going and looking for what's coming next, good or bad. To me, life is more or less like standing in the middle of the Colosseum as a gladiator. Taking on whatever comes next that's going to tear your ass apart. It could be a person just trying to throw a net over you and kick your ass that you have to put some effort into beating, a target you could easily spear, or a lion that's going to fuck you up and you have to accept it. Whatever happens, happens. Get over it and keep moving. This is a very long analogy for "suck it up and meet your girlfriend's parents."

She breaks the news to me quite gently though, I am at work tapping a kid's desk to focus when the bell rings and they all go to lunch. I am sitting in the lounge texting when there's a phone call to go down to the office because something is waiting for me. My anxiety peaks, hoping to God it's not a lion. I head down and notice it's just my girlfriend. So it's an easy target, but one that's fine as hell. She has even brought me fast food, something I haven't had in weeks. The only thing better than this is if she was going to feed it to me like Caesar with someone to fan me. Should have known it was bait to a trap.

"Oh my God, what a nice surprise. What're you doing here, babe?"

She hands over the bag with a big kiss. "I can't visit my boyfriend after class at his big job?"

"Of course you can! Just have to find this big job you're talking about." She punches my arm at the joke and takes me to go outside. "Let's go sit, it's beautiful out." Ladies and gentlemen, it's February on Long Island, the most un-nice out time of the year. This time of year it's nothing but grey skies, freezing temperature, but more than enough ice and slush to make anyone say "This sucks." We sit on this bench dedicated to who-gives-a-fuck and I start eating in the cold. I unwrap my chicken sandwich as a small bit of secret sauce gets on my shirt. But I have lost ten pounds so it still looks good on my dad bod-less body.

"So what're we doing for Valentine's, I ask as I wipe my shirt with a spit-filled napkin.

She takes my hands and says "I want you to meet my parents." I nearly dropped the sandwich. Nearly, I'm not a fucking noobie. I am, however, shaking my head already without words. She starts patting my hands and saying "Douglas, stay with me here. Douglas, babe." I hate it when she full names me.

"Babe, I'm not sure if I can do this." She gives me the "grow up" face. I swear she's like that thing from Avatar: the Last Airbender that revolves faces for something-or-another. I don't know what to say. I'm upset, pissed off.

"Babe, it's been three months. They're excited to meet you and they're really nice. I promise."

"You said the same thing about your friends," I retort with fear. By the way, her friends were boring as sin and thought I was too sarcastic. Humorless little twerps.

"My parents are different. They're very inclusive and a joy to be around."

"I think I need to lie down."

I pretend to faint so she rips my dramatic ass back up and says, "Don't be such a bitch." Now I know she's serious.

"Babe, do you love me?" She added sincerely.

"You know I do," I say, almost spitting out a pickle at her.

"Then we're doing this. Friday at seven, bring wine for them, and you drink water. Got it?"

"Got it, babe." I might as well have said "Yes, dear," and hung my head low, I felt so defeated.

"Alright. I'm going home. I'm getting cold."

"Why the hell did we come out here for this talk?"

She whipped back with a death stare and said: "I knew you'd throw a tantrum so I wanted no witnesses if I had to kill you." Smart woman, that Angela.

Why am I throwing such a fit, you may ask? Because I'm an immature jackass. Yes, you already have that answer. But no musician has ever had a good encounter with parents of a significant other. It's just a fact of life. You see it in every sitcom. The dad's daughter brings home a boyfriend who's a leather-jacket-wearing, Harley-Davidson-driving, hair-slicked-back pretty boy who plays in a band and smokes cigarettes. What they all fail to realize is that in this day and age, musicians who grew up with the Internet can barely accept criticism, let alone be badass enough to walk into their spouse's parents' house and say, "Yeah, she's with me now, bro." I couldn't even text that to someone.

But that's just it. Time to grow up and start taking this relationship seriously. It took me six months to meet the ex-fiancee's parents. Although she was humiliated by me, so there is that.

I talk it over with Mom and though she understands the hesitation in taking such a leap, she has no understanding as to why I have such low self-esteem about it. I get done with my whole monologue—I told you about the TV version of me—and I hear from her for the first time in my life, "Cut the bullshit, Doug." That'll wake you up, huh?

"Mom, what do you mean?" She starts to pet the silly creature that now wants attention. As she scratches Bruce I hear his little bell around his collar ring and also the sound of my mother telling me how much she believes in me.

"Doug, look at who you are compared to who you were a year ago. You were fat, unemployed, pining over a failed relationship and still thinking you were God's gift to music. I always had your back, but you were acting like a fool with no direction. It was humiliating. But you got back on your feet, got a job, and now you're healthy and full of drive and ambition. I've never been more proud of you than these last few months. You go to that dinner and you show those people the amazing son I raised." All the while a panting dope lays on his back for a belly rub with his tongue out full of joy. Pretty badass of her to tell me all that. I didn't know I was such a burden on them, for lack of a better word. But she is right. I've been kicking ass and taking names all year and I have something to show for my work. It's not an idea in my head or a riff that won't leave the basement. It's the true showmanship of a hard-working man. I worked my fingers to the bone to show people I'm not a loser and I can do it. And, hell, if I can do it, you can, too.

Although I really wish I had Mom's pep talk recorded. I could put it on my phone and play it as I drive down her street in khakis and a button-down shirt. I got wine and flowers on the passenger seat with sweat dripping down my face and into my eyes causing them to burn. Is this what my fuck buddies felt like? Pay attention, Doug. I park the car in front of their house like I've done so many times when they weren't home. I still hope they don't know I've been in their house, or their daughter. Sweat is rolling down my arms and I'm gripping the wheel as though I'm about to have a coronary, looking at my GPS, wondering how far Tijuana is. But I look in the rearview mirror and realize she has come out to the car to help me with carrying things in. She opens the passenger door, see's the flowers and says, "These for me?" I nod and she doesn't even smile, but says, "It'll look better if they're for Mom." She really is on my team.

I get out and on the walk up I see their yellow Labrador I've bought so many bones for without their knowledge. Sitting with excitement next to a stand with no vase next to it since we knocked it over getting so crazy making out and walking at the same time. She told me she blamed it on the wind knocking it over as she was opening the door. Is she a keeper or what?

We walk up her steps, since her house is one of those houses that has a scissoring staircase with an apartment in the basement. I'm greeted by her dad who actually has a smile on his face. What the hell is this? I shake his hand and I'm not nervous at all. I hand him the wine and it turns out to be his favorite. What fucking planet have I crashed on? I pet my friend, Lucy the yellow Lab, as I cross the threshold. I hand her mother the flowers and she pecks me on the cheek after giving me a hug. Is this what having likable people in your life is like? Hell, I'll come here for breakfast, lunch and dinner, if so.

All my notions about coming here tonight were wrong. And I couldn't be happier about it. It made every bad experience with the exes go away because I think in my heart of hearts I have found my people. We all sit and eat for hours around their big kitchen table. When meeting a potential mate's parents, it's almost like a job interview.

"So tell us, Doug, tell us about you." Mom's pep talk got me psyched to have the confidence to answer truthfully.

Instead of stretching the truth with "I'm an up-and-coming musician with an album in the works," I tell her plainly, "I'm a teaching assistant at one of the local elementary schools while I'm in school for early childhood education. I have two lovely parents and a poodle named Bruce. In my spare time, I like to play music and write when I have the time." Her mom seems really pleased.

"Oh, Angela writes her own songs too! It's like June and Johnny Ca—"

"Mom, stop!" Ang damn-near gets up and covered her mother's mouth.

I looked over saying, "You never told me that."

"They aren't as good as yours and I can't play any instruments. It's more poetry, thank you, mother." She's blushing red and I wanted to laugh but don't want to embarrass her.

"Why don't you show me one of—"

I am cut off again when she shouted, "Show them yours." I took my phone out and show them "It's All Over" and "No Pressure." Her parents actually ask for a physical copy for their car.

I then ask Ang "Can I see your poems now?"

The little cheater goes, "I never agreed to it, so you lose." Jesus, she ought to be my contract manager.

Dinner is over and I stick around to help with the dishes. We all joke around telling old family stories and embarrassing tales from when we were kids. I did it. I faced the dude with the net I thought I was facing and kicked his ass. Ang and her mom go to the next room to grab a few cleaning supplies to which her dad grabs my collar and said, almost Batman-like, "I like you, you seem like a good kid, but if you make my daughter unhappy, I'll be sure you don't live to write another song about it." They are walking down the hall and he pushes me back up, both of us acting normal when they walk back in. Apparently, this lion still had claws.

9

"Oh Brother"

So after we have washed dishes and my neck is less red since I got pulled by my collar like Bruce when he poops on the rug, Ang walks me out. I stand in the garage and use my automatic starter before I go out. My night has been great so I'm not freezing my ass off in the meantime. "I think your parents like me!" She walks over and gives me a hug and a peck on the cheek. "I think they like you more than me. At least you can write a song." I pull her off gently.

"Yeah what's up with that? Why didn't you tell me you write songs?"

"I like yours more, so I don't want you to judge my crappy ones."

"They aren't crappy!" I said earnestly.

"You haven't even heard them!"

"Yeah but they're by you so I bet they're great. If not, I'll help you."

"I don't want your help."

"Why not?" I said almost accusingly.

"Because they're mine. You, of all people, should know what your own sense of self-expression means to the writer. If someone comes along and goes 'I know you better than you know you,' it's kind of a dick move. Let me do what I want with them and if I need your help, I'll ask you for it." My car starts warming up; I give her a big hug and kiss on the forehead and say, "Fine I won't help. Only on the condition of you help me when I ask you."

"You mean *if* you ask me."

I gave her a kiss on the lips and said, "No, when I ask you. You mean a lot to me and I value your take on things." She blushed like the first time we met. "Okay fine." And off I go.

As I drive home I realize there are very few times in my life when everything has gone according to plan. This went even better. Who knew that all you have to do is calm the fuck down and things will sort themselves out? I can't help but notice on the way home that I'm driving with one hand on the wheel and my seat reclined back. I'm driving a little slower and I have a positive disposition. This is new, and quite frankly, I like it. I think I found the new Doug. Now back to our regularly scheduled program.

I pull up to the house and notice a familiar car in the driveway. A brand new out-the-showroom something-something sport with all the bells and whistles. It clicks in my head and my head falls on the steering wheel when I realize the inevitable shit hitting the fan and my good day comes to a screeching halt. My brother is home.

Now, my brother isn't a bad guy. Far from it. He's actually my best friend next to Tim. He's comforting and warm, with a kind sense of humor. Not a mean one like mine. It's just that he's successful and I'm—well me. He's the head of emergency medicine at the hospital Dad works at. Yeah, he got Dad the job. He stops over every once in a while to check on things when he has the time. Not that he doesn't want to, but he's booked solid while living at least an hour away. He's got a wife and kids, so it's not like he can just bail and come see us whenever. But every time I see his something-something parked in the driveway, I just know I'm going to inevitably feel like shit. He doesn't mean anything by it, it's my problem, not his. In fact, he's my biggest supporter. No matter how busy he is, he always makes time for my shows, listens to whatever I send him and gives me feedback that's constructive. It was actually his idea in "It's All Over" to switch the verses. Tim just backed him up.

I walk in at my normal height of six-foot-two inches, I will inevitably go to bed at a height just under the sidewalk—he makes me feel that small. Instantly as I walk through the door he's on me with a big bear hug. "How's it going, bud!" God, I love him.

"I'm good, Chris. Just got back from meeting the girlfriend's parents."

"Did you remember the wine I showed you?" See? The fucker is good.

"Yeah, it turned out to be her dad's favorite."

He claps his hands in approval "Told you, dude. It always works. Not too much burn just enough flavor. Just like Robin." Robin is his wife. God damn, I wish I had his jokes. "Christopher!" Mom damn near throws a book at him. Yeah, he's an adult who saves lives every five minutes, but he's still her kid. Mom's house, Mom's rules.

"Hey how about we all sit outside with a fire?" Mom says with enthusiasm.

"Whatever you want to do Mom," Chris says. "Let me go get some old newspaper and we'll meet you both outside." Mom and dad get up and head outside all giddy. Not aware of the quiet storm about to brew between her sons. We watch them both leave. Chris takes a swig of the wine and says, "You have no idea how much I want your life, dude." Ding ding, that's the bell and round one starts.

I start with, "How dare you. You have everything I could ever want and everything I do, you do better in no time at all. Do you wish you had my life? Fuck you, man." He doesn't even get mad. Just shrugs his shoulders and says, "You don't think I'd rather mold the minds of America instead of saving the dumbasses that walk in every day?"

Oh, now I'm fuming. I go off with, "I basically point a kid's nose at his paper and say, 'Pay attention' for eight hours. Do you really think it's rewarding? You can do it walking in there with no experience. You save and improve lives every day." He starts to raise his voice a little.

"Drunks who decide I'm not worth their time or money, hypochondriacs who think they're dying of cancer because they farted a little louder than usual, and the chest pain who need a stent put in. Yes, it is a high-maintenance job but at least people appreciate what you do. Most people go on the Internet and try and prove me wrong like I didn't go to school and put myself 250 thousand dollars in debt. At least you lived a little. Playing and writing music that everyone loves."

I kind of look at him funny. Not in a "Fuck you" way, but in a "Really?" kind of way. Like I never thought of it. Then he continues. "Not to mention you get to see Mom and Dad every day. You help them into their later years while I'm helping everyone else's parents. You get to see the fruits of your labor. If I do my job right, I don't see them again. But if I do see them, it's because they didn't listen."

I sit back; I never really realized he felt so unappreciated. It really hits me hard. This guy does nothing but gives while I take. And often, I do get more praise while he gets criticism. Like I'm supposed to whine about something that someone at a show once said about a song that took me ten minutes to rehearse? This poor fuck deserves more. I think I'm going to write a song about that.

I run outside and say, "Mom, I'm going to bed. Feeling kind of tired since that dinner." Chris heads over with his apology of "Look I'm sorry, I didn't mean to snap," but I am in full songwriter mode saying "Yeah, yeah. Sure, it's fine." I shut my door and pick up one of the acoustics. When I have a message and not a riff, I use the typical G-E minor-C-D chord progression just to hammer lyrics out. Over time I realize I want him to know it's okay and that he has responsibilities he can't help but have. He lives so far away and— "oh brother, how are you? I know that you're far away," yes a melody will outright interrupt a sentence.

Oh Brother

Oh Brother, how are you?

I know that you're far away

I know everything's so strange

Nothing is quite the same

Don't worry I get it, you don't have to say a thing

Life may not go your way, but you're stronger every day

But always remember

I'm just a phone call away

And remember

I'll always stay the same

Oh do you, remember

Our long drive through the north

You rested on my shoulder

We'll always be back and forth

Don't worry, you'll get it

Please don't change a thing,

I know sometimes you're angry

I love you all the same

But always remember

I'm just a phone call away

And remember

I'll always stay the same

We never wanted this way, but thats the way that it is

We can't be always thinking of wished for outcomes

We can't pretend that its easy, I think I got it from here

I'll all be worth it in the end

But always remember

I'm just a phone call away

And remember

I'll always stay the same

MOVING ON, I never really write songs about other people's struggles or their views. I always write my own views, even political songs. So I realize after I get this line, this is going to be a letter to him, for him, and about the struggles I now know he faces every day.

I send a rough demo to Tim. We developed a new system for recording. We only record on Thursdays so that Fridays are for Ang. But I am so nervous about how this will come out. What if Chris doesn't like it? What if it comes out like crap? But alas, just like before, my anxiety is subdued by the result of it coming out even better than "It's All Over." I show my parents and they cried, Ang and her parents think the same thing. So I send it to Chris. The thing is, I don't hear from him for a week. I nearly shit a brick. I call him after another studio session. "Hey, you never told me what you thought of the song," I say a little shyly. "Oh, God, it never sent!" he says in a panic. "I've been listening to it all week crying as you did after —" and I don't even hear him finish I am so elated. Jesus, what one song can do for another person. Not nearly as important as proper medical care, but it's really something. It just goes to show you never know someone else's life until you walk in their shoes. Hey, what a title, maybe that's something too!

10

Introducing Jackie III

So walking in my shoes turned out to be a bust. But it happens often. Nice of me to leave you with optimism then take it away, isn't it? Anyway, Tim and I have been working on a bunch of songs every Thursday after work. We have about eight or so finished but we're only going to do four —for an EP. In case you didn't know, EP stands for extended-play. It's a collection of songs more than a single with a B-side, but not enough songs to qualify as an LP or long play. A lot of artists do that these days to save money and to see how the first batch of songs performs. If they like it, more come. If not, well you get the idea. We know "It's All Over" and "No Pressure" for sure are going on it. I'd really like the song I wrote for Chris, "Oh Brother" to go on it, but it's up in the air. We have a lot of options to work through. Many bands make damn near up to fifty songs for an LP of about twelve songs. Artists like John Mayer, blink-182, and Green Day all come to mind. It's better to be over-prepared than to go forward and be told we don't have enough. A goal I always set out to accomplish is that every song you put on an EP should have the potential to be a single. No songs that you could skip over or say it's an "album song." And I have to say I'm pretty proud of what we have as a product. Even Tim is getting more enthusiastic than usual. So enthusiastic that he did something I damn near killed him over.

I got a call from him the other day saying "Hey, man, so I really like how this is going." I replied, "Hey, dude, me too." He went on to say "So I've been showing a lot of people it and I'm getting nothing but positive feedback."

"That's great!"

"Yeah, I sent it to a few people I used to work with." Now if you're not into the business aspect of songwriting I can understand why you wouldn't get why I was enraged. To send a song out that isn't copyrighted is extremely dangerous. Anything that isn't copyrighted runs the risk of being stolen and not having proper legal backing to say, "I own this, this is mine." So for Tim to be so careless, was to me, blatantly distrustful. And I let him know it, too.

"Are you fucking crazy? You know none of these are copyrighted and there are one of two people on your roster I've heard use one or two of my riffs, Tim. I cannot believe you'd do that." But he was all cool about it.

"Don't worry. None of them would fuck with my productions or steal from us. In fact, they asked if you'd have the time to sit down with 'Jackie Ill' and help her write the hook for her new song."

"I still think she has the dumbest name."

"She's offering to pay you."

"Tell her she's got a deal." I'm a sound whore, what can I say. The only hangup I have is, Jackie Ill is a 21-year-old girl whose becoming something of a local legend. She has featured on all these artists' songs and is really starting to blow up and has all this sex appeal. And as a 26-year-old man, I have no idea what it's like to be a pretty 21-year-old girl. So I go to the prettiest 21-year-old girl I know.

I call Angie up and ask her to send me a few of her lyrics. And boy, that wasn't an easy fight. "Ang, I really need to see a few examples. I have no idea what it's like to be this girl." Her response was "because I do?"

"Ang I have no idea how to sound like a 21-year-old girl with boy problems. I don't know if I can relate to her or write in her style." And thank God she's the brains between the two of us because she lays it out for me. "She doesn't need another song that sounds like her. If she's coming to you, she wants to sound like you. So just let her talk about her life for a little bit and make what you can make of it. If she likes it, she'll take it —and I'm sure she will. She wouldn't be paying you money if she wasn't." God, I love this woman. So Jackie comes to Tim's studio in a limo. Mind you, she lives four blocks away. Fucking divas.

She comes out of the car with a security guard and a Maltese in a crop top, mini skirt, and sunglasses. Keep in mind, it's raining. I have no idea what a lot of artists like this are thinking. But then again, maybe that's why I'm still here. But this is a recording session, not the VMAs. I go to sessions in the plainest and most comfortable clothing I can find. Hell, I'll go in sweatpants and a hoody if I can still sing. I'm not out to impress anyone with anything but talent. She doesn't walk in at first, she has the security guard circumnavigate the perimeter of the studio, all three rooms, making sure there isn't anyone conspicuous. Fucking ludicrous. Then she walks in soaked but acts like she meant for it to happen.

"Which one of you is Doug?" she says to the two of us, fully aware of who Tim is. "That'll be me, dear," I say through my teeth, full of frustration. "I like that one song you do with the guitar and I wanna have lyrics like dat." Keep in mind, she's putting a Latino accent on and this girl is whiter than Dove soap. I lost it after that. That's right, two sentences are all it took. "Okay listen, I know you want me to write a song for you but I am not going to put up with this horse shit image. I don't know you, but I can see right through this crap and know this is not who you are. Maybe your self-esteem is shit and you're trying a new image because you're terrified of showing your real one but you must be a real asshole to suppress the real you. No way are you getting one of my songs." She busts out crying and shows who she really is. Someone exactly like me.

"Fine. I'm sorry I wasted your time. I really liked your song and it sounded like something I've always wanted to do but never had what it takes. I'll leave; goodbye."

Tim looks at me as she runs out the door and goes, "What the fuck was that? Are you trying to be an extra-special asshole? Go get her outside or you and I are done."

So I haul ass after her. "Dear, please stop. I'm sorry. I didn't mean it." I'm shouting this as I chase her the four blocks back to her mother's house. She goes to her house and slams the door. I knock to be greeted by what I can only describe as a brick wall with limbs, an earring, and a really pissed-off expression that speaks with an Italian accent.

"What did you do to my Jacqueline?"

"Sir, I apologize. She was speaking weird and I lost my cool. I'm here to say 'I'm sorry' and hope that she'll come back and get some work done."

"She's not going anywhere with you now. Get off my property." I go for broke with this guy. "Sir, she was acting in a way that didn't sound like who she was at all. I don't know her, but I know when someone is doing something they don't want to do. If she doesn't want to come back, fine, but at least let me tell her I'm sorry." She calls from inside the house

"Daddy, it's okay. You can let him in." He gives me that same weird stare Ang's dad gave me at their house over dinner. I walk in and she's in their living room with tears running down her face.

"Hi, Jackie Ill. I'm sorry if I was a—" she interrupts and says, "Don't call me Jackie Ill. That's not my name."

"You don't like your own stage name?" She gets real as hell with me.

"My manager picked it out. I'm not even a hip-hop fan. The only way he'd manage me is if I changed everything about myself and went under this title and image. It's not what I want to do at all."

"Well, what do you want to do?" She has me sit on the couch.

"I want to be the next Stevie Nicks. I want to play music like Fleetwood Mac, Tom Petty, and Bob Dylan. Stuff with a message that matters. To be there for other people like they were for me. But they told me maybe when this hip-hop faze wears out I can do what I want. But until then, it's all about going with the trend. That's why I loved 'It's All Over.' I told my manager you were the writer of that song about bouncing asses off the wall so maybe you can write a folk song that was so good he'd change his mind and let me do my own thing."

I take a big breath and exhale. "Jackie, let's go write your new song. I've already got a theme and a verse in mind." She gets excited and gives me a big hug. I couldn't have been more wrong about her as a person. We get back to Tim's and we get to work.

Turns out she has been at war with herself and her own image ever since she started trying to make it as a singer. Like many pop and hip-hop artists, her label and management want them to be what's trendy, to have sex appeal, and to make songs played in clubs that people drink shots to. After she says the words "at war," it came to me. I play this very Neil Young acoustic riff with a harmonica and sing, "Oh the last time I left for war, I learned a thing at my hell's front door. Those who do not know their own worth, are living in their own hell on earth." She starts tearing up and runs into the booth to sing it. We have to remind her we need to lay down all the instruments first. But it is so nice to see someone be herself after such a long time being someone else. She is damn near squealing she was so excited to have it her way. We go on to write the whole song, but my favorite part is "live your life, but not too fast, you never know how long you'll last. Be your one and only self, you're the only one, there's no one else."

Tim sends it off to her manager and it is almost like he ordered a salmon and got a steak. He is so irate he called Tim in a fervor. Tim tells them they already spent their money on it so they might as well put it out. Scenarios like this usually call for a lawsuit big enough to make a grown man cry, but everyone at the label loves it so much they don't have the heart. It technically is their property, so they make it a little faster, add sampled drum beats instead of Tom's outstanding playing, and take out the bridge of our harmonies and made her do a rap verse over it. It sounds more like "Over and Over" by Tim McGraw and Nelly. I hate this business.

11

You Sure You Want to Be Famous?

Wow, I did something productive with music. That's a first. It didn't go to number one on the billboard charts or anything, but it's been getting some airplay on college radio stations. Better than anything I ever did on my own. I kept getting calls from Jackie saying, "We did it! It's on the radio. Thank you!" It was cute at first, but after the tenth time, it gets under your skin. But I can't really bitch. Since they didn't get rid of the audio of me harmonizing and the one or two vocal lines I threw in, it is dubbed "I'm at War" by Jackie Ill featuring Doug Manning. I am getting phone calls from relatives I hadn't talked to in years because it was played on a college radio station that broadcasted on the same channel as a national sports team. Isn't that nuts? From a guy who was slowly backing out of the business, I sure as hell seem elbow deep in it.

Speaking of which, Mom and Dad were not so thrilled. Seeing that I'm working and going to school full-time, it seems like I'm not taking everything seriously. Mom approaches me nicely about it. "Heard your song, Dougie. When did you have time to write that?"

I countered with, "Kind of just wrote it in an hour, Mom. She hit me with a wave of inspiration I was feeling at one point, too. So it just came naturally." That went as well as could be expected.

"Well have your grades been coming to you so easily?"

I rolled my eyes while her back is turned. "I just have to finish a paper on the progress I've made since starting my first semester. A real hand-job of a paper, Mom."

"Will you just take this seriously!"

"Mom, you're not in the class, it's easier than you think it is."

She almost drops the boiling pot on my head. Deservingly so, since I am being a little snot. "You know what, I'll just go out for a while. I'm taking everything seriously. I wrote a song for someone, that doesn't mean I'm quitting my job or dropping out of school. Please chill." Please note, you should never tell anyone angry to chill, because they will erupt with anger. Especially the woman who gives her entire life for your existence. Yeah, I've earned a piece of shit, gold medal.

I get in the car and start driving. I have not even traveled two blocks when I get a call from Dad. Oh boy, did I fuck up now. I answer with a pleasant, "Hello?" In return I get, "So this is what's going to happen. You're going to turn around and drive home to apologize to your mother for your shitty attitude. You know you haven't been giving work and school your full attention and it's about time you do. We have been beyond patient with you about music and I'm putting my foot down. You've gone too far." I went from pleasant to enraged within .05 seconds. "What the fuck did I do here? Yes, I'll apologize to Mom but I didn't sell drugs or wreck the car. My grades are great, work loves me, I'm doing better with my health than I ever thought I could. Get off my back. It's my life," and I hang up the phone.

And if you think Ang is on my side, oh you'd be dead wrong. More times than not, my girlfriends have always taken my parents' side. Win, lose, or draw, they'll never be on my side. It gets quite annoying, actually. I pull up to her house and she's waiting outside for me. Jesus are they all on a conference call? I'm not even out of the car when she's at the window with her hand out with a phone in it. "Call your mother, now."

"Babe how did you—"

"She called me," she says, interrupting. I don't know if I can get a word in edgewise in my own life. "Ang, I'll call her later I just want to blow off steam and get my head straight." "You don't get to cool off with me until you call both your parents and apologize." Now I've lost all my cool. "I don't want to hear it from any of you. Don't forget, you told me to write to her and gave me some pretty great advice on how to. This 'hit' is on nobody more than you, Ang. I'm sick of everyone talking to me like they're in charge of me. It's my life and I'm going to live it how I want to."

"Then drive off because I'm not talking to you for the rest of the day, asshole."

I didn't even say "bye". Just put the car in drive and drove off.

I'll talk to mom and dad later, and I'll apologize to Ang tomorrow or something. I don't want to go home, but I can only think of one place left to go. So I stop by Chris' place. I am greeted at the door by him but with a look of absolute disappointment. He shakes his head silently but saying everything. We say nothing to each other as I got back in my car and head down his driveway at full speed. I have nobody on my side. The support system that sent me hurtling toward this world is now pulling me back because it has become bigger than they thought it would ever go. It's almost like they are all saying, "He's having fun, why ruin it for him? It'll never happen, so what's the harm in him having fun?"

I'm not allowed to go home, but I have no place left to go. So I stay in a hotel for the night. I can't believe what I'm reduced to. What a cliche I've turned into—a lonely artist in his hotel room. I have some bouts of inspiration, but nothing concrete comes of them. I've never been kicked out of the house before, but here I am.

The next day I go off to work in the same clothes I wore the day before. Yes, I have washed them. I'm not a total pig. I get a call from the class I'm in to go down to the principal's office. I've never been to the principal's office, even as a kid. So obviously, I'm petrified. I walk the long walk of shame down the main hallway past the guidance counselors, the school nurse, and the auditorium. And maybe it is the sheer panic of this possibly being my last walk down this hallway that has scared the shit out of me enough to realize that I don't want to lose this job. It's a good gig while I'm in school and It'll only get better as I grow older. Why blow it on a gig that'll get sick of me and throw me to the scraps when they find the next-best replica? Jobs like this value wisdom and experience, they don't discard them. Everyone's right, I have to get my head out of my ass and into the sun where I can see what's coming next.

I walk into the office and have to re-introduce myself to the office assistant. Now I'm not against hiring the elderly to do clerical jobs, but I think to qualify for this job, you should have to be able to see the person coming in for assistance. Have your bifocals ready, Darleen, we have shit to do.

I walk in and Max, the principal, who I graduated with by the way—over-achieving prick—sits me down to have a talk. He's nice enough but feeling inadequate in everything you do in life sucks. Having someone speaking to you in a shallow and pedantic way doesn't help.

"Hey, Doug, have a seat." So I sit like Bruce waiting for a treat.

"How's Mom and Dad?"

"Everyone's good. Getting together with them later for dinner," I reply obviously lying.

"Girlfriend good?"

"Yes, sir. Just got back from a vacation."

Artists lie every day to make it look like they aren't scrounging.

"And how's Chris?" "Everyone is good, Max, what's—" he gives me a look with the intent of letting me change what I just called him.

"Sorry Dr. Veitman, slipped into old high school jargon."

He doesn't say anything, just nods his head. "So I was listening to the radio and I have to tell you about this song I heard. Seems like you finally broke through and I have to say I'm proud of you."

I'd be smiling and saying 'thank you' if I didn't expect it to be followed by some bad news. He could have said this in the hallway, why call me to the office? Then he turns around and sits in his chair. "It's really great. I love how it sounds, but I don't like the sound of my students talking about one of my TA's being a pop star on the radio. It's a distraction and gets rumors started."

I squint my eyes with disbelief. "What rumors are you talking about, dude?"

He rolls his eyes, seeing I'll never fully respect him. "How about that you wrote that song snorting coke off her ass, or you're leaving to go on tour with her? Or how you both are hosting SNL as a couple."

"Wait, you know none of that is true."

"Yes, Doug, I know. The point here is you can't keep doing both. The school board is pressuring me to fire you."

I damn near fell out of my chair. "Fire me? For what, having a hobby?"

"I told them the same thing, I can't fire you for something legal you're doing in your spare time. But, we can fire you for causing distractions to students and displaying inappropriate behavior."

"It's not even my behavior!"

"Rumors can overshadow the truth and you know that."

"So I'm just letting you know, it's going to have to be one of the other. Teaching, or music. I'm sorry. I wish I had another choice. Head back to class and try to have a better day."

I walk out, stark white and pale. It wasn't just a metaphor anymore, I have to make a choice: have financial security and be stable doing something I love, or do what I've always wanted since I first dropped the needle on a turntable.

I drive back home and pick up flowers for both Ang and Mom while I grab candy for Dad. I think I flipped between the right choice and the wrong choice at least a hundred times today. But then again I also think I made the right choice. I'll never know until I pursue my pick and see in the end. Jesus, I know people make hard choices like this every day, but this is never something I was prepared for. Regardless, time to man up and apologize to the people I love. The people who, no matter how angry they make me, are just looking out for me—regardless of how much they're being a pain in the ass. I roll up to the house and to Ang's car parked in the driveway. Are they hanging out without me? What the hell? I walk in with everything and they're on me in a second with hugs and kisses.

"What the hell is going on?"

Dad put his head on my shoulder. "Doug, Tim died early this morning."

12

"Long Long Gone"

Y ou could have knocked me over with a feather. It was almost like a part of my soul was ripped straight out of me. My best friend, the 23-year-old genius producer, dead. You ever hear something that devastates you and it's so unfathomable it's like you didn't hear it? After Dad told me, it was like he had said it in Latin. I just made a face and acted like it wasn't what he said.

"Dad, w-what did you say?" He gave me a big hug, let go and said, "Tim was riding his motorcycle when a 90-year-old with dementia blew through a stop sign and hit him. He was pronounced dead at the hospital after they tried everything. It happened just up the road about a mile away." I fell to the ground. I just lay on the floor without any intention of getting up. The guy who truly believed in me as a human being cut down in his prime by someone who shouldn't have been on the road. What the hell is wrong with this world? The good really do die young and we leave the assholes to live forever.

I lay on the floor crying for about an hour and 17 minutes. It could have been 20, but my watch had tears on it so it was tough to read. I tried to call Tim's phone at least 10 times in that hour. I'd heard of people doing it, but I couldn't help hoping that he would pick up and it was just like a death hoax from the Internet. I even messaged him some old riffs to see if he'd respond. But no, he was long gone. I did get a message from Jackie, though. She was as distraught as I was. I got a bunch of messages from all the artists he worked with. All stuff about how he was an outstanding producer and just really good to artists. But honestly, Jackie and I were the only ones talking about Tim the human being. The guy that would call an Uber for you if you were short on money for a ride. The guy that boosted my self-esteem if I was ever feeling down on myself or my abilities. It really goes to show that you'll only be shown the respect you deserve when you're gone. Only when you can't hear are nice words said.

The funeral was a week away. Tim's mother was so distraught she was in denial up until two days before. She kept saying things like, "That can't be him. He's on vacation," or "He's at his father's house all week." Unfortunately, Tim never knew his dad and he had only ever taken one vacation in his life, three years ago. Even then he brought a guitar along with him just in case something sparked.

I pulled up to the funeral parlor with Ang. She hadn't let me out of her sight since I got off the floor. I was gripping her hand like a kid so I wasn't showing much progress. Walking in we realized were about 10 minutes early. If there were too many people I probably would have bailed because oddly enough, I don't do well with big crowds without being in charge of them. So maybe it was a blessing in disguise. We walked into the room where the funeral was to be held and only a few people were there: This one cousin I had met once before and his parents. I gave my respectful greeting, sat down and just waited. The doors opened so we stood arms folded. Turned out to be his mother being escorted in by two other family members. She looked like she was about to fall to the floor and had to be held up. I'd been there already so I was about to join. Then they wheeled in the coffin. I was so not ready for this. He was wheeled in by about 5 family members. One of them seemed to be about 14 or 15 and he seemed awfully scrawny and emotional so the casket was listing to the right while going down the aisle. So I walked over Ang's legs, walked up, and straightened it out while walking him down the rest of the way. Tim had guided me God knows how many times, time for me to return the favor.

We lined him up the way you do at open-casket funerals. They popped the top open and he laid there still. Even hanging out with the guy he always bounced his leg as he had restless legs. Seeing him this still almost made me not believe it was him. They put in the belongings that meant the most to him. A childhood blanket he stuffed his bass drum with, a picture of him and his mom from his first concert. And the AC/DC wristband he'd had since he was a kid, allegedly the only thing his father ever gave him. Lastly, they put in this china cymbal he made out of a kids toy from the church he played at. This friggin' bizarre-looking thing. Every time we jammed I'd make fun of it but he always had the same answer. "Yeah, it sounds like shit, but I made it, man." I stood over him with my head down and hands at my front and said, "Rest in peace, man. I love you," and I walked out. I couldn't handle this.

I had Ang drop me off home and told her just to go. I needed to be alone for the weekend. I went to my room and shut the door. I didn't come out for a good 10 hours. I came out just to eat dinner, then went back in. I didn't go to the basement once. Why write songs anymore? I can't captain a ship without my first mate.

I got out of bed finally around Sunday afternoon. I started to walk and I had to catch myself for fear of falling over. I caught myself on my dresser that had my stereo on it. I accidentally hit it on and all of a sudden the stereo jumped to this track of us screwing around into the microphone. Just yelling and cursing with funny accents with Autotune. Just being crazy kids, having fun in the studio. I couldn't help but giggle like a little girl. I knew I would always have these recordings and memories of us making music, but I wished I could have one more minute with him to just say thanks. Just to write one more song, one more memory, and tell him how much he meant to me. My brother from another mother. Since I don't have him, I'll write one for him.

Tim always got on my case about trying to branch out with new instruments. Even if it was a piano.

"Everyone's heard you play guitar, dig deep, bitch, branch out once and awhile." So I ran over to the piano with my guitar, playing these four chords he always liked. I looked on the neck where the notes were and figured out the tempo on the piano. I started playing the chords whole, but it sounded too busy, "Maybe it'd be good for the chorus? I don't know." But then I remembered he always liked it when one hand stayed the same while another played the bass notes. So I gave that a shot and I figured out the verse then and there. As much as I liked these chords, the song seemed really bland and kind of boring on its own. No matter what words I put over it, it was kind of bare. Any guitar part I write for it just sounds too busy, so maybe the drums will be constantly changing and that would almost be the interesting part. Like never having the same drum part in any verse or chorus. Regardless the best drummer I ever worked with had recently died, so I guessed it was up to the few drum lessons he had given me to get me through this quagmire.

After I had got up and made a cup of coffee I got a call from an unknown number. Same area code, maybe a town or two over, but I answered anyway. "Hello?" as you typically say.

The voice on the other line was a woman who sounded familiar. "Hello. Is this Doug?"

"Yes it is, who may I ask is calling?"

"Hi, this is Ms. Fallon, Tim's mother."

"Oh, um, hello, ma'am. I'm so sorry for your loss and to be acquainted this way. How may I help you?"

"Well, I'm sorry to be a bother, but it seems you're one of the few numbers he had in his emergency contact book. Did you two record often?" Tim's basement was soundproof so anyone playing was never heard upstairs.

"Yes, ma'am I was over every Thursday for about the last three months. We'd go out together on the rare occasions we'd both have the energy to get up and we've been friends for many years."

"Oh, well it seems like I found the right person to call, then."

"What do you mean, ma'am?" I was seriously confused.

"I was wondering if you wouldn't mind taking his recording equipment out of here. It's become far too painful to look at and it'll do no good here by itself with me. So I figured if anyone should have it, it should go to someone he deemed important enough to write down for an emergency." This took the air out of my chest, I had barely any idea how to work any of that crap, but if this poor woman is suffering, I really ought to take it off her hands. "Yes, ma'am I'll be over within the hour." I called Jackie and we both went over to dismantle it all.

As we walked in we're greeted by her in pajamas, a robe, and no makeup on. She'd probably cry it all off anyway but you could tell she'd been in a world of pain by the redness under her eyes. They matched mine. So we walked down and she said, "Take everything out except the drum set. That I want to stay with me."

"Yes, ma'am," we both said at the same time. We went through everything, the crap wires he'd kept in an attempt to fix them, the headphones from the mid-nineties he thought were vintage, and God knows how many broken drum sticks he, at one point, had tried to hot glue together to make a chair. Spoiler alert, it broke instantly and had sat on the ground broken ever since. We picked it all up and took some of the posters of the bands he was in off the wall. Thought it would be nice for his mother to have them framed.

We chucked the broken sticks in a garbage bag, took the drums upstairs to vacuum the rug they were on and the rest of the basement after everything was done. We loaded the cars up with box after box. Then we went back in and said goodbye to Tim together in the basement. We went upstairs and said goodbye to his mom. As I pulled away I couldn't help but look at his house in the rearview mirror. It was the final moment of realizing my friend was long, long gone. Oh, wait a second . . . what a title.

Jackie and I went back to my place, plugged in the bare essentials and hammered out the song very quickly. I still had Dad's drum kit so I figured out some ambient beats to fit the straightforward patterns. It was almost like drumming when necessary and in good taste. Jackie and I made it a duet. I almost couldn't make it through when she wrote: "now you'll always be 23 years old, now you'll always be out in the cold."

Long Long Gone

I know you've heard it from your mother before

Put it down once you close your car door

It can wait for a second it can wait for a minute

My life way way better when you were in it

Now you're long long gone

Now you'll always be 23 years old

Now you'll always be out in the cold

I just had hope I could make the wrong things right

Guess I'll try to stay awake through the night

Now you're long long gone

You can peel the rubber from the streets where you were

Just a mile up the road I hope you just weren't hurt

My friend for so long and now its come to an end

You were way too young you were way too young

Now you're long long gone

Jesus, even now it makes my bones ache. We had something that would immortalize our mutual friend: the friend that brought the two of us together as artists and souls with the same dream and ambitions. I'll always love my friend and miss him more than I can bear. I just wish I had one last moment to tell him one thing. I could write it down a million ways but I'll always come back to, "What the fuck is up with that cymbal, dude?" Some things will just never change.

13

God Dammit Champ

J ackie and I decided to produce the song ourselves with what little knowledge we had between us. Tim and I had written and recorded together for years so every once and a while I'd hear him mention things like, "Double tracking each instrument to make it sound fuller." Or "If you play with the Les Paul, do a second guitar track with the tele-caster." And also "Apply the EQ to get some clarity." It all amounted to the last song I'll ever record. Oh, that's right, I didn't get to mention my decision about what to do with everything involving Tim. I am throwing in the towel after I releasing this one EP. I am going to make this a tribute to Tim and put it out under the alias "Panic Under Pressure" to be sure work doesn't find out.

I liked the way the song had come out, I have to say. I even showed it to Ang and she thought Tim had done it himself, so that was a good sign, right? Even though we all know I'm not continuing on after this, I want it to be right. God forbid I ever have kids, they can hear it so they know their dad doesn't totally suck. He is actually pretty tolerable. Ang and I ended up getting together to decide which of all the songs sounded the best. Even though there were some good contenders, "It's All Over," "No Pressure," "Oh Brother," the new one for Tim, "Long Long Gone," came out the strongest. I guess we burn brightest near the end and want to show we did our best when the inevitable end is coming. Whatever the case, if this was what I was left with at the end of the day knowing I could do no more, then I would be satisfied with what I have.

I'd written the best I could for myself, Tim, and Jackie. I'd been unhappy with life before and I guessed this was the highest note I can go out on. I wished I had my friend to see it end with me, but what can you do? That's life, unfortunately. Sometimes those who stick by us through the worst won't get to see the end result. It's an awful feeling, but it happens. Tim had told me he was proud of what we were making at the end. So in hindsight, how can any review hold up to that?

About a week after we got everything mastered by a few of Tim's old associates, I got a call from an unknown number. I answered and instantly thought I was either on a game show or that the other person was mentally ill. I picked up the phone and heard, "Hello, Doug. This is Champ Beats with Management Unlimited. How the Hell are you?" I damn near gave my own phone a stink face. "I'm fine, sir. How are you?"

"Well, I'm quite fantastic after hearing this EP of yours." Now I was mad. It wasn't supposed to be given to anyone outside of myself or Jackie.

"Excuse me. Those songs are not for release."

"No, I'm not releasing them, sir. I'm here to represent you."

This was really bizarre, although not unlike the luck that I usually have when it comes to life decisions. I would get out, and they would pull me in. "Mister, um, Beats? Is it? How did you hear these songs?"

"Well your friend Jackie was holding onto them and I listened to the mastered tracks on her computer. I'm her manager, you see."

"Sir, I haven't even heard the masters. I can't help but feel this is a complete violation of my privacy."

"Well, don't get so upset sport. You'll be rich and famous with these songs. I can guarantee that."

"I don't want to be rich and famous, these songs were made for my release and on my terms. The answer is no. Piss off."

Managers and people who do the representing in this industry are notorious for going too far, making promises they have no intentions of keeping, and ripping people off. I have zero trust in someone who has no respect after hearing "no," and continuing on anyway. Fucking pigs.

And just as expected, it wasn't the last I heard of him. I got a call two hours later from him to sign a 360 deal. I immediately shot him down. Two hours after that, I was asked to sing on another song with Jackie under my real name to keep with the hype of "I'm at War."

"Forget it. Go away. If it's not on my terms, I'm not doing shit. Goodbye." Four hours after that, he went for broke. "Alright, kid, what do you really want? Nobody makes music like this because they're bored. They must have something in it for them." Wow, now he had caught my ear. Besides the big "fuck you" I would inevitably give him before the call ended, I did have one request before I packed it all in. I wanted to do one show at the biggest theater in town, the Roundhouse. It's a 2000 seater that only national acts get to play. No locals allowed ever. I would have loved to play that with the songs on this record there, plus a few with Jackie, and a cover or two of mine and Tom's favorite songs. After that, I would be gone. I said that to him and he said he would give me a callback.

The next day I did my routine and headed home from my last final I'll ever take. I walked out to my car and heard my phone ring. I picked up the phone and said: "What's up Champ?" "You'll be playing the Roundhouse in two months. Enough time to finish your obligations and certification exams, then play this one last show, Sparky." I dropped my phone and then a load into my pants. Holy shit, this is it, folks. I picked it back up.

"They're willing to book me without a record out?"

"I sent them the masters and they liked what—"

"You sent them the fucking masters without my permission, little fuck?" I told you, they do one good thing and expect the hundred other bad things to go away. He tried to defend himself with, "Hey, I'm just doing your friend Jackie a favor here, buddy. Don't get mad at me. This is mostly for her benefit, not yours."

"Oh, yeah? Well, fuck you, Champ. Find someone else." Not five minutes later I get a call from Jackie. "What the hell are you doing?"

"Jackie, he's being a dick and not listening to me."

"Doug, he said you called him the c-word and you never want to work with me again. Is that true?"

Lying sack of shit, wasn't he? "Jackie, I'll work with you until my days are done, I told him to fuck himself because he sent my masters that are not copyrighted out to different people." "Yeah, that sounds like him. Sorry, Doug, I'll make it right."

As I sat outside with Mister Bruce I got another call. "Dougie, baby, still want to do that show?" I deeply exhaled, "Champ, I will do the show on one condition."

"Name it, buddy. We'll add it to your rider."

"No, Champ. It's a contract negotiation. I will only do the show if I never hear from you about being in this business again. I'm doing this show to go out on a high note. If you hear from me, it will be about writing under my alias for Jackie or for someone else. I will not perform or record my own music again. I'm doing my set the way I want to, with people I audition. You have no say or hand in what I do." Champ might as well have put me on silent. "Yeah, we can get that last minute. No problem." So after I re-explained my conditions, three times over, we came to agreeable terms. I would only deal with him for the release of this one EP, this show, and then I would be gone.

Running everything past Mom and Dad went over rocky at the start, but in the end, they realized this was an opportunity I couldn't pass up. To play this theater was a dream come true. The modicum of success I would be achieving was better than I thought I'd ever actually see come to fruition. The only problem is I couldn't talk about it to anyone I met in the future. I couldn't risk my job over it. But I also couldn't turn my back on a lifelong obsession and not be sure I had conquered everything I set out to. So if anyone ever talked about how good Jackie's show was, the mystery opening act would remain that: just a complete mystery, but a badass one at that.

Things started going well with the plans for the show, but the EP release was a nightmare. Champ wanted to release it on Jackie's label, but I wanted to be as anonymous as possible. I didn't want to be put up on billboards, commercials, or anything like that. I just wanted to put it on various streaming services and be done with it. Let people find it and have it as their indie thing that only they knew about. Then over time, have people find each other and let it be something to connect over. Though that stuff sounds well and nice, Champ thought it would be best for him to buy it outright and have all the control over the songs and the masters. To which, I'd rather spit in his morning coffee than give into him.

He saw the ideas about my album art and just said, "No, no, no. That's not the right direction for you."

"Hey, Champ, you don't own any of it, so keep your mouth shut."

"Yes, Dougie, but my artist is associated with you."

"Your artist's biggest hit is because of me so I'm pretty sure my direction is doing just fine. Get fucked." I don't do well with being told what to do. Never have, never will. My idea for the artwork was very simple. There's this picture I have of Tim's studio all full with his gear after we had cleaned it top to bottom. Then a picture of the room the last day we were there; all empty and bare. It showed how I was full of all the spirit of music, and now I'm just not there anymore. Along with it, on the back was going to be an explanation of the EP and who it was for. I thought it was great for the direction of my life and the fact that this was a one-time effort. Obviously, Champ thought of something original: me sitting in a diner with a guitar. Oh wow, breathtaking, isn't it? I told him we don't want to do it, so he sent his print ahead to get EP's made. I saw the test printing while I was in their office discussing what we wanted to do for the show. I crucified him for that and told him that if he made another adjustment without my consent, I'd drag him to the lobby and beat his ass in front of his clients. A month before the show I got a call from Champ: "How would you like your songs on the radio?" Now we're talking, but of course, my rules or nothing.

"I pick what gets played and you're not in the building."

"Done. You have to be in Chicago in three days to be at the station for the interview." Well, road trip time.

14

Sweet Home Chicago

I tell Ang the news about the radio interview and she really is skeptical of the idea at first. We had a talk about pulling out of music and sticking to only writing under my stage name. However here I am moving forward advertising the music. After we talk it over, we agreed that playing one of our songs on the radio is a chance that neither of us would pass up. And after I agreed that we can stop off at the Rock and Roll Hall of Fame in Cleveland, it is all systems go.

From Long Island to Chicago is a 12-hour drive, so this whole conversation happens mere moments after I get off the phone with dickhead. Figuring that we leave in a couple of hours after we pack, we can pull off in Ohio, see the rock hall the next morning, finish the drive that evening as we pull into Chicago, get some dinner and sleep, then do the interview the next morning. And aren't I just the best boyfriend in the world to spring this all on her in just five minutes? But as luck rarely so has it with me, everything works out and we are on our way. Anyone else thinks this sounds fishy to you, too? A born skeptic like myself is on pins and needles saying, "This is way too good to be true. Something is bound to happen."

So I'm told by Champ that the radio station is a big-time Chicago station that focuses on an artist for a couple of minutes, asks them a few questions, plays the single, and then I'm out the door. Let's see how much of this is true by the time we arrive there. Well, we are not even off Long Island before Ang has done some research and found out it's not a radio station, it's a podcast. Though they are few and far between, podcasts are usually hours long and play very little of the music. Immediately Ang gets on my case with "I knew he'd lie to you, I don't know why we're doing this, if you keep this up after the show, I'm gone." And she's right, I have jumped the gun again. I trusted someone I shouldn't have trusted. "Ang, if you want me to turn back, I will. But let's just call the podcaster and ask if he'll play the music. If he's not playing the music there's no real reason for me to be there." So she doesn't let me call, she calls for me. What a woman. "Hello, is this the 'Nonsense at Noon' podcast?" I can't hear what the poor guy on the other end of the line was saying. Kind of just sounds like the teachers from Charlie Brown. "Yes, hi, this is Angela Bryson from Panic Under Pressure's management. How are you today? I'm good, thank you. Now, I had heard this is a podcast, not a radio station, correct? No there's nothing wrong with that at all, in fact, we prefer them over many stations. We were just told that it was a radio station so we were under the impression his songs were being played. Can you tell me if you guys do that?"

God damn does she do this in her spare time in secret? Or is she a call girl because I'm…sorry, back to Ang.

"You don't play songs on the show. Yes, I understand." I start to put my blinker on to go to an exit ramp and turn around when she pushes my wheel back to the lane and tells me to keep going. "Now, is there any way you can play the songs and then discuss them on the podcast?" I understand it's not something you do but we have several other artists lined up who we'd like to put on the podcast if that becomes an option, including Jackie Ill. Yes, she's a good friend of ours. Sometimes a little too close." She bashes my knee with the side of her fist giving me a big hint. "The thing is, we're coming a long way for the show and the trip is beneficial to us if the songs were played. You understand, don't you?" There was a long pause until I heard, "Fantastic, we'll be at the studio in two days' time. Would anyone like coffee? Great, we'll bring some. Have a nice day!" She hangs up the phone and says, "The coffee is for in case they want you back."

It doesn't take long for me to utter, "Babe, I know we're pressed for time but I'm so willing to pull over for a quickie. You turned me on so much." She smiles but then it quickly turns to, "That's what happens when you use the people who love you to help you."

"Babe, what do you mean?"

"I understand how Tim dying got you in a daze, but with this Champ guy, you hardly pay attention to me or your parents." Oh boy, here comes the lecture.

"I get that you love this and I get this is all you've ever wanted, but why are you trying so hard for something you're just going to give up and let be the past? Put your efforts toward something you know will last forever and be important to you. Like school or your girlfriend. If this was what you wanted forever then fine, I'd get it, but if it's not what you want, after these obligations you have to let it go."

I say it over once in my head to be sure I don't say something stupid. "I know we both love music the same amount and we love to relate, but this is the one thing I want to accomplish in life, hell, the only thing that I've ever cared about. I just want to make my mark. Even if it's such a small mark it goes largely unnoticed. Haven't you ever wanted something so bad enough and now you're on the cusp of making it a reality?" She sits on her legs and says something that knocks me dead. "Yeah and now I have it, you. I've wanted someone to love and care about me above anything else, and until these opportunities came up you've shown it to me. Have I been showing you the same amount of love?"

"Ang you know you have-"

"Then why am I background noise? I'm right here, right in front of you. Willing to show you all the love you could ever get from entertaining people who will move on from you. Why can't I be enough?"

Goddammit if that didn't make me feel as low as Chris does. "Ang, you're absolutely right. You are enough and you're all I need. I swear on all things art, that after this podcast and the show at the theater, I'm done. I'll walk away. I will only write for others. Not go out on my own, because you're all I want for my own." She puts her hands on mine, kissed my cheek, and we just sit in the moment of love and affection we have for each other. Why bother getting the approval of others when you got it from the only person that matters? It never clicked like that for me before. Now, I'll never forget it.

That all happens as we are leaving New York. After a bunch of twists and turns and tickets to take for pay roads, we get on the expressway and head west, west, and west some more. Now back in the day with Chris, we'd make mix CD's to take in and out of the CD player. Since those days are over, Ang and I pass the aux cord around for our playlists from Spotify that we both already have. Needless to say our taste in music is the same, but bizarre, and jumps around more than House of Pain. We started with some Slipknot since it's our band as a couple, I have already said we're odd. Then we jump to The Beatles, Incubus, John Coltrane, Underoath, and Talib Kwelli. After a while, we got to Warren Zevon, mom's favorite. She turns on his song "Keep Me in Your Heart For a While," and then this conversation comes up.

"I'm really excited to see the Rock and Roll Hall of Fame, but I'm also a little pissed off at how many people you'd think are in it, but aren't." "What do you mean?" Ang asks. "Well," I say, "Warren Zevon, a songwriter like no other, at this point of 2019, is not in the Hall. There's a staggering number of people who aren't in it who should be."

"Like who?"

"Well, just off the top of my head, Warren Zevon, John Coltrane, Judas Priest, Iron Maiden, and Motorhead." Ang is drinking water at this time so I have to say, I'm pretty proud to have been able to get her to do a spit take.

"What the actual fuck? The people who helped shape most of what is considered the foundations of modern rock music and songwriting today aren't in? Why the fuck are we going, then?"

She has a valid point, but then again I also want to at least stop by it. "I have an idea, let's go stop by, then stand in front and take a picture of us flipping it off."

"Yeah, let's do that!" Ang is bouncing in her seat like I just told her we can go get ice cream. We are still trekking through Pennsylvania so we have quite a way ahead. On the way we bounce around on our playlists, play car games—to which I lost everyone on purpose in order to be a gentleman—and even attempted to drive with my feet. It is a success up until a state trooper almost pulls me over. Not for driving with my feet but because of the stench coming off them. Kidding of course; on why he pulled me over. My feet are still putrid, mind you.

We pull into Cleveland around five pm so it's only open for another half hour anyway. We pull over and park illegally for only a couple minutes, get out, and had a stranger take a picture of the two of us flipping off the museum. We're so classy I don't know how we do it. Champ has told me because of the mix-up, dinner is on him when we get to Cleveland as long as it isn't too expensive. So I take Ang to the most expensive restaurant in town, order two lobsters, which I ate none of, as a big "fuck you" to Champ, order a bottle of champagne for each of us—and I pour mine down the drain since I'm still sober—and tip the waitress the bill. Don't fuck with me and make my girlfriend have to do your job, bud.

We go to bed and wake up pretty early, and have more or less the same road trip activities all the way into Chicago. It feels pretty cool to see the Chicago city limits sign while Ang blasts "Sweet Home Chicago" by Eric Clapton. We pull into the hotel, get some lunch, went to some local venue to see some live music, then go to bed, all the while realizing Ang was right, I don't need the audience anymore. I'm grateful for them, but I'm putting on the biggest show of my life being around her.

15

Nonsense at Noon

So the Nonsense at Noon podcast is run by two chuckleheads named Johnny and Ronnie, both of which are music junkies like Ang and me, although, they are both two slacker-stoners who run this podcast out of their home. They live to not work. The fact that this podcast is as successful as it is shocking even to them. They're really my kind of guys, particularly since they weren't happy when Champ called after Ang demanding to know why they listened to her and not him. Their response was perfect to me, "She offered to buy us coffee, brahhh," which we have remembered, and have even brought in doughnuts. They were already stoned when we walked in so it was like Ang had walked in holding a piece of God Himself. Made it all the better that she walked in through a cloud of smoke so it was kind of like her finishing a long race emerging the champion.

"Alright, so are you Mr. Panic Under Pressure?" says Ronnie through a mouthful of Boston cream. "That's me, man, just call me Doug when we're off the air." "Informal, I like it." says Johnny exhaling from his cock-shaped bowl. "Look, man, Johnny's smoking from your manager: a dick." I roar with laughter, goddamn if that hasn't made the trip worth it, I don't know what else will. "So, bro, if you want to be on the podcast you gotta spark up with us." And here lies the dilemma. I haven't smoked weed in four years. I have to start applying for jobs in a couple of weeks, but I have to be on this podcast or else I can get in serious trouble with management. I look over to Ang and we have the same look on our faces. We have a telepathic conference and after several seconds of stares, she shrugs her shoulders and says, "You heard the man, take a load from the dick bowl." Ronnie falls out of his chair laughing so hard. "Yo, I never thought of that. Holy shit, it's like I've been swallowing . . . hey, does that make me gay now?" Stoned people are really a trip. I spark up and cough until my lungs turn green. Here we go.

They pass the bowl over to Ang, "Mrs. Panic, will you be joining us today?" She didn't even say a word. Just took it, sparked up, and took a bigger hit than I ever have—even in my time of smoking—I really ought to consider how much three months of my salary is.

The boys set up the mics, mix the sound and hit record. "Hello, everyone, and welcome back to Nonsense at Noon. It's your hosts Johnny and Ronnie and we're here with someone all the way from New York." Johnny starts out strong then continues. "They here from New Yahk, prick. Hey, I'm walkin' here!"

"Johnny, he may be walkin' here but, man, he ought to be playing here. I gotta say I love this EP we got from him. He's here in the Nonsense Podsense studio with his Mrs. and better half. We got Panic Under Pressure here. How are you today, sir?"

"I'm doing great, boys, I just walked in off the street from my favorite pizza joint after catchin' a Yankee game. Hey, how ya doin'?"

"Johnny, he gets it!" Ronnie says putting his hands in the air like he has scored a touchdown at the football stadium for either of the New York teams, neither of which are located in New York. "In all seriousness, sir, I love these songs you got for us today, but we're kind of bummed this is the only collection of songs you plan on putting out yourself. Is that true?"

"Yes, sir. I'm afraid it is. Nothing against performing but I'm just more of a writer. I'd rather write songs for others to perform. These are the only songs I felt like I wanted to release myself and showcase my talent. After this, it's peace out for Panic."

"Well if that is true I'm happy to say that you'll put out something I'll probably have in my headphones for the next couple of weeks, if not the rest of the year." My heart is doing backflips.

"Now, Mrs. Panic, how do you feel about him doing only the one-time deal? Would you ever want to see him do more, or is it the right thing for him to do?" Ang picks her leg up and folds her arms. "I think he's truly the best writer I've ever met, but he's an even better person. I'm standing behind whatever decision he makes but I think this is the right idea. Good things should have expiration dates, not dolled out until it starts to suck." Yup, I'm finding this woman a white dress. Ronnie lays back in his chair like he has just had his mind blown. "That is a valid point. It's always annoying when you know the party is ending and there are still people eating chips at the bottom of the bowl. It's like, go home, get out of here."

"I feel personally attacked. Why do I?" Johnny asks in an accusing voice. "Because you always do that, bro. You always end up with the bowl on your face licking the bottom cuz you want all of it."

"Only on the lime-coated chips. That shit is the bomb, bitch. Anyway, we're gonna go track by track on what each song is about and how they came about, but before that, are you happy with the way the record came out?"

"I'm very happy with it, yeah. I love the feel and the flow of it. The production is top-notch to my ears and I can't wait to put it out once all the artwork is together and ready for release."

"Yeah, man, I'm sorry to hear about the producer passing away. What was his name?" I take a deep breath. It's still hard to talk about.

"Tim Fallon, yeah. He was a dear friend of mine. The EP is dedicated to him. We had some great times over the years but making this was just the utmost peak of our creative integrity together and making music without him seems kind of weird. The last song is about the incident. Hit by a 90-year-old man with dementia while Tim was on his motorcycle." Johnny choked on his dick bowl.

"What the fuck man. That just killed my vibe."

"Crap, I'm sorry, haha. No, it's obviously sad but I'm just happy for the time I had with him. We found out a lot about ourselves writing and producing together so to finish it in his honor just seemed like the right thing to do."

"Johnny, I'm tearing up at this shit. Start playing the songs, goddammit."

"Boys, I swear to God I'm not this depressing off the air! Just saying the truth."

Johnny looks at me and says, "Never apologize for the truth, brother. Respect, man, respect."

They pull up a playlist with all four songs on it. Seeing it up on their monitor was pretty cool. The songs that were just ideas in my head are now talking points for us to fuck around with and deconstruct. Life is good. They start with "It's All Over." They hit play and it runs for the whole 3:43. "Boy, did that one sound like you were anxious."

"Haha, a little bit, man."

"Ronnie hasn't been that anxious since he earned his nickname 'leaky dick'."

"Fuck you, dude. Don't talk about your sister like that." Johnny throws a pillow at him and misses by a country mile. They're podcasters, not athletes. "So how did that song come together? What happened to make that one fall out of your noodle and onto the page."

"Well, to be honest, guys, my noodle is not usually working, but when it does it makes shit like that. That song actually came about the day I met Mrs. Panic. Literally about three hours after I met her on the way home from class it started churning, but really came out when I went down to my basement and started jamming." Ang looked at me with her why-didn't-you-tell-me-that face. "I swear, I met this young lady while at school and she dropped a book on my head. So I guess you can say she made it fall out. Right, babe?" They both laughed like hyenas while Ang was blushing. "It slipped out while I was air-drumming—you know that!"

"Whoa, whoa, a babe who air drums? Do you have a sister?"

"Piss off, Ronnie. That's my Mrs. Panic."

"You right, you right. But what did it end up being about, because it seemed like you were uptight over something"

"I was very uptight, yes, you could say that. I had met the young lady and on the way home I was freaking out about how this girl seemed like she was the one for me, but I was thinking back at all my other failed relationships. Between the month-long shitty relationships, the booty callers, and the ex-fiancee' I was sitting in my car on edge going 'I can't do this.' So I went to the basement, came up with the riff, and thought about why I was freaking out and how I could get over it. I came to the conclusion that I had got to be confident that this would be better, and whoever was in my past would not see the great person I would become and they'd have to eat my dust as I strode far ahead of them."

Ronnie doles out a high five. "That's what it's all about, brother. Put the past behind you and keep on trucking. Rock on, sir. Mrs. P, how do you feel now knowing the song is a reaction to your early connection?"

Through ugly tears she says, "IT FEELS GREAT JUST PLAY THE NEXT SONG!"

"Whoa, yes ma'am." They load up "No Pressure" and play all through the 3:52 run time.

"I have to say I think that one is my favorite," Johnny says sparking up and exhaling into the microphone. "I love the opening and how simple it starts then goes into this fucker of a song."

"Yeah, but what were you drinking to get that fucked up?"

"What wasn't I drinking? That's the real question. This was all about one bad evening where we were at a . . . um." I have to pick my words carefully so I don't say "work party." "I was at a family party with Mrs. P and I made an ass out of myself. So much so I got sober, actually."

"What did you do to Mrs. P?"

"Ronnie, it's okay, we're fine. But no, he made an ass and a hole out of himself. He got so drunk he was falling, belching, and disrobing all over the place. He was so bad I left him at the hotel the party was at and told him to stay in the room until tomorrow morning."

"Hence why roll me over, I'm not sober and so on and so forth. The part where I'm saying "There is no pressure here just want you to know, these are the stories that I've been told," was me hearing how much of an asshole I was the next day. I had to calm down after I recounted my shenanigans and got a hold of myself. It's a song I wanted the message to be right with, but at the same time have something instrumental that sounded interesting. Not just four chords, but do something funky with the pedals. So I used a loop pedal and just overdubbed everything."

"Overdub is what we call my fat sister after she passes out from edibles." "He ain't lying, guys. John's sister eats edibles like they're....like edible." Goddamn, these guys are fucked up.

Next, they cued up "Oh Brother," Chris's song with a 2:40 run time. "Before we play this song, Johnny, this is the one that made you cry."

"Holy shit! You cried at my song, man? I'm honored!" Ang rubs his arms with sarcastic support. "Does Johnny want to cry some more?" Johnny actually wipes tears from his eyes and says "I love my brother too, man, why are we all crying on this podcast what the fuck."

"Hey, only half of us half, sir. You and Mrs. P. stick to yourselves while us men go chop down trees and make fire from scratch. But, yeah, man obviously with this song you love your brother, but was there something that sparked this song? Like did something happen or was it just built-up feelings you needed to get out?"

"I wrote this after my brother and I had a pseudo-argument about how lucky the other one is in comparison to the other.

We both apologized mere moments after it happened, but it did start as an argument. I still live at home with my parents working on life and he's a full-licensed doctor in an emergency room out on Long Island."

"Yeah, I already feel like shit compared to your brother."

"Nah man, he'd be flat-out be jealous of you guys. You make money doing something you love. By smoking weed and talking a blue streak about pussy and music no less. He's dealing with the worst kind of shit you can see. And he has to do it with a smile on his face."

"Hold the phone, dude. Ronnie. I never tell you enough how much I love you and appreciate what you've helped me do here, man. I love you for it." Ronnie starts to sniffle and hold back a tear.

"Got you, bitch!," yells not Johnny, but my own girlfriend. The woman is nuts, folks, chocolate-coated and nuts. "Are you two finished enough to let me finish?" Ronnie sniffles back but gives a hand gesture that I take as meaning "go for it."

"So, he always has to be in the absolute worst kind of humanity at all times with no sign of it ever getting better. He works his ass off making sure other people get fixed, and then there are people screaming at him that he's not doing enough. Like that shit always bothers me. This guy worked his bones to the dust to get to where he is. When he was an undergrad, he worked two jobs to be sure he, and the family, were getting by, all the while studying to take the MCATS—the test you take to get into medical school. After he got in, with damn near top marks, he went to medical school and took every opportunity to get better at his craft. If he was up 16 hours a day, he was studying at least eight of them. Stopping only for food, bathroom, or to go to class. He got the residency he wanted, too. A dual residency, meaning he does internal medicine and emergency medicine at the same time, all the while managing a girlfriend and being blinded by student loan debt. The world gave him no quarter, and he asked for no quarter. The least someone could do is write a song telling him "I'll handle our parents, I got it from here, all your hard work will pay off in time."

"Can you all please hold yourselves together?" As the entire room is sobbing at the thought of "I love my brother, here's his song."

They finally hit "play" on the fucking song and it runs out with no interruptions, but we stall going into the next one so everyone can dab their eyes with tissues and blow their nose. Maybe I'm all cried out from Tim, but, common people it's not a movie about a dog. Suck it up.

"Hoooo, I haven't cried that much since I watched Brian's Song." "I don't want to hear it, nah-nah-nah'" I say putting my fingers in my ears. The two jackasses smirked.

"Oh, you don't like Brian's Song do you?" My hands are now covering my ears. "I'm not listening." But of course, these two pull up the end of the flick, the ultimate guy-cry experience. When Billy D. Williams's character says, "I'd like to say a few words about a friend of mine named Brian Piccolo." My head falls into my knees as these fucks start chanting, "Cry! cry! cry!" When the scene ends with "I'd like all of you to love him, too," poor Ang is sitting there watching, saying "I've never seen this and now I never will turn it off!" At least they listen to her.

"Now obviously we touched on the last song a little bit already, and going from that movie to this is kind of fucked-up, but let's dive deep on this. You told us about the circumstances surrounding his death, but when it comes to your Brian Piccolo, Tim, is there anything you'd like to say before we start the last song?" Now I am going to start crying. "In all honesty, if I had anything else to say it would just be 'I love you, buddy, thank you for helping me find my voice.' Play the song, please."

He cues it up with the run time of 3:29 and let it run. It finishes and respectfully the boys raised these shot glasses full of God knows what, and say, "Rest in peace, Tim Fallon, you did good." They slam them down the hatch, put them upside down, and flicker their faces. Not big drinkers, I see. We keep talking on the podcast for another two hours after that. We talk about shitty movies, a smidge of politics, and what we could do to clone Ang.

"Now, before we get you two out of here, we got to mention this show you have coming up at the Roundhouse in Long Island." I hold up my hand, "First I got to say thank you for having us, gentleman, I know we've taken up plenty of your time, but you're class acts and I appreciate you both." Ronnie gives me a big hug and says into my microphone, you two can come back anytime, podcast or not. Just don't bring that lick bag of a manager."

"Oh! Sick burn, Ron. But yes, Panic Under Pressure will be opening up for Jackie Ill at the Roundhouse Theater on Long Island. On, in, which is it? You being locals and all." We both say "on" at the same time. Goddamn, it's frustrating when people get it wrong. "Sorry, but yes, buy tickets to the Round-house on Long Island to see this awesome show with a lineup of more to come." Every time someone mentioned Round-house Theater, Ang gave them a swift roundhouse kick as a sort of punctuation mark. "This is the Nonsense at Noon podcast and as always I'm Johnny." He gestures to Ron. "I'm Ronnie." Johnny continues, "Keep your Nonsense Podsense with you at all times and remember, don't Panic Under Pressure."

They lower the faders and stay silent for five minutes. I have no idea talking so much would be so draining. Afterward, we decide not to go out to dinner, but to hang out with the boys at their house, get in their hot tub, order some pizzas and have a chill night. We get an Uber back to the hotel later and after we have taken our showers and lain in bed, we are burnt the fuck out, man. We are as crispy as a mother fucker. Nevertheless, my good lady gave me a kiss goodnight and said: "I'm glad we came."

"Really?" I say, knowing she means every word.

"Yeah, it was fun playing hooky from responsibility for a while." We both rolled over and started to fall asleep. Mission accomplished. All that's left is my crippling anxiety about whether this is the right move or not. But hey, don't panic under pressure.

16

Meet the Band

We wake up the next morning and life couldn't be better. I am in Chicago, one of the most important cities in the country for art and culture, with the girl of my dreams, who I love more and more each day, with a job in education. I love my life. I really do. I roll over and give Ang a kiss on the forehead, smell her nasty morning breath that I've grown to love, get up and hop in the shower. I can't help but notice though, in the shower with me is a tight grip around my waist. It's hugging me and giving me kisses on my back. Could it be? But it is! It's Ang coming in the shower with me. Hold on, I have to do something quickly.

Sorry, she had this itch she needed to be scratched. She hops out and goes back to sleep so I go down for some coffee and breakfast from the buffet to bring back to the room. On the way out from the buffet, I couldn't help but overhear the hotel clerk's phone playing the podcast. The boys must have done only quick edits and put it up overnight. Now realizing it's 12:15 and they put it up at noon. Goddamn, I sound funny, and the songs sound great. Can I keep this high forever?

We get dressed, get our bags and go downstairs. On the way out I can't help but tell the hotel clerk, "Hey, you know those guests on Nonsense at Noon? That's me and my girlfriend." He must be a huge fan because he has glassy eyes and starts tearing up saying, "That shit was awesome, yo." I guess the fans of the boys live similar lives. The ride home was more of the same—us being our goofy selves. Until Ang says, "Are you sure it's a good idea to back out of this music thing?" I mean it to be bad because I am thinking the same thing. "Ang I don't know anymore. Yesterday was so much fun, wasn't it?"

"Doug, imagine a life lived like that. Just living in the moment and having fun with people doing nothing but being silly. I know we're really good at our jobs, but this could be a career that makes us happy. You doing your thing and me being there by your side to help if you need it."

"Ang, I'd be there for you too. This is a partnership, not my enterprise." She gave me a big kiss for that. "Good, you've been listening. But in all seriousness, now I see why you chase this life. It's so much fun." I keep my eyes straight ahead after that. "How about we take a week and think about it."

We don't stop off in Ohio this time. We drive straight through, so we get home around one o'clock in the morning. I pull into the driveway to see Mom jumping up and down and Bruce wagging his tail. We get out and give her a hug. "Did you hear the podcast?" She looks at me with confusion then realized what I meant.

"No, sweetheart. I don't know what a podcast is. I checked your student portal and you aced everything. You're a certified teacher!" I felt elated. Far more elated than I ever felt in my life. Ang jumps on me and gave me a big hug. She runs inside and checks her online portal and sure enough, she has aced everything too. We are a teacher and a nurse. The whole world is in front of us on two fronts. And now, the sudden panic sets in. Mom lets Ang stay the night because she knows we have a lot to discuss the next morning and doesn't want to waste any time.

We wake up to sheer horror as I have a sore back and she is cranky pre-coffee. We go out to the porch and talk about everything. We know we want each other, but what do we do to support ourselves? The decision becomes much clearer after I get this voicemail: "Hey, Doug, it's Champ. Give me a call about paying for the trip." I am red from anger. I call him in my usual way. "What the fuck do you mean—pay for the trip?"

"Hey, Doug, good to hear from you. Well, you see, the trip wasn't free. You have to pay for the room, business support, and the bill from any use of the credit card I gave you."

"You told me it was on you, shrimp dick!"

"Well, for the moment it was, but then you have to pay me back. This music business costs money, Doug. I don't know if anyone ever told you that."

"Why the fuck would you offer to pay if it would just be on my dime, anyway?"

"Well, we didn't want to have you worry at the time. The total bill for the trip is about $2485.89 but we can put it on a payment plan if you want." The phone slips out of my hand but Ang catches it. She strokes my arm with a face of "Let me handle it." I let her do it.

After quite an argument, she comes back and says, "Because you're not signing with the label you're going to have to pay it. They also said that since you don't have that money, they're just going to take it from your pay from the show. Which was only about $500.00 so we'll still owe a little under $2000. Baby, I'm so sorry. If I knew—"

I'd never take this out on Ang; I'm just going to have to pay it. Whatever it takes, I'm never going to sign with him. I've dealt with some annoying-ass students, but if I had to work in an industry full of people like Champ, who leave out the truth just to make a profit on your back, then I'll be happy to never go into this business. Jesus, I need a drink. I'm not going to, relax.

"Ang, we'll pay it off. I have the money in my savings. It's not a big deal." She gives me a stink face and says, "Where the hell do you have money between going out and the money you make now?" I guess I have to spill the beans here. I returned Annie's engagement ring and got half the money back. I was saving up to buy Ang one, but I guess that'll have to wait. It's only been just shy of six months, but I know I have found my best friend for life. After I tell her, she drops to the floor in tears, so, I consoled her, and tried to comfort her.

"Honey, it's fine. It's just money. I'll make more." "It's not that, I'm just so happy you started saving up for one. I love you so much." I thought yesterday was a good morning. This one, I'll always remember.

Later in the day, Ang goes home to rest and celebrate her passing with her parents so I have some time to get my act together with putting out applications and making a few calls. As luck has it, I get a call from Max, the principal of my school. I let it go to voicemail because I have no desire to talk to anyone today. "Hey, man, congratulations on passing. I'm pushing your application through for next year. We'll figure out your subject closer to that time, but you have a job. Welcome to the big leagues." Jesus Christ, life is good.

As that message ends, I get a text from Jackie. "Hey, sorry about Champ. He's a dick, but business is business. Let me know if I can help." I shoot her a text back.

"Yeah, he's a dick, but I get it. I wish he'd been upfront about it because I wouldn't have gone at all. Guess that's what you have to do to keep the product going." She responded with, "Yeah it sucks to suck. But look on the bright side, tomorrow you're auditioning players for the live show!" Someone needs to fucking call me with this shit. "Is this your way of giving me a heads up?"

"I guess so. They said they shot you an email."

"Jackie, they don't have my email. I refused to give it to them."

"Well, be at the business office tomorrow. There's a studio in the basement for you to audition and interview the players. Want me to be there?" Though I'd really love her to, I think Ang might cut my throat if I did.

"Nah, I'm good. Thanks though, bud." I let Ang know, of course. I get a bone for good behavior. And I'm not talking about Bruce's bones if you know what I—moving on, sorry.

I pull up to the studio, take out two guitars, the pedalboard and amp, and a dolly to move it all with. I bungee cord them to it and head in. Ang follows behind me on her phone, taking pictures since she's never been to anything like this before. "It's like going to camp!" At least she's excited. I've never been more nervous. These aren't my guys. I've played with Tim for the last five years, what if none of them click? Well, only one way to find out. I set up and plugin like I've done a thousand times. It might actually be a thousand times come to think of it. And I wait for the first guy. Here goes nothing.

We cut the auditions into three days. Day one drummers, day two bass, day three lead guitar. Each person brings in their own stuff except the drummers. For drums, we have all the hardware like bass drums, floor toms, but they bring in their own cymbals and snare drum. They have all been given a copy of the EP to learn the songs along with a couple of covers they think would sound pretty cool, if I do. They chose "Simple Man" by Lynard Skynard, "45" by Shinedown, "Use Somebody" by Kings of Leon and "Show Me How to Live" by Audioslave. I can sing loud as a mother fucker. We start out with the originals and then move into the covers. The first drummer comes in and is nice enough, but every time he gets into it, he keeps jumping up too high and missing his crash cymbal. It's kind of important to stay in time and, you know, hit things as a drummer. The second guy is pretty good but has not practiced the covers. So half the songs he doesn't know. Great. The third dude comes in and tears it up, though. He doesn't really speak so I am interested in what'll happen in the interview.

We sit down to talk, and after I say, "Hey, man, you tore it up. Sweet job," he cracks his fingers, twists his neck, spits on the floor and says "Alright, so who's paying me?"

"Excuse me?"

"Listen, man, I know I played the songs better than anyone else who came in so let me tell you how this works. I get paid upfront with no hassle or I don't play. I know this is just one gig and is fun and games to you, but this is my trade and stock, okay? I'm a professional and this is my job. So unless you have anything else for me I'll be seeing you." He gets up and leaves behind the drums for someone from his little entourage to clean up. I don't get up from my chair because I'm in shock to think that anyone would speak to another person like that. Ang, however, almost breaks the door down in the control room to beat his fucking ass. That lovely lad is Jason, and is my drummer for hire for one show, if he survives my girlfriend.

Day two: bass players. The lovely Jason returns to help with the auditions, holstered only by the promise of a hundred dollars and coffee brought to him every time his cup is empty. Bass players can be a tricky lot. I've noticed bass players can be really good, or flat out suck. Players one, three, four, five, and six are really great players. Two and seven are atrocious. Two decides to dress up like he belongs on the sunset strip in the eighties and only plays the root note of what I am playing instead of the real bass parts. Seven outright doesn't know how to play without spinning and losing his chord. We found the ace in the hole in Maggie, player number eight. She knows all her parts, but is really fun and bubbly to be around. All smiles and positivity. She interviews really well, too. After we put our instruments down, she starts in on her pitch. "Okay, so what do I have to do to be sure this isn't the only EP you put out?" I started giggling, "I'm sorry, dear. This is a one-time thing."

"It's really fun to play, though! It's simple but the parts to be played are the perfect fit. The bass is like Goldilocks, not too much, not too little, but just right."

"Well thank you, Maggie. I appreciate it. Mind if I ask your experience level?"

"I've played bass for about five years and I play in a cover band called Speakeasy. We play at a lot of cosplay events and last year we played Comic-con." I'm impressed, I didn't even know live music was at Comic-con.

"Where at the con did you play?"

"Oh, well, if there's the center of Comic-con, we were nowhere near it. We were in a bar about ten blocks down but a couple of cosplayers and even an actor came down to see us play!" I love a self-deprecating sense of humor. "Do you know which actor saw you play?"

"Yes, he said his name was Nathan. He acted like he liked the band then grabbed my ass after stealing our EP."

"Oh, Jesus Christ. Maggie, that's awful." She shrugged and said, "Yeah, but the worst part was he never called me back." Holy crap, she's funny. I got a death stare from Ang for laughing too hard.

"Do you have any trouble playing the songs?"

"No, not at all, I'm ready to go on stage now if we have the time. Put me in coach, I can do it!" I think I found my new best friend. "Well, Maggie, you got the gig, please be back here tomorrow. We'll be auditioning lead guitar players." She let out a squeal that reminds me of an anime character. I can't remember which one, but I'm pretty sure tentacles were involved.

If you think bass players are a tricky lot, they've got nothing on lead guitarists. We had to go an extra two days auditioning about 20. Everyone has their own style, sound, or take on how the song should be played. All are either fine, good, or "head and shoulders above" professionals. We end up taking a break and go across the street to grab a cup of coffee and some fresh air. While there, we find this dude on the sidewalk playing with his case open. I throw a couple of bucks in before I get my coffee. While in line I can't help but admire the fact that the dude doesn't need a venue to play. He just plays because he loves it. That's how it ought to be done. I end up chatting with him outside for a bit before heading back across the street. "Hey, bro, my name's Doug. You sound excellent." He lets his guitar rest behind his back like he is Johnny Cash. "Hey, man, I saw you guys been coming across the street for a couple of days. You in a band or something?" He shakes my hand by covering it with his other hand. You don't see that kind of kindness anymore. "Yeah, man, I'm playing this one show opening for Jackie Ill at the Roundhouse and I'm trying to get a band together."

"I don't know who Jackie Ill is, but if you're playing that barn you gotta know what you're doing. God bless, brother." It was like talking to a young Bruce Springsteen, what a down-to-earth guy.

"Hey if you're not still playing, want to come across the street and hear the record I'm putting out?" He got his money together, put his guitar away and picked up the road case like he was trying to catch a train in a hurry. He must have been doing this for a long time.

"Let's roll, bro." We head across the street and before we even play him the songs, we get to talking about life. Turns out his name is Nick. He's from Brooklyn and moved out here to live with his aunt and get away from the craziness out there while he regroups and finds the sound he's been looking for. We play him the tracks and in his own words, he yells, "Alright. I found the sound, man." It breaks my heart to tell him this is a one time deal, but he replays all the tracks just so he can audition. We let him borrow one of the old electrics with a Line 6 amp that we put on the pre-set distortion. He plays those songs like he wrote them himself. God damn, I think I just found another guy I should have been writing music with all along. It's crazy how you can find people you're meant to be around. I'm not sure in anything about God or the afterlife, but I do believe people gravitate toward certain personalities. Which is exactly how I think you're supposed to find lead guitar players. You don't go with the outright most talented, you go with the one who is picking up the vibe you are putting out and gets the direction you want to go in.

Spoiler alert, I don't continue with music. Ang and I get married, stay kid-less, and we just do our jobs while writing music for Jackie and Nick until they feel like stopping. Nick is even my best man. I knew he'd be my inevitable best friend when we told him he got the gig. We tell him as such and he puts his hand out and says "I don't want money, I just want to play. Donate the money to a charity of your choice." Ang gives him the biggest hug I've ever seen. Bigger than any she's given me. I'd feel jealous but I give him one just as big.

So my band is together, I'm playing the Roundhouse Theater in a month, and I have a career in teaching ahead of me to look forward to. Cue the shit hitting the fan.

17

The Aforementioned Shit Hitting the Fan

So I have a band, a show lined up, and a list of songs that need to sound even better live than they do on the record. I have a month to get it perfect. Nothing I haven't done before. Though it has been a while, the ambition I usually keep hidden is in full swing. Time to get to work. So each song has the parts that each member will be playing, but there are also a number of parts that we made with either a piano or a synthesizer used on a computer program. Since there's not a lot of time left, we decide it would be better just to have any parts with keys to be pre-programmed and timed to the show to be played through the PA system. All we need is one person to hit play when the cues come up. Simple right? Guess again. That's just one delegation for one person.

On any crew of people working on a set, there is always a crew manager and stage manager along with all the workers making the show run smoothly. Everyone has their job and it is not to be interrupted unless there is an emergency. Though it sounds serious, some of it can be absolutely silly. "Hey dude, you're supposed to be pulling the curtain."

"Fight me, bro. I gotta put out the stage props."

"Tough shit, Noodles is gonna do it, you gotta do the curtain, then help do the third costume change." None of my stage shows are anything close to that, but some can be.

Cut to the week before the show, we have two people helping the entire production: one to run errands in case anyone needs anything, and one to do sound. That's not including what needs to be done as far as lights, instrument techs, stage management, striking crews to change bands one after another, and the runner to do errands. Forget one person to do the keyboard sounds, we need an overhaul of people to get this shit done. And since Champ's so lovely, it has all been delegated to me since he has finally had enough and said, "You wanted this show so bad, you set it up. You ain't paying me." It sounds like a curse, more like a gift. My show, my way.

Before anything gets done to get this show set up, let me tell you about everything that has gone wrong in one day and that almost got everything canceled.

We were posting the job on a social media site that advertises for stagehands. In return, they get beer or entrance to the show for free. All of a sudden I get a phone call from Champ. "Champ, to what do I owe the displeasure?"

"Just wanted to let you know you're being sued for copyright infringement." Cue armpit sweat and a migraine.

"What the hell? Who's suing me and for what reason?"

"You're being sued by a band in Chicago over the song 'It's All Over' and it's over the entirety of the song. They say it's far too similar to one of their songs called 'Over and Out.'" I have never heard of this band or the song so how can this be? The dick sends me the song and I have to say, it makes me nervous. The structure is similar, the lyrics run the same way, with a similar message, and even the guitar solo sounds the same. This is bad, really bad. I called the lawyer for the management company to call the band and ask certain questions. If my phone call was at 10:00 in the morning, the phone call that would save my ass comes at 4:45 in the evening. Fifteen minutes before he closed up for the day.

"Doug, you're all in the clear."

"What the hell happened?"

"Well, you can blame Champ because he called the band about the song and thought they'd want to hire someone to pursue a suit against you so he can get some money as a finder's fee. The band wasn't interested in suing you. Even if they were, they didn't have their song copyrighted so, if anything, they just found out that they're the ones in an actionable position. Not you."

"Can anyone go to Champs office and beat his ass into the ground, please?"

"You only have to deal with him for another week. Let it go." I thank him and even pay him a small amount of money for having my back. Anything Champ can do to get extra money he'll fucking do.

Next, I get a text from Max. "So what's this about Panic Under Pressure, hmm?" My heart almost falls out of my chest. I play dumb. "I thought I just wasn't allowed to use my real name. Not just cut music out like a tumor."

"Well, Doug, you're my tumor. One of the students was playing a song from your record in the cafeteria the other day. I've been hearing you play and write since middle school so I know your voice when I hear it. What were you thinking?"

"I was thinking I could do something under a different moniker." I saw the three little bubbles come up and disappear God knows how many times. After a while, it resulted in this. "Look, the school board doesn't know. I only know because I got you to confess it through here. So I guess it'll be our little secret. Tell me you aren't playing a show at the Roundhouse, though."

My response was, "I heard that band Panic Under Pressure is opening for Jackie Ill, you want to go with me?"

"Goddammit, Doug . . . sure I'll go, but you need a disguise to have plausible deniability and you don't know me. You don't speak to me. Got it?"

"You got it, boss."

After I have almost lost my song, money, and career all in the span of one afternoon, I decided to change my underwear after almost shitting myself enough times today. That is until I get a message from Jackie. "Hey, how quick can you learn a song?"

"Depends. How hard are we talking?"

"All four-chord songs."

"Jackie, you said a song. What's wrong?"

"So my guitar player quit and I'm playing for an hour and a half. So I need you to learn twenty songs by Friday night." So I change my underwear again and realize these last-minute deals with music will give me a peptic ulcer sooner than I want. Jackie sends me the list and though they aren't hard, it's a fucker of a setlist to learn in a week. So I get put on a schedule of practicing every day with my band, then stay for an extra four hours to rehearse with Jackie. I can't wait for this to be over.

So if all this happened on a Monday, Tuesday through Friday were by far some of the most exhausting times of practice I've ever done. I play for about 45 minutes, then Jackie gets her hour and a half. Every day we go to practice, Ang has to drive me since I am so tired and stressed out. And all that week if it isn't one thing, it's another. Every day there is a new problem.

Although I love two-thirds of my band, God damn, they can be frustrating. One day Maggie forgets her music, then spends an hour running home getting her music and then an extra 45 minutes getting food. By the way, catering was brought to practices. A gift from Jackie no less. Another day Nick forgot his capo. A song that requires a capo is already a song that needs special attention. The strings have to be put on properly and sometimes they break, Sometimes an open string with a capo can be nowhere near where you're supposed to be on the fretboard. So when Nick forgot his, the two songs that needed it sounded like absolute garbage. And if that wasn't enough Jason was, well Jason.

Every day before he started playing he'd hand me a newly edited version of his rider. A rider is something a performer needs—or in his case demands—in their dressing room or on stage to be done, or else they cannot perform. Mine is the shortest by far. Bottled water and wet wipes. Maggie asks for water, chips and guac, and adequate WiFi so she can be on her phone. Nick asks only for peace and quiet for meditation. Yes, his is cheaper, but peace and quiet backstage is damn near impossible. Jason demands at all times to have his coffee-filled, a massage station with a masseuse, the furniture to match whatever wall decorations, catering for his entourage, his entourage to have matching jackets for the gig, and for him to have full access and be able to make changes and final say to the setlist. I am willing to give him a cup of coffee from across the street. I'm not paying for any of this and neither is Champ. Every day it was given to the stage managers we hired from off the street and every day we find it in the trash. This is all going to backfire unless something is done.

So on Thursday, he comes in with his newly revised rider, and his new inclusion is to have sunflower seeds peeled and fed to him on the couch while he wears a robe. Not already de-seeded seeds, but seeds in the case, to be peeled in front of him by the lead singer's girlfriend. Oh boy, where do I start?

I don't know where this little shit has the nerve to demand these things. The nerve to be fed things like Cleopatra on a couch, let alone by my girlfriend in this absurd power move. Nevertheless, I did nothing but laugh. I showed it to the entire band and crew before showing Ang. She saw it, took a deep breath and jumped behind the kit punching the shit out of him and cursing his ass out. "You little mother fucker, who do you think you are, you misogynistic little shit, I can't wait to see you die alone." Oh my God, I couldn't breathe I was laughing so hard. He tried to get up and quit but Nick stood over him, making him cower in fear, and said "you're doing this show if you want to keep your legs. And now you're doing it for free." He sat his ass behind the kit and didn't say a word until he stepped off stage on Friday, the nasty little shit.

18

How to Put on a Show

N ow I have briefly talked about the low amount of staff we had available for the show, but let me tell you what it really takes to put on a show. Not in metaphors or fancy pseudo-intellectual descriptions, but what it takes financially, in manpower, and the mental toll it takes on someone.

So let's start with the venue. Whether it's a club, theater, Coliseum, or even an American Legion Hall, there is always a flat fee to rent the space to play. Each place will vary and the bigger you go, the bigger the cost. In our case, the Roundhouse Theater costs us just shy of $10,000 dollars. So if you're playing a theater, you better be sure people are coming and that ticket prices are set to the appropriate level. Since Jackie is the biggest act on the bill, and not even really that big, tickets are being sold for $75 dollars. We, therefore have to sell 200 tickets just to break even before other expenses are even mentioned—already hard enough when we're relatively unknown. So that's why we're booking other acts besides the two of us to be sure the other bands can bring people in. Though I'm opening for Jackie, opening for me is that band

Arrowhead from Chicago who Champ almost tried to get to sue me. Since I had the upper hand, as an apology I got them booked to be my opener. Opening for them are two other bands. Rattattack from Long Island, and Sleeper Agent from Fairfield, Connecticut. The three opening bands are given 20 tickets each to sell in pre-sale. You can either sell them to people or just fork out money and give them away. Unfortunately, pay to play is the only way that places are guaranteed to get their money back before people start ordering food and drinks. I have to sell 40, and Jackie has 100. Her being the headliner, all eyes are really on her. The amount of responsibility can really get you sweating. The financial burden alone is ungodly.

So after the venue is booked, it's up to the promoter to get the show heard about and to put asses in seats. Promoters usually take a fee of anywhere from 3-10% of the ticket cost which is why they usually set the ticket price. The one at the Round-house takes a fee of 5%, therefore taking in revenue of $3.75 per ticket. If the show sells the 200 ticket minimum, he makes $750 dollars. They have to spend a lot of money on advertising, too. For instance, to promote on a local FM radio station, it costs $2,000 upfront for spots to be run for the month. We only have about two weeks of promotion so they knock it down to $750. That's basically him giving his paycheck for someone to talk for two weeks about a show that few people even care to go to. So they make every artist on the bill post to their social media about the event and damn near barrage us to be on top of it. Though the venue holds 2000 people, it's highly unlikely a local band is going to sell out this place. I thought I'd be nervous playing guitar, I'd be losing hair by the fistful if I had that poor sap's job.

Now the road crew we mentioned: but they rarely, if ever, get paid for small-time shows. Usually, the roadies are parents of the band or reluctant best friends who are paid by free admission to the show. As a joke sometimes they may be paid with fast food. The people we got from the site are pretty good though and are dictated to by Dad and Chris, making sure everything is set because I'm such a bundle of joy. Not.

House lights and sound guys are usually paid a flat rate fee by the venue, but oddly enough, a lot of bands bring their own PA systems and pay them themselves to lower ticket prices so it's easier to get people to come. Sometimes they can be expensive, and sometimes you get someone who just wants to be on the road and will volunteer to do it just because they love doing it. Those are my favorites, those who work well, and are cheap.

And if you have bands or artists coming from out of town, costs can start piling up in terms of hospitality. Think hotel rooms, busses to take them from gig to gig, amenities for people who're high maintenance like Jason. Now obviously where they stay, the number of people, and how diva-like they are is taken case by case. But even the most conservative number can run up to about $500-$1000 bucks a night.

This all comes before artists get paid. Some get about $50 dollars each, some get $50 for the whole band. Some get absolutely nothing. But if you have a good manager—as I don't— the more you play and the more your reputation develops, the higher you get paid. And that's how people like the Coliseum players get paid hundreds of thousands of dollars for, at max, four hours of work.

What I'm trying to say is, touring and doing these shows is expensive as hell. The amount of pressure, and how deep under the microscope you're analyzed, is immense. Obviously, it isn't open-heart surgery to call a phone and fork over the money, but the balls it takes for an artist to walk into a venue, do what they do best, know it was a total success, and not have it be an absolute financial disaster, takes a set of cajones. When I find mine, I'll let you know. I'll be in my classroom with absolute ignorance on what it takes to keep a school running. Just show up with my cup of coffee, shut up, and teach.

19

You Better Have Show
Etiquette

W hen I was 15, Dad took me to my first open mic at a
coffee show in town. I had what I was going to wear
all picked out, my set was ready, and my friends and some girls
were coming. I had everything ready, or so I thought. What I
failed to realize is that every live performance, from coffee
houses to Woodstock itself, has show etiquette. I, being bright-
eyed and bushy-tailed, got to the place early, and put myself
third or fourth. That's not so bad. Other people needed to go
first so they could play and go to work or go to another open
mic that night. What I failed to do, was to show any form of
respect to the people going on before me.

What I did was this. While everyone had their guitars and
other instruments in cases lined up on the wall and labeled, I
kept mine out and was playing in the corner while the other
performers were on stage. I then started making out with a girl
in front of the performer, not to mention shouting "Free Bird"
at each performer. Just to let you all know, the "Free Bird" guy
at the show, is the most hated guy at the show. I then went up,
did my thing, and came off. Dad snatched my guitar out of
my hand, threw it in the case, and said "get in the car"

through his gritted teeth. I thought it was because I messed up a chord change. I was thinking in my head, "Oh no Daddy, I promise I'll get it right next time." But, oh no, this is way worse than missing that Em7 change.

In the car on the way home, totally leaving my friends behind, I was berated on what I had done wrong and how my behavior was deplorable and embarrassing. "You're not coming back to any one of these until I tell you you're ready. I've never been so disappointed in you." So while all of you get to be spared Dad's wrath, here are some of the basic rules of show etiquette. On and off stage, audience member or performer.

Performing etiquette has its own set of rules. It's like having two sets of crowds. When you're the performer, headliner or opener, you're on display. Your behavior and the way you present yourself at shows are indications of what it's like to work with you. If you're not listening to the rules, nobody's going to want to work with you.

Starting with rule number one, treat the roadies and staff with respect. Everyone is busy and stressed out trying to make your show a success. You're basically their boss. If you don't treat your workers with respect, they won't listen or will outright sabotage you. Thank them, ask how they're doing and if they need any help. Get them some water or beer if they need it. Oh, and to any singers in bands or solo artists, just because you don't play an instrument doesn't mean you get to sit out at load in. Without your brand, you're singing karaoke. Do you know when your band is considering their solo careers the most? When you don't help. Get to work.

Rule number two, unless you're a stand-up comic, or as interesting as the boss, keep your stories on stage short and sweet. Think of it like this, your joke or story better have, at max, six lines total. Three or four of which to set it up, give a punch line, say "This song is about the last girl who broke my heart, sing along if you know it," then play. Nothing is worse than the singer who doesn't know how to get out of a story he's telling. You sing for a reason, you suck at talking.

Rule number three, to follow suit with rule two, if you're not a politically charged act, like Rage Against the Machine, Bill Marr, Louis Black, or Stray From the Path, and you go political, expect to have people boo you or be disinterested in you. Politically charged acts can be badass, don't get me wrong. But if you're notoriety is based around a song you have about a girl, dogs, or a pickup truck and start talking about something else, you're digressing away from what your crowd is there for. Your job is to play what they want or what they're willing to hear. They have jobs too, and if they can be possibly fired from that job by expressing political agendas at work, you should be held to the same standard. Yes, court jesters and minstrels did it back in the Dark Ages, but it's no longer dark, and you're being paid quite handsomely. Play the one about the girl.

Rule number four, if you're done performing, get behind the merchandise table and mingle with the crowd. Or go into the crowd and be an extra body to support the next band. It's cool to see the person you just saw on stage acting like a normal person, mainly because you are normal. Get rid of that barrier of you being better or disengaging and say thank you to the people who bought a ticket to see you perform. Or, get in the crowd and be there for the next act because they were either there for you or they were warming up the crowd doing merchandising, too. And if they were being dicks, show them how it's done. Be the example you want to set out at these shows.

And lastly, no touching the instruments of the other bands. They're set to how they like it. Nobody cares what you want, except your people. I was doing a talent show a couple of months after I was allowed to play live again and as I was in the cafeteria tuning up, away from other people, all of a sudden, I see a buddy of mine pick up the next act's guitar and start de-tuning it from standard tuning to a whole step down. Forget the fact that he has his own that I had already tuned up for him, but he picked up something that doesn't belong to him and changed it mere minutes before someone else had to go on stage. He de-tuned it, played maybe a minute, put it down, then walked away. The guy came out to get his guitar and as he played it, he was so distraught about it, having no time to fix it before going on stage, I came out, explained what happened, loaned him mine, then fixed his so he could use it in his next song. I even brought it out to him on stage. It is so mind-numbingly stupid to think you can touch or change anything you want on someone else's instrument. I told my buddy that if it happened again, I was letting him get the ass-kicking he deserved. As should anyone who does that.

Now, audience members, you're not excused from this conversation. You do some dumb shit, too. So let's go over some basic survival tips and do-goodery you can do at shows.

Rule number one, while there's a performance going on, keep your mouth shut unless it's short, sweet, or funny. Nobody cares about your commentary unless it is on a DVD bonus feature or podcast. Unless it's an emergency, save it for the car. You don't see people talking in a movie theater. And if you do, what do you do? You "shoosh" them. Except you don't shoosh at a show, you politely ask someone "Excuse me. Can you shut the fuck up? Your lack of basic decency seems to be interrupting my enjoyment of the performance. If you cannot shut the fuck up, please leave. Thank you and have a nice day." Actually, that kind of negates my whole point. You know, just say "Shut the fuck up."

Rule number two, have a sense of decency in the mosh pit. We could do a whole chapter on etiquette in the pit, but stick to these things most importantly: Don't drag in people who don't want to be dragged in, if they fall down, pick them up, and no elbows. Back in high school, we had a guy who ignored all these rules. Since he had to be taught a lesson, we let him go in the middle and then we all bum-rushed him. We didn't kill him, we just wanted to have him "maimed or gravely injured." Bless you, Dobby, you're a free elf.

Rule number three, if you have to smoke, just go outside. I don't know why you would do it, anyway. This has been stamped onto everyone's head since grade school, so why should it suddenly become okay at shows? Not everyone wants to breathe in what you're smoking. Weed or otherwise. Go outside. By the way, if you leave and can't go two hours without smoking, you have bigger problems at hand than showing etiquette, my friend. Often enough, if you leave you can't be let back into the venue anyway unless they have a designated patio or door that goes outside. So put the butts away. Unless you're at a rap concert. Get it?

Rule number four, don't hold up the merchandise line. We all know the girl behind it is hot. It's probably a band mate's girl-friend or sister. Just buy your shit and go. No, they don't have changing rooms. If you don't know your own shirt or pants size, you're far more useless than you know.

And lastly, put the phones away. I don't know how else to say it. Forget about the performer being distracted, it's annoying when you stick your phone up and block the views of people who can't see. Or when they stick it in the air and hit tall people straight in the chin. And to those people who like to record a snippet of a song and post it on social media, that's cute for maybe one song, but stop clogging our feeds with your shitty camera angle and bad singing. It's like a big "fuck you" to everyone who watches. If I wanted to see the concert, I'd have bought the tickets myself. There's a reason performers are starting to lock up phones at live venues. You're not responsible enough with it.

Now obviously these are satires and musings of how people should be at shows, but in all honesty, just don't be a dick. It's that simple. If you can't be pleasant, just stay at home.

20

The Big Night

Before we go any further, I just wanted to say the show went over without a hitch, it was by far the best experience I ever had with music and I went out on top with a bang. We sold the fucker out and we had the time of our lives. I could've dropped dead after I finished. If it never gets better than that, so be it.

I woke up, and all day I was going through my checklist of what had to be packed and how it had to be loaded up. Ang came over and was re-checking everything I was doing since I was a nervous wreck. Load in time was 3:00 pm, so all morning I was checking my watch saying "Okay another six hours. That's six episodes including commercials of 'Breaking Bad.' Okay, another four to go." I then took a nap and woke in a panic. Have you ever fallen asleep and forgotten what day it is? I do often. It scared me so much I almost started crying because I had thought I had missed the show. Ang told me to get back in bed I have another 2 hours. She woke me up and we headed down. We were the first ones there followed by Jackie and the other bands. Oh man, did these bands not hear Dad's speech. Besides the fact that they didn't help any of us with load-in, they passed on meeting the owner backstage and went across the street to get some barbecue sandwiches and dollar iced teas. They didn't tip any of the bartenders and they got smashed before 5:00 pm. The doors opened at 7:00, the first band was on at 7:30 pm. If you start late, you don't get that time back. That's just the time that you lost. Sorry, don't be so shitty next time. Although I have to say, those guys sucking made me look ten times more professional and show-cased how decent the band and I were.

The reason I included that part about start time, is because the first band, Sleeper Agent, missed theirs by about 10 minutes. If we give you a half-hour, you just blew a third of your time. They played pretty decently, but they were more about the show than sound. If you were a movie maybe I'd have your back when it comes to sights over sound and dialogue, but come on, man, act like you've played guitar before. They came in dressed looking as if Aerosmith and Johnny Depp had a love child with the number of scarves and bracelets they wore. They walked on with their tallboys and started sniffling and spitting on stage like they were suddenly stricken with a postnasal drip. Fucking gross.

Rattattack was my pick from Long Island. They were an art-house band who, until today, were really nice dudes. They were short and snippy with staff and demanded things for a chorus of people that were supposed to come on stage during one of their songs. Maybe they were nervous, but I didn't care enough to ask, I had my own shit going on. Let them destroy their own reputations. They played three songs, all of which came out fine, but had so many bizarre parts that they made the audience look at each other with confusion. When you're met with polite applause instead of "Woos" and "You rock," something has gone wrong and you need to fix it. But then they had this chorus for their last song. They all came out in these robes that were multi-colored and had the band's symbol on it. They were a three-piece band so after the chorus came out, the singer/guitar player put his instrument down and took a maestro's baton and started conducting the audience. Of about 2000 people, they had their own fan base of about twenty, all of whom knew the words. It looked bizarre and like something that belonged in the Hollywood Bowl. But here it was tonight at a rock concert. Whatever, guys.

Finally, Arrowhead went on. The worst of the bunch. The guys I technically could have sued and got them this gig to show them no hard feelings decided to go on a tirade for five of their 30 minutes about why I sucked and they shouldn't buy my record. Which only drove people to buy my record. I should have sued for slander but they destroyed their own reputation, anyway. They flat out sucked. They invited friends on stage to dance and they'd stop in the middle of a song saying, "Oh I don't remember how that one went." By the way, that was a Metallica song they stopped in the middle of. They were crucified for that and booed off the stage. I would have been embarrassed for myself, but I was smiling ear to ear. I couldn't have had a better intro if I wanted. They were the worst opener I've ever seen in my life. It was a guideline for how to be mediocre.

It was time to go out; it's my turn to make a statement. I had my rules, I had my set, I had a job to do, and I was going to do it well. The lights dimmed down and I had my introduction done by the boys from Nonsense at Noon. They made the crowd crack up and put them in good spirits. After that Arrowhead horror show, they needed it. I got myself together and let the show start the way we rehearsed. Jason went out first and started the drums to "It's All Over." Maggie came out second and they started an eight-bar bass and drum duet. Then Nick came out. Already the crowd was in much better spirits. They were getting palatable music. Nicky comes out and kept one note going palm-muted at one rhythm so

Maggie and Jason can keep up the duet if it went well. After that was done, I took a breath and walked out with my hand in the air to say "hi" with a big shit-eating grin on.

The place didn't know who I was, but they knew already I was for real. I kept things light on the mic. "Sorry about that before, that other band gets a little cranky when they haven't gotten their daily spanking." the whole place laughed. "Don't worry. We'll give it to them. I just wanted to say thank you to everyone coming out and for all of you to know it means the world to us." I let them applaud some more. "Make sure you stick around for Jackie Ill, alright?" Let them applaud some more. I reached my line limit so I walked back to Jason, had my ass to the crowd and started playing the riff that started this whole thing. I was shaking my ass in time and having fun. After they had eaten up the song, I knew this show was going to be amazing. We didn't waste time and went straight into "No Pressure." I started the song with the loop pedal so I had the camera zoom in on me while the lights dimmed low. Ang told me after that the moment made her . . . um . . . flood her basement? I guess if that's accurate. But the synth matched the timing of the band and it killed.

After that, I took a swig of water and vamped. "We sound alright out there?" The crowd was loud but sounded soft. "I said we sound alright out there?" The crowd got even louder. "Because you sound beautiful up here." I put the water down. "This next song is one of my favorites, hope it's one of yours, too." Then we kicked into "Use Somebody," to this day, one of my favorite songs. That went well, then nobody spoke, but we put our capos on and played "Oh Brother." Chris didn't have a dry eye the whole night, and neither did I, in truth. The whole time I felt like I was on the verge of tears.

"This next one is gonna be a little bit more serious in the message, and on my vocal chords. Regardless, it's Nick's favorite. While you're at it, make some noise for Nicholas Basquiette huh?" The place went nuts for him. He started playing "45" and the crowd went wild. The same thing with "Simple Man," except I had to make the obvious joke, "Maggie, if you play your cards right and listen to the words, you too could be a simple man." We were greeted with applause and a middle finger from Maggie.

After that was done I thought I was going to pass out. Next was "Long Long Gone," the song I wish I hadn't been given the chance to write. I said as much on the mic. "This next song is a tough one, folks. This song was written for the man who recorded this EP and, to be honest, I'd give it up just to have him back for another day. He did all the drums on the EP and I gotta say, he'd have torn this place up." The song started and we were greeted with lighters and cell phones with the flashlight on waving back and forth. I made it through, but barely.

Lastly, I played my favorite song and the one I taught myself to sing to. "Ladies and gentlemen, this is a night none of us will ever forget. Thank you so much for coming. You didn't give me life, but you showed us how to live. Rest in peace. Chris Cornell. Nicky, kick that shit off, will you please?" While Nick started the riff I threw Jackie some love. "Who here is excited for Jackie Ill, huh? The place went ballistic. "Show Me How To Live" is a mother of a song to sing, so after I did that scream at the end, I simply said "You guys are incredible, we're Panic Under Pressure, we love you, goodnight," and just dropped the mic on stage. It was badass.

I went to my dressing room to take a shower and change before playing Jackie's set, but Ang was waiting back there in need of me to fix the flood problem. I went back out all sweaty and gross but I played my ass off. We did our duet and Jackie did something that knocked me dead. She said "Ladies and gentlemen, Doug Manning." The place went ballistic chanting "Doug, Doug, Doug!" It was amazing to hear, but I had an even better view. I saw my beautiful girl staring at me with all the praise and honor I couldn't have gotten from 10 of those crowds. I had 2000 people in there, but I was really playing for an audience of one. I know this whole time I've been saying "fuck this business it's good for nothing," but everywhere is like that. I'm not leaving music because I hate it, I'm leaving because I love teaching and being with Angela more. If you want to make it in music, go for it. The road ahead is filled with the traffic of others doing it as well. But if you can figure out the path to get there and do it with earnest-ness, integrity and, most important of all, legally, then godspeed and good luck. I'll be here, listening.

Curveball

1

Stuck in a Rut

M ick awoke from his bed at 7 am. He was woken up by his cell phone's ringtone, which was playing a song his friend, Doug, wrote a couple of years ago. He loved his friend's music and showed his support by making his ringtone a song called "Bite My Tongue" play at full volume to wake him up in the morning. Mick woke up the first time it went off, but he let the song go just to hear it a little bit. *Well just know that you're not alone. Fight for a cause you know* The phone played on. *You don't know about the outcome yet, it's better to try then always regret.* Mick looked around his bedroom. He had been living in his apartment for 2 years after leaving his parents' house. He looked around at the desk he doesn't use, the music collection he acquired after years of hanging around Doug, and the walls that were vacant of any decorations. He had no pictures on the wall, no posters, no artwork. His apartment lacked any form of individuality except for a picture on his nightstand of himself as a baby being held by his father in his fireman's uniform. He reached his favorite part of his ringtone and hit the snooze button.

He looked at his phone to see if he had any texts or missed calls. He noticed no missed calls, but he did have a text from his friend and co-worker, Richie. Richie is the antonym of Mick. Richie is a fun-loving, crazy, jokester who always has a comment or a joke. He spends his days quoting pop culture and just wants everyone to be happy. Even as a paramedic, he'll always try to make his patients laugh. That was not how Mick operated at all. Mick, is a hard-working, ruthlessly dedicated, and immensely talented paramedic. He chooses to be the bad cop to Riches good cop. A role he gladly bestowed himself since someone had to be the professional.

He looked at Richie's text and saw a picture of Richie looking confused at a portable suction unit and the suction catheter. He also sent along a caption that read, "You think I could fit the whole catheter in the mouth or Nah?" Mick rolled his eyes and sent back. "I think you should stock the rig and clean." Mick is the captain of the ambulance and has chosen not to reprimand his friend.

He goes back into his phone and goes to the dating app he has on his phone and starts to swipe to the right if he finds them attractive, left if he finds them ugly. He continues to swipe as he thinks over what he has to do today. "I have to go for a run, shower, drink some coffee," he ponders, as he continues to swipe left on girls he's already talked to. "I have to call the city about my application, remind Doug I'm coming over tonight after work." He swipes right on a girl he had a crush on in high school, but never got the chance to ask out. "I have to call up about my car insurance, maybe watch some TV before work …" he then swipes right on a girl who wore a tape to a police scene as a bra to an ABC party, an Anything-But-Clothes party, and they matched. Mick's chest was flickering at the idea of someone matching with him. He sent her a polite message: "Hey! You seem really sweet," the message said as he hit send. The message sent and hung there in the conversation bars for a few seconds. Mick didn't move in case she responded immediately. The message hung for a few more seconds until her profile was removed from his matches. Ugh! This has happened to Mick before—the girl had removed him from her matches, and it sent a wave of rejection that shivered up his spine. He became overwhelmed with frustration and unplugged his phone, grabbed his headphones and got up to go for a run.

He opened his closet with frustration and mumbling to himself. "Stupid naked bitch un adding me. Probably has a hundred guys lining up her inbox and I can barely get 1. Probably took plan B after that party. I'll probably have to pick her drunk ass up one night in the rig and have to be nice to her." If you haven't noticed already, Mick's tolerance for rejection is lower than that girl dancing at that party. She did in fact drop it low and had a great time without having to answer to a man who'd try to reel her in and not have her be herself. Mick is looking for a wholesome girl who can be there for him the way nobody seems to be able to be. To fill the void in his life he can't seem to fill with job satisfaction, friends that love him, or his lifelong dreams of being a paramedic in Manhattan. But until then, he has to deal with what he has.

He puts on his compression shorts, pulls a pair of shorts on top of those, puts on a long sleeve t-shirt, and leaves his apartment to do his morning 5k around his neighborhood in the crisp atmosphere of Long Island in the fall. Mick lives in the town of Riverview, a town that is filled with nothing but bars, schools, hospitals, and the bare essentials to living. Everything else is wide open fields for farming, woods for hunting and ponds for fishing. Mick started his playlist of songs that he hypes him up and started his run. Mick runs at a pace of a 12-minute mile. He's not fast, but he covers the distance at his pace. Which is also applicable to his life. He graduated high school, went to community college, volunteered in his spare time, and worked his way to becoming a paramedic. He would take trips when he wanted, hang out with his friends, and do what any normal person does when they graduate high school and experience the real world; he'd make mistake after mistake. Relationships would fall apart for reasons that were foreign to him, he'd get too hammered and throw up the next day, crash a car because he wasn't paying attention, and all for the betterment of developing a thick skin and experience he could take with him into the world. If only he'd learn from any of them.

He took a right turn from his neighborhood development and ran straight through an open field that would lead to town. He ran through at his own pace but was overwhelmed by the scent of fresh-cut grass. The air was filled with hair from the horses on the far side of the field. He narrowly avoids a sprinkler hitting him as he continues to run, undeterred by anything going on around him. He runs through the field and makes it to the other side to a small cut in the woods that leads to the town. He pops out on the other side and waits for cars to pass to continue. While he waits, he switches songs on his phone and checks his dating app. No matches have surfaced in the 7 minutes it takes to run from his home to the road. He mumbles "fucking dating app" under his breath. The cars pass, and he has a clear shot across the road. He looks at the yellow line in the road, recalling a time when he pulled the driver of a car out of its wreckage and onto a stretcher. That was the time when he found out that the reason the guy wouldn't just get on the stretcher was because the accident had left the driver permanently paralyzed from the neck down.

He makes it to town, where he proceeds to run around the park and small stores. The owner of the smoke shop stands outside to hand him a cigar on the house because Mick brought him in the ambulance due to the shop owner's COPD from smoking since he was 16. Mick didn't smoke, but he took the cigar mid-stride, smiled back, and said: "Thanks man, feel better." The shop owner smiled, waved, and went back into the store.

He reached the statue of the town local who went on to do who gives a fuck, turned around, ran the same route back past the smoke shop, through the park, across the road, through the field and made it back home at a pace of an 11-minute mile. He noticed it and smiled slightly. He then went back into the dating app and continued to see nothing. His smile went back to his normal face of contentment and went back into the house shaking his head. He then hopped in the shower and contemplated if his life is really going on the track he wants, like everyone does in the shower, gets out and dries off. He wrapped his towel around his waist and started brushing his teeth. While he brushed his teeth, he swiped some more. "Ugly, ugly, underaged, ugly, hot," he said to himself until he stopped at one profile and started to explore it. The profile read that the girl was in an open relationship but she was looking for another man for the relationship. "Fuck no," he said out loud. He closed the app and went to make himself a coffee.

He closes the Keurig and walks over to plug in his phone. The coffee started to pour into the cup and he plugged in the phone and trips over his own laundry on the way back. He stops to be sure all of his work clothes are ready and makes a mental note to grab a pen before he goes out. He puts in two sugars and pours in his half and half, then makes his way to the couch to watch TV. He turns the TV on and immediately falls asleep.

He wakes up from his nap in a panic, hoping he didn't miss his shift. He ran to his phone and realized he had two more hours before his shift starts. He breathes a sigh of relief, then starts swiping the app again. He's delighted to see a match and a girl already sent him a message. The girl was very beautiful and seemed to have a bio he especially liked. The bio read: "23, tatted, in school for nursing." The bio also had an emoji of two beer glasses clinking together. He was very optimistic for about 2 seconds until he read the message. The message said, "Add me on this snap channel and subscribe to my Patreon for xxx pics." He quickly unmatched her and returned to the couch. He watched the same episodes of "The Office" he usually watched when he was bored until he realized he had another hour until he had to be at work. He was incredibly bored so he said to himself, "Eh, going in early never killed anybody." He then grabbed a pen and got in his car for work. He started driving his usual 10-minute drive to work but he drove slowly to make it last just a little bit longer. He put his friend's album on in the car and even sang along to it.

He parked his car in his usual spot and walked in. On the way in, he realizes that he is just terribly lonely. He has no hobbies he enjoys in his spare time, no places to go that he's been dreaming of going to, he has nobody hitting him up on the dating app, he's entirely alone. He walks through life unafraid because he's seen it all, but nobody to walk through it with. Many people would say he's horny because he has more than one dating app, but doesn't it also say he's lonely? Sex is great and all, but without an emotional connection and someone who wants to be with you, all of life gets pretty lonely.

He unlocked his locker with the thought of loneliness in his head, put on his work shirt that had his name and rank on it, closed his locker, and went to sit at the bar in the dining area. He poured himself a soda and sat and watched TV until his shift. He sat there and watched the same office episode he watched at home end, then on to the next show. He sat there and started to have slight tears in his eyes at the thought of going home alone after a night of work and hanging with his friend that it just killed his self-esteem. That is until his co-worker and friend Richie came running out of the bathroom to give him a big hug. "Ready to save more ungrateful people today buddy?" Richie said in sarcasm. Mick chuckled and said, "Yeah, I'm ready to do too much work for too little money." "Ain't that the truth," Richie said taking a seat next to him. "Mets game on Saturday. I know you off so you in?" Richie asked trying to check in on his friend in an inconspicuous way. "Nah, I hate baseball. Plus I don't know how you keep rooting for those losers." Mick retorted. Richie is used to Mick's negativity, so he shrugged his shoulders and said: "Hey, I'm a loser too and you keep rooting for me." Mick giggled again and continued watching TV. "You go down and check the rig yet?" Richie asked Mick. "Not yet," he replied. "I was waiting for you since you're the lowest man on the pole." "I'm only the lowest man on the pole in that ambulance. I only have Diaz above me in the seniority list so when he fucks up, I'll be swooping right in as your Lieutenant." Mick scoffed and said "That'll be the day. And please don't anticipate your co-worker screwing up and getting fired to climb higher on the ladder please, huh?" "Tell him that, Mickey. He's the one who put an IV in a patient with a double mastectomy." Richie walked out of the room, but Mick spit back into his drink he was so annoyed. "He did what?"

2

Reprimanding the Crew

Mick and Richie made their way out to the ambulance bay 10 minutes before the start of their shift at 3 pm. Richie made his way into the ambulance and took out the checklist each crew needs to do before they start. Mick decided to hold the checklist, sit on the couch in the ambulance bay, and let Richie check the ambulance while he continued swiping on his dating app. Richie began opening up doors and latches counting how many of each item they have and relaying that to Mick, who is barely paying attention. Mick was too busy opening doors and latches into his love life to care. "We have about uhh 6 Nasal Cannula," a small tube that goes into a patient's nose to get low doses of oxygen, "about 5 NRB's," or Non-Re-Breathers, a mask a patient wears to get a higher dose of oxygen, "and about 4-6 OPA's," or oral-pharyngeal-airways, a device used to maintain a patients airway while they're unconscious. "Wanna meet in the middle at 5?" Mick asked without looking up from his phone. "Yeah that sounds good," Richie said continuing to shout to Mick in the ambulance bay.

Richie emerged from the ambulance to check on Mick and ask "did you check the fluids?" "Uhh," Mick said not looking up from his phone. Richie started to get annoyed at his friend's lack of participation. "It's not exactly a multiple choice answer dude," he said stepping down out of the ambulance. "Then no," Mick said still not looking up from his phone. Richie sighed and continued. "All right, I'll do that too, will your highness be joining me today? Or should I go play hide and go fuck my—" Mick finally looked up and said "Hey! Language! Now can you please go check the fluids?" Richie mocked him saying "Yes sir, right away sir," quoting a Star Wars movie. He walks toward the front of the vehicle when he stops, looks at Mick, and has a smile from ear to ear, and says "Man are you swiping?"

Mick rolled his eyes and let Richie know he was annoyed by letting out a long groan. However, Richie didn't seem to care and strolled over to tease his friend. "So what's their name?" "I'm not getting any matches except for your mom, Rich." Richie is still undeterred and replies "good, she could use a nice boy like you. Someone to cry like a pussy with ya know?" Mick laughed it off. "And what do you mean you aren't getting any matches? You're the Rolls Royce of bitter young men who act like they're 40!" Richie continued. Mick rolled his eyes again. "I don't know man, they just aren't coming." Richie smiled since he found another opening for a joke. "You have to get a match before you disappoint them by not making them cum, Mickie." Mick got tired of this and got up to check the fluids under the hood of the ambulance.

Mick opened the hood and secured the latch. Richie followed him, to continue busting his chops. "I mean, if you think about the dating app you're on, you might be batting out of your league. Girls in their 20's aren't always looking for a guy who's mentally unstable and cranky. I think a woman in their 50's or an old veteran type guy in his 70's would be more your speed. I mean, you can bitch and moan about the young people while eating dinner at 4 pm and go to bed early together. Whatya think?" Richie said while butting Mick's elbow. "I think I should close the hood on your head, Rich." Mick went to the side of the ambulance bay to get a roll of paper towels. He came back and took out the dipstick to check the oil. It was filled sufficiently, and he wiped the paper towel on it. "That's the length a real woman wants, not your stub ya know?" Richie said continuing his banter. "I thought it was the motion of the ocean, not the size of the boat. "Or did your ex tell you that and you're just quoting her?" Mick said contributing."No, she was much meaner than that. I believe she said 'I'd probably fit you in my mouth more than I could a Tootsie roll.' She's creative, though, I'll give her that." Mick and Richie continued to laugh at the misfortunes of each other's dating life.

"You ever think we're wasting our time with this job? People are almost never grateful and always have criticism for us like we're running a Macy's," Richie said as they finished up their checklist. "Every day, Rich. Every day," Mick countered. "But hell, if we're not there for them, who will?" "Probably another poor sap who thinks he's making the world a better place. Honestly, sometimes when we have a patient who's a pile of shit, I think about what I could be doing at home. Like if I didn't have to pick this fucker up, I could have been fixing a nice sandwich with a cup of coffee watching cartoons." Mick didn't look up at him since he had the same thoughts from time to time. "The only thing I don't relate to is the cartoons," he replied. "Some of us broaden our horizons, Mickie. We can't be watching reruns of *The Office* for hours on end like some people." This, Mick was annoyed by. "Hey, find me a funnier scene than the CPR scene, and then we'll talk," Mick said pointing a 20 gauge angiocath at him. "Don't you point that thing at me. Show me any 10-second clip of a Looney

Tunes cartoon and that beats your CPR scene." Before Mick could form a counter-argument, the morning crew came in to join them.

"Well, thank you for coming in early gentleman. Captain Thomlinson, good to see you today," Ex-Chief Fauler said. "Hmm," Mick said continuing with packing up the paramedic bag full of medication. Richie looked nervous when Mick did not greet the Ex-Chief, so he took over. "You'll have to excuse him, Chief. His feet are nailed to the floor again." Next to Ex-Chief Fauler, stood a young girl who was a probationary member, Violet. She was also the daughter of one of the local Fire Marshalls, so around her, everyone was on their best behavior. Apparently she didn't get the memo of "snitches get stitches." "No, it's fine. Don't say hi to the Chief in charge, it's fine," she said in a caddy voice. Mick looked up without thinking and said "I don't think I asked for your opinion, Violet. By the way, your request for a day off has been denied since you owe us 3 make up days and you need to re-take your CPR class." Violet was dumbfounded. "The day off is for the CPR class," she replied trying to lie. "Then maybe you shouldn't have written "I gotta get Lipski" on it. I know it's for a night out, don't lie to me. You work the morning shift, do it on your own time," Mick countered in a stern voice. "I'll call my dad if you don't give me the day off," she said in the same caddy voice. "Sounds good to me. Maybe he can tell you about the time I saved him from dying of alcohol poisoning on the side of the road while you're at it." Richie covered his face with his hands. You are never allowed to give patient information to anyone, even family members. Violet walked away stamping her feet.

"Winters, why so tense man? Is it because your old crew-mate, Diego, got into the medic academy in Manhattan and you didn't?" said the third member of their crew, Diaz. Diaz was a lengthy and thin man, about 26 years of age, with wild, long, curly hair that needed to be held back with a hair tie. "Diego is an astounding paramedic and I'm not jealous at all. Getting into the paramedic academy is about waiting until you're called, not whose best. You'd know that if you did anything besides go home and jerk—" "That's enough," Ex-Chief Fauler said. "Captain Thomlinson, you need to learn how to talk to insubordinate members." Mick snapped back at the Ex-Chief saying that "maybe if their crew chief knew how to ring them in I wouldn't have to snap at them." Richie threw gauze in the middle of them all. "Flag on the play, I want all members involved to go back to what they were doing and leave this situation in an orderly fashion. Ex-Chief, lovely to see you and your charming crew, Captain Thomlison I think you need to shut the fuck up before you get us both in trouble. End scene," he said.

Confused by Richie's buffoonery, they all calmed down and tempers eased. At that moment a call over the radio interrupted the silence. "Riverview Ambulance Company this is central fire calling at—" the entire ambulance bay had their fingers crossed. Hoping that their crew would not be called and the other would have to go instead. The call continued "—03:01 PM. The patient has a chief complaint of—" the morning crew clapped and let out noises of excitement that their shift was officially done. The rest of the call was unclear due to their excitement. "Sorry about the bad luck boys. Maybe it's someone who needs a cranky-ass and an idiot," said Diaz, poking fun at the crew while exiting the ambulance bay. "Your mom seemed to love the idiocy I gave her last night, Diaz. Maybe you can use that big mouth of yours under the chief's desk and get a pay-ow!" Richie said, while Mick hurled a pen at him that hit him between the eyes. "Take your own notes and shut up," Mick said. Mick got in the passenger seat and picked up the two-way radio to call back central. "Central, please repeat the last call, the call was fuzzy on our end," Mick said in a pleasant voice.

Central came back to repeat the call. "Riverview Ambulance Company, central calling at 03:01 PM for a patient with a chief complaint of hypoglycemia and injury from a fall. The patient is located in the Hunters Park blue trail. There is an officer waiting for you at the scene." "Copy that central 4-3-4 ambulance responding," Mick said back to central. "Hypoglycemia huh?" Richie asked. "Yes, it means low blood sugar Rich," Mick said. "I know that, you jerk. I was about to do the old rhyme for it." "What rhyme is that?" "Cool and clammy, give them candy, pink and dry, sugar high," Richie said in a voice imitating an old EMS teacher. "Is that how you learn things? By stupid rhymes that sound funny?" Richie hit the button to open the doors and started the ambulance. "Look at me and tell me you didn't learn the cardiovascular system from that Happy Days episode without making a face." Mick shrunk in his seat. "Good point. This time please don't take off without undoing the—" Richie stepped on the gas without unplugging the cord to charge the battery to the engine. Causing it to follow them and break again. "Whoops, sorry Mickie." "No, it's fine. I love driving in an ambulance like a Winnebago who took off too soon from the gas station." "Right?" Richie said apologetically.

3

A Difficult Day

Mick and Richie continued in the ambulance toward Hunters park to respond to their patient. "I never understood why they call them 'patients.' I've never met one who had any," Richie said, turning his face to Mick to try and make him laugh. It didn't. Mick was too busy pre typing into the digital PCR, patient-care-report, the information about the EMT's in response to the scene, the ambulance ID, and the call number.

"Did you say something funny?" he asked.

"Yeah I said the one-liner about patients not having patience."

"Okay, then no you didn't. You say that joke before every call," Mick said in a stern tone.

"I'm sorry 'Grumpelstiltskin', just trying to put a smile on that face," Richie said imitating Heath Ledger's Joker.

"Hmm," Mick said continuing his work.

They approached the parking lot for Hunters Park when Mick contacted central communications to get more information on the patient. "Central this is Riverview Ambulance come in, over." Central took a minute to respond. "Riverview this is central, over." "Central, I'm calling for more information about the patient in Hunter Park. The patient is 1.5 miles deep on the blue trail. PD is on the scene providing appropriate care, but you can't take the ambulance in because it's too big for the trail, you'll have to proceed on foot." Richie and Mick both rolled their eyes and groaned. "Central, are you sure the neighboring district can't respond seeing as they're far closer than we are?" Central responded quickly this time. "No, it's technically in your district, regardless of how far they are in the trail. The park medical personnel are unable to help due to another call in the park that the neighboring department mutually aided." Richie got out and opened the back door of the ambulance. Mick groaned once more but replied "Thank you Central, we're on scene and making our way to the patient."

Richie took out the stretcher while Mick took out the medic bag and wore it like a backpack. With Mick in the front and Richie in the back, they walked the stretcher through the park's blue trail to find their patient. They were about half a mile in before either of them said anything. Richie decided to cut the silence with a knife with "you ever wonder why they say the patient 'expired?'" Mick didn't look back at him but responded anyway. "It's to be sensitive to the patient's family."

"Then why don't they just say he died? It's been said for thousands of years before health care became a business. So why do we all of a sudden say they expired like he's a container of french vanilla in the fridge."

Mick stopped in his tracks. "Do you mean the french vanilla creamer in the fridge at the station?" Richie had a smirk on his face. "Yeah, why?" "I used that this morning! Why didn't you throw it out?" "Because I knew you were going to be a dick today and I wanted to drop that on you. You're welcome." Mick immediately started to spit on the ground as they continued walking.

They saw the patient lying supine with the officer trying to coach him to get up. "Sir, I understand you're having a medical emergency, but can you not speak to me that way?" The patient stuck his fingers in the officer's face and screamed "I wanted a male officer, not some equal opportunity pussy like you. You'd be better off in the kitchen at your station."

Richie and Mick stopped in their tracks. They saw the officer losing her patience by taking a deep breath. She saw the guys approaching her, then threw her hands up in the air. "I've had it. You deal with him."

The guys approached the patient, making sure it was safe and he wasn't going to throw a bottle on the ground at them. "Hello sir, my name is Mick, and this is Richie, we're from the ambulance company and we're here to help." The patient exclaimed "well it's about time! I've been waiting for 45 minutes!" Mick and Richie both swallowed their anger and put on a pleasant face for the ungrateful patient.

"We were told you're diabetic, is that what emergency you're having today?" Richie asked as he put a non-rebreather on the patient's face.

"Yeah, and I didn't eat anything in the last twelve hours."

"Is there any reason you didn't want to eat today?"

"My wife sucks at cooking, and I told her I won't eat anything she cook

"Understood," Mick said taking the glucometer, a device that checks a person's blood sugar out of his medic bag. Richie helped the man to a sitting upright position and was checking the back of his head for secondary injuries from falling down. "Are you allergic to any medication sir?" Mick asked taking out the finger pricking device.

"No, but I enjoy morphine."

"Yeah, don't we all," Richie said back. Mick looked back at him with a piercing stare. He hates when Richie fools around on calls.

"That being said, sir, may I see your finger?" Mick said politely. The patient looked at Mick and gave him the middle finger, both providing him with a finger to prick as well as a 'fuck you'. "Terrific," Mick said with a smile staring straight at the man. He took his finger and wiped it with alcohol then pricked his finger without taking his eyes off him. That was his little 'fuck you' back to him.

"Ow! That hurt you jerk off!" the patient said angrily.

"It doesn't bother me when my mother says it, it doesn't bother me when you say it," Mick said being unfazed by the patient. He wiped the first drops of blood away, then used the second drops to use on the glucometer. The glucometer processed the blood and his blood glucose was at 40, which is an obvious sign of hypoglycemia.

"Sir, your blood sugar is way too low," Mick said.

"Hence why I called you idiots," the patient said back.

"Sir, you're doing awful damage to your body. We need to get you to the hospital immediately. You're hypoglycemic." Richie said, backing Mick up.

"Hypo-my ass," the patient said, getting up indignantly. He started to walk away, stumbling as he did, and then went to his back pocket and pulled out a cigar. He unwrapped it and took his lighter out of his front pocket. "Wait, and you smoke too?" Mick said. Richie leaned into his ear and whispered "he can smoke this dick the way he's talking to us right now." Mick giggled but regained composure.

"Sir, you're doing incredibly hurtful things to your body. You need to come with us to the hospital now." The patient was in a daze and let out a roaring "uh-oh, medicine men!" letting out a sound that sounded like a siren. "Woop-woop-woop, medicine men up in here. I've been living like this since you were doing laps in your daddies sack, son. Why don't you go to hell, and—" down he went, fainting once again. Instead of freaking out that a patient fell, Mick and Richie were quite relieved that he shut up, although, they would never say that out loud.

"Well, let's get him on the stretcher and get him to the hospital," Mick said.

"Grab the stretcher, Rich." Richie lowered the stretcher and the boys lifted him onto the stretcher. But when Mick went to raise the stretcher, it wouldn't go up. He kept pressing the 'raise' side, but nothing would budge. He looked down and saw the red light flashing 'change battery.'

"Rich, give me the other battery."

"What other battery?"

"The one on the back of the stretcher, where you are."

"Mick, it's charging in the ambulance. Didn't I tell you that at rig check?" "

No, no Rich, you didn't."

"So what are we going to do?" Rich asked, really hoping they don't have to bring him a mile and a half back to the ambulance on the lowest possible setting, at ground level.

"We have to bring him out like this. Let this be a lesson to both of us, I guess."

"For me to always change the battery before each call, and for you to help with rig check?"

"Basically," Mick said dreading the next 15 minutes.

The pair of EMT's brought the patient out of the trail and made it to the ambulance before he woke up. "Where am I?" he said. Richie opened the doors and switched the battery out. "We're bringing you into the ambulance, sir. Just hold still so —" the patient immediately started thrashing around to get out of the stretcher. "No! I don't want to go! I'm refusing care! Where's the officer?" the patient demanded.

"I think she's back in the kitchen. Isn't that where you sent her?" Richie said to intentionally patronize him. The officer was on the side of the ambulance laughing her head off, and she had no intention letting this man off without a hospital visit.

They brought him into the ambulance while he was screaming "Attica, attica, attica." Richie shut the doors and got in the driver's seat while Mick sat in the back with the patient.

"So sir, I need to raise your blood sugar. To do that, I'm going to need to see your arm." Mick said patiently.

"Why?" the patient asked with a curious look.

"I need to start an IV and give you intravenous glucose." Mick thought to himself: "I know he's not going to let me give him an IV." He was proven right when the patient said "fuck that. Go away."

"I can't go away, but I will let you refuse."

"Why couldn't I refuse back in the trails? You guys are kidnapping me, technically."

"Technically, we're not." Richie started saying from the front seat while pulling out of the parking lot. "You're hypoglycemic, which causes an altered mental status. If you have an altered mental status, you are not allowed to refuse medical treatment. And also, we don't want you, so again, not kidnapping."

Mick chortled when Richie said that. "Oh you think this is funny?" the patient said. "Just wait until I call your chief of you for this mistreatment."

"Want her number? I got her on speed dial."

"Yeah, I'll put it in my phonebook next to your mothers," the patient said.

"Very clever, sir," Mick deadpanned. Mick sat next to the radio to call a nearby hospital to warn the emergency room they were coming. "Long Island General, this is Riverview Ambulance, please respond." "Help me! Help me!" the patient screamed to try and interrupt Mick. The hospital gave no response. "Once again, Long Island General, this is Riverview, please respond."

The hospital gave no response, again. "They must be with that first patient from the other ambulance, Mick."

"Yeah, probably."

They proceeded to the ambulance bay at the hospital. Two nurses were outside smoking and frantically put them out to go in and prepare for the incoming patient. "Rich, I'm opening the back. Put it in park." Richie parked the ambulance and proceeded to go to the back and help. Mick opened the ambulance doors and went to unlock the stretcher, but the patient started hissing at him with rage. "What?" Mick said to the patient.

"I'll give you one more chance to let me out and go home."

"That's not happening."

"Very well," the patient said in a mysterious voice. Mick unlocked the stretcher, pulled it out, lowered it so it touched the ground, and lifted the latch to bring him in. As he unlocked the stretcher, the patient spit in Mick's face. "You mother fu—"

"You deserved it," the patient said calmly. Mick raised his fist but held back. "Get him in there, Rich."

Richie brought him in while the patient continued to spit at him and miss every time.

"Call security," Richie said to the EMS nurse. The patient continued to spit at them and say "fuck all of you. You don't deserve to help me. You all suck and I'm not listening to you." A nurse came out from behind him and pulled the stretcher into the trauma room. They held his arms down while Richie undid the restraints and they pulled the patient over. Security brought it soft restraints and tied him to the bed. After he was restrained, a nurse put an IV in him while he screamed frantically. They attached fluids to the IV and gave him a shot of a combination of Benadryl, Haldol, and Ativan, and the patient fell asleep minutes later.

Richie exited the hospital and joined Mick in writing the PCR in the back of the ambulance. "Talk about a money shot," he said to Mick. "Fuck off," Mick retorted.

Behind Richie, was a nurse who knocked on the door not to interrupt. "Hey Richie, you don't want to visit me anymore?"

The nurse was young, average height, with blonde hair. Just Richie's type.

"Oh my goodness I'm sorry. I got caught up with that lovely patient who was spitting at us. How've you been?"

The nurse was biting her lip at the sight of Richie. "I'm good. I was wondering when we're going out again."

Richie jumped out of the ambulance and closes the door so Mick wouldn't hear him flirting. "I'm off at 11 tonight if you want to do late-night drinks after your shift," he said sweetly. "Maybe at that bar you were telling me about last week?"

"That'd be great. Text me when you're not on a call?"

"You bet! I'm sorry to cut this short but I have to help my partner out. I'll see you later!"

"Bye!" she winked.

Richie got back in the ambulance to help Mick, and it was his turn to bust Richie's balls. "She dehydrated? She's thirsty as fuck." Richie laughed and actually slapped his knee. "Hey man, she was sweet. Better than any of the girls you met off that app."

Mick looked puzzled. "What do you mean?"

"Oh please, let's go through them shall we?" Richie held up his hands and started counting off girls Mick met off the dating app. "Amanda, wouldn't have sex unless you flicked the lights on and off three times, Carissa would be messaging on her group chat while she was on top of you, and Mary, the Jesus freak, wouldn't get down without Jesus looking down at you. It's like she'd look up going 'heavenly father, should I throw it back?' and he'd look back like 'no, my child.'"

Richie looked at Mick with the "are you kidding me" face while putting his arms down after imitating Jesus on the cross.

"What's your point?" Mick said trying not to let Richie be right. "

Man, you have a stiff mind." Richie laid on the newly done stretcher, and at that moment, the radio went off. "Central calling Riverview, please respond." Mick and Richie both groaned. "I'll go get this signed and then we'll go." Mick sulked inside, sulked back, and got in the passenger seat to take off to the next call.

4

Department Drama

M ick and Richie responded to two other calls before
they arrived back at the station. They had an old
woman who fell out of bed and hit her head on a nightstand,
and they had to give Narcan to a heroin overdose in an alley
behind a liquor store. All went smoother than the diabetic
emergency they had earlier, but none of them said thank you,
acknowledged that they needed help, or were grateful at all.
The old woman only had an ambulance respond because she
hit her life alert by accident, and the heroin OD was phoned
in by someone passing by. None of them wanted help but
were given it. The ungratefulness can really wear on someone
after awhile, so it was no surprise to Richie that Mick was in a
horrible mood when they were on their way back after the
heroin OD. They said nothing to each other, but they work
together 40 hours a week, so Richie knows that Mick is silent
when he's angry. Richie said nothing, but he handed Mick the
aux cord to put on whatever he wanted. He angrily grabbed it
and plugged his phone in to play some of his friend's music.
He only looked up to say "thanks" to Richie, and Richie
understood he felt a tinge better, which is all he would ever
ask for.

Richie looked at him and said, "You know I love you right?" as the song started with a drummer set a steady beat for the band to work off of.

"Yes Rich, I know," Mick said while looking for the stash of cigarettes he keeps in the glove compartment of the ambulance.

"Then why do you get so upset every time we have a miserable day?"

"I don't know," while lighting a cigarette.

"You can't control how people act. So why let annoying people bother you? You go back to the life you live outside of work and you have a support system they most likely don't."

"If I had an answer I'd give it to you, but until then, I don't know bro." The song continued playing as they drove.

They pulled up to the door of the ambulance bay and Mick hit the remote to open the doors as the chorus of the song became louder. The door opened as it did 20 years ago, and Richie almost pulled into the spot where they park the ambulance, but Mick said, "hold up." He took one last drag of his cigarette, then flicked it outside, then started air drumming to the chorus of the song. Richie laughed, pulled into the spot and they got out a little less annoyed than before. They went over to the time clock and punched out, but went into the kitchen for a quick cup of coffee before going home. As they walked into the kitchen, Mick noticed the mess of blankets not put away, food left out for hours, and a stain left on the counter left behind by someone who couldn't be bothered to clean up. He went from less annoyed to seething in a matter of seconds. He was so irate that he took his mug and chucked it at the wall. "These people are so goddamn useless that they can't be bothered to clean up like they do at their own homes.

I'm not their mother, I'm their boss. All I ask for is the slightest bit of respect and they can't even do that."

"Dude, I love you, but this is simple shit you can't help but have to deal with when you're the boss. I'm really getting tired of the attitude you carry with you. We had one bad call, but the two others you were a rock star on. You need to learn to chill," Richie said getting in Mick's face as he's done many times before.

Mick was about to continue with his diatribe of how annoying the staff has been, when all of a sudden, Diaz stumbled out of the bathroom mumbling "Yeah Thomlinson, you gotta learn to chill." Both Mick and Richie were puzzled beyond belief.

"What the hell are you doing here?" Richie said beyond confused seeing Diaz today.

"Our crew is covering the night shift cuz they wanted off," Diaz said as he sat in a chair and closed his eyes.

"I didn't approve a switch, Diaz," Mick said.

"It's an even switch it's cool," Diaz said with his eyes closed and motioning his hands in a way that reminded Mick when he'd shoo his dog away from putting his paws on the table.

"No, you're picking up unapproved over time and now I'm going to have to write up your crew and the night crew for not submitting a request. Good job, Diaz."

"Just put it on my tab," Diaz said as he put his hands behind his head to relax.

At that moment, Violet walked in shyly. "Captain Thomlinson, can I have a word with you?" Mick looked over to her in anger he hasn't experienced in a long time. "What is it, Violet?"

"I'd like to apologize for how I spoke to you earlier. I told my dad what happened and he was furious. So I'd like to say 'I'm sorry' and 'it won't happen again.'"

Mick didn't have the time to discipline her, so he said "it's fine, don't let it happen again. I was in a poor mood and I apologize as well." through his teeth.

"Not like you're ever in a good mood anyway?" Diaz said, still acting like he owns the place.

"You are on such thin ice that you are about to be out on your ass, Diaz."

Diaz stood up and stumbled toward Mick. "Shhhh capt, I think I hear your mom calling. She wants you home to apologize for raising an asshole."

Mick was so irate he almost left over the counter to strangle Diaz. "Diaz, shut up and sit down," Richie advised. Even Violet had realized their behavior earlier was pathetic and now they've gone too far. But at that moment, Diaz's face had gone from a smirk to a realization that something bad is about to happen, so he stopped mocking Mick and ran to the bathroom.

The entire room could hear Diaz throwing up in the bathroom. Mick had no idea what to feel. He was angry, disgusted, and sympathetic to Diaz, but he only could show absolute anger. He walked toward the bathroom and shouted: "Jesus Christ, are you drunk?" There was no response from Diaz. He then turned to Violet and repeated himself. "Is he drunk?" Violet said absolutely nothing because she was so scared of the inevitable consequences. Mick had enough of the nonsense going on and screamed louder than he had in years, "IS. HE. DRUNK?" He screamed so loud that even Richie had jumped, and he wasn't even under the gun. The scream made Violet break down in tears, and was even heard out in the parking lot, where Ex-Chief Fauler overheard the scream and ran inside.

"What the hell is going on here?" Fauler exclaimed. Mick was unstoppable in his anger. "I'll tell you what's going on. Your crew member is drunk and as the crew chief, you should've let me know of the situation to handle it. Not let him come on the crew."

Ex-Chief Fauler made a face of annoyance. This, to him, was not a serious problem. "That's it? Thomlinson, he's a fireman and an EMT, what do you expect from him? Firemen drink while on shift all the time. It's a part of the culture."

Mick was now boiling. "Are you out of your mind? He's working at his job, and therefore cannot be consuming alcohol or any other drug."

"Alcohol isn't a drug, Mickie."

"Ethanol is a legal, yet recreational drug. Regardless of your relaxed view on it, he can't be working. Have you had any this evening, Chief?"

Ex-Chief Fauler rolled his sleeves up. "Yeah, we had a couple of beers before we came in. So what?"

"Then both of you are not riding tonight. And everyone on this night crew is being written up for being intoxicated during their shift."

"Who's going to work for us tonight then huh?" Ex-Chief Fauler said.

"Mickie and I will work in your place," Richie said backing his friend up. Mick looked back at him with a face of gratitude and respect for having his back in this situation. Ex-Chief Fauler was furious inside, but he did not show it. He checked under his nail beds then looked up at Mick. "It's a shame you're such a stickler for the rules, Thomlinson. When your dad was here, we'd get loaded, take the ambulance out, and pick up a couple of girls to party with back here for the night. I think that's how he and your mom met, isn't it?" Richie had tensed up to the point of no return. He had no idea what Mick was going to do next. Mick stood there with a smirk on his face. "Yeah, but he grew the fuck up didn't he. He didn't live a life full of one party after another. He settled down with a wife and kid. And that kid went on to be a better paramedic than you. He went on to be your boss and is now telling you to stand the fuck down," Mick said in a tone that was louder than a whisper, but not by much.

Ex-Chief Fauler was growing impatient. He took off his glasses and set them on the table. "Is that right, Mickie?" Mick didn't move from his spot. "Yeah, that's right. I went on to be a better medic than you ever were. And when I go home, I don't sit around wondering what I could have been if I had had the sack to get up and move. Unlike you, I bust my ass for this place and I don't cry myself to sleep thinking about where I could be with one hand down my pants and another holding my phone. You lazy, repressed, little shit. I can't wait to see you get fired for this. Because I'm going to laugh you out of the building my dad built and you couldn't." After Mick spent time breathing Ex-Chief Fauler down, Fauler took his right hand and punched Mick square in the jaw.

Fauler didn't knock Mick out, but it knocked him down. As soon as Richie saw Fauler make contact with Mick's jaw, he ran and tackled Fauler to the ground. He pinned him down and told Violet to call the current Chief of the department to deal with the situation. After Mick rubbed his jaw and came back to, the Chief's assistant was walking in, impatient and furious at the situation, and said "Fauler and Thomlinson, Chief's office now." Both Fauler and Thomlinson put their bullshit aside and went to speak with the chief.

5

The Chief's Office

M ick and Ex-Chief Lautner went to open the chief's
door, but it was locked. Everyone in the department is
taught if the chief's office is locked, there is no entry, that she
is working on something important and cannot be disturbed.
There is no second key, and if there was, nobody would dare
try to open it. So Mick and the Ex-Chief sat in chairs outside
like 2 kids waiting to see the school principal for starting
trouble in the halls. Mick has no experience in mischief what-
soever. The Ex-Chief however, has a long history of starting
trouble, so this is no big deal to him. He is so nonchalant
about the incident, he decides to slouch in his chair and start
whistling "You're Gonna Live Forever in Me," by John Mayer.
If Mick wasn't already in a fiery ball of rage, he was about to
become an inferno at this lack of care.

"You're absolutely pathetic," Mick said.

"And you're a cocky twerp. I can't wait to be suspended for
this so I don't have to see you for weeks."

"You're looking forward to this?"

"Mickie, I've been suspended many times. I've gotten into fights, screaming matches, and had an unannounced bachelor party here once."

"You've never been married so what're you talking about?"

"Well, I wanted a hot woman to jump out of a cake, so why split hairs?"

"I repeat, you're pathetic."

Ex-Chief Lautner sat up in his chair. "You know what your problem is Mick?"

"That I have an impending black eye and I'm about to be suspended for doing the right thing?"

"No, it's that this job is your entire life. What do you do when you get home? Go to bed, wake up, go for a run, sit around until work, and the cycle starts all over again? You have no life. Don't worry about your black eye, worry about your life going to waste."

"My life is fine, thank you very much."

"It may be, but if you want something worth living for, have a little danger."

Mick looked at him for the first time since they sat down. "Was having crabs from that stripper dangerous enough for you? Or was watching her alone enough since you don't have a friend to tell it to?" Lautner lunged at Mick again and knocked him off his seat.

The scuffling continued until the Chief's office door swung open and flew off the doorstop. Lautner had no regard for what could happen when the Chief saw him. Mick, however, knew not to hit back since it'd only hurt his chances of staying at work more. Let Lautner have all the discipline. It took the Chief one hand to pull Lautner off Mick and drag him back 2 feet. She pulled him back and looked down at him. "Get it my office and don't even think about a sarcastic comment," The Chief said without an ounce of expression on her face. The Ex-Chief finally had nothing to say, he got up and went into the office and sat down. The Chief went over and helped Mick up and helped him to a chair. She went to a cooler in the corner of her office and wrapped ice up in a bandana and put it to his forehead.

"So an ex-chief and an ambulance captain get in a fistfight in my station, making me come in at midnight to discipline them like children. Great, really great." The Chief took out a binder, flipped to a blank page, and clicked her pen. "So Mick, tell me in your words what happened."

"Well, he was being Mick and told me to—"

"Ex-Chief Lautner if I wanted you to speak, I'll tell you." The Ex-Chief was stunned. He rarely gets told to not talk. He sat quietly while Mick spoke.

"Thank you Chief," Mick began, "Richie and I started doing rig check when the morning crew came in and gave us a hard time about—"

"We were busting your chops, none of it was serious," Ex-Chief Lautner interrupted. The chief picked her head up from her binder. "What side of the desk are you on, sir?" Ex-Chief sat back and cleaned his nails. "Continue," she said as she put her nose back into her binder.

"They were giving us a hard time about being a man down for this crew. We then got a call for a diabetic emergency out in Hunters Field that was difficult, but we got him securely to the hospital."

"You call a grumpy patient difficult," the Ex-Chief inter-rupted one more time.

"Which side of this desk are you on? Observe that, and keep quiet!" The current chief gave him a stare warning him one more outburst would be fatal to his career. "Right, right," he said in a grumpy manner. He sunk in his chair a little more in embarrassment; realizing he's being told to be quiet in the office that used to be his.

"Anyway, Chief. We had a geriatric patient who fell out of bed and didn't use her life alert, and we narcanned a patient who overdosed on heroin behind a liquor store after. All of which were reluctant to see us or be treated, so admittingly, I came back from my shift with an elevated temper," Mick stated.

"And when did you see crew member Diaz?" The Chief inquired.

"I saw him stumble out of the bathroom and he was very out of character."

"How so?"

"He was slurring his words, he had dilated pupils, and was very confrontational."

"Did you think he was drinking?"

"I realized that after he went to the bathroom to throw up. I would have called you, but Ex-Chief Lautner had punched me in the face after threatening himself and Diaz with writing them up for drinking on shift."

"Well, wait just a minute. We weren't on shift yet, we were walking into it. It was only 2355, we still had 5 minutes," Ex-Chief Lautner interrupted for the last time.

"Lautner, let me ask you something. In your time as Chief, have you learned anything?" the Chief inquired as she tapped her hand with a pen. "You and your crewmate arrived after drinking alcohol, and one of you was over the legal limit, you talked back to the captain of the crew when you did not let him know about a switch in the crew, and you used physical violence to resolve it. Since you like to interrupt and speak up, tell me right now why you shouldn't be fired before you leave this office." Ex-Chief Lautner and Mick were speechless.

"Well, uh, you see Chief, uh," Ex-Chief Lautner started.

"Well spoken, get out, and take all your possessions out of your locker with you," she said firing the Ex-Chief and now Ex-member of the department. His words came flooding back to him. "Now wait just a minute. I'm an Ex-Chief of this department and deserve to be treated with a little respect. I've worked my ass off to get this department to where it needs to be, and if someone disrespects me the way this little bastard has, I'm going to do something about it." The Ex-Chief was teetering between anger and fear. The fear of losing the job he started with when he was 21 and gave him his confidence and financial security.

"Let me give you some advice for your next job," the Chief said sitting back in her chair. "To get respect, you give respect. I've seen you on calls. You're sarcastic and make fun of the patients. Frankly, I've been looking for a way to send you out of here, and you gave it to me with blood and bruises on Mick. Your position has been terminated, please leave my office, thank you."

The Ex-Chief was on the verge of tears, but he got up shaking as he did. "Wait, one second," the Chief said.

Lautner stopped in his tracks, hoping this was all a ruse to get him to behave better. "Chief, you are really good. I mean wow, I almost believed you for_"

"Leave your badge on the table. You're not allowed to be on this premises from now on. See? Isn't it annoying to be interrupted?" Lautner was devastated. He took his badge off and threw it at the Chief. Mick got up in his seat to defend her, but she said quickly, "You'll be out of here with him if you do it, Mick." He sat down and waited for his punishment as Lautner stomped out.

"So, I'm sure I'm not off the hook, huh?" Mick said trying to sound optimistic.

"What was your first clue?" The chief said without smiling or indicating she finds this at all funny. She reopened her notebook and clicked her pen. "So you getting hit is not your fault, the unapproved switch is not your fault, and the crew being rude and inappropriate to you while they were also under the influence is not your fault." Mick had a sigh of relief when he heard this. "I'm not done," she said looking up at him. "What is your fault, is the manner in which you handled it. It was not becoming of an officer and it was something I'd never expect out of you. You're on the fast track to becoming my successor and this is a big step backward. What the hell were you thinking? We both know you're better than this."

"Chief, I wouldn't have acted this way if they weren't being so incredibly rude."

"You can't control how people act, you can only control how you react to the situation. Insulting someone doesn't get your argument across. Just because you yell, does not make you right. Now I'm going to forget you said that, and ask you one more time, what is going on with you?"

Mick adjusted himself in his chair. Although he had a million things that he'd like to say is wrong with him, he thought about what was relevant to what's going on, and what could destroy his career. She saw the look he expressed on his face. Like his wheels were turning trying to think before he spoke. "Take a minute, I'm going to get a water bottle from the break room." She left the room for maybe 2 minutes. He took deep breaths and thought of what outcome could come of what he's saying. There's how you're feeling, and then there's how to say it appropriately.

The Chief returned and went to the cabinet near the ice cooler. She took out a glass and filled it with ice. Mick looked back at her and thought that was a valid representation of how he felt at the moment. Just shoveling something out to get to where he wants to be without spilling the real contents. She came back to the desk and poured her water into the glass. "Well, let's hear it." Mick cleared his throat. "Chief, in all honesty, I'm having trouble putting words together that are appropriate and wouldn't insult you. You're too smart to accept anything less than that. I'm really having a hard time in life right now. I'm unhappy, I feel alone and dejected, and I'm worried about my future. I think I'm lashing out because of the anger inside and I don't have someone or something to channel it at. I just feel depressed right now." Mick thought it was the stupidest thing to say. Who cares how you feel inside in EMS work? It's not relevant. It's about the job you're doing. Turns out, those words saved his life.

"Do you feel depressed in a way that makes you're unhappy, or do you think you'd hurt yourself or someone else in the process?"

"Chief, I could never hurt myself or anyone else. I guess I just feel like I'm in a rut. I don't know how to feel and I feel like anything I do is a mistake taking me further away from my end goal." The Chief pushed her chair out and went below to her file cabinet. She rifled through the drawers as if looking for the solution to his problem. She took out a card and closed the cabinet. She pushed her chair back in still holding the card. "So, you will not be suspended or face disciplinary charges," she said. Mick could tell she wasn't finished, and he feared what could possibly be on the card. "You will, however, be put on a medical leave of absence." He opened his mouth to lash out, but the chief gave him a glance that made him think otherwise. "You will report to a licensed master of social work for treatment. You can return to work after your sessions are done in two weeks. I'll make a call to set the whole thing up, and you report to this counselor tomorrow evening." She handed him the card. He took the card that read "Christopher Lazlo, LMSC."

"What's the crew going to think about this, Chief?"

"They all know you got punched in the face, and once they found out he assaulted you a second time, they'll think it's for the trauma and rest. I also recommend you go to the doctor and get that all sorted out with a cat scan or an MRI."

"Richie will be alone though for two weeks," Mick said thinking about his friend in need.

"No worries, I'll be riding with him until you come back." Mick thought about his shift tomorrow and the look on Richie's face when the Chief shows up to ride with him. That put the icing on the cake. "Alright Chief, I'll go Monday."

"Good, now get out of my office. And try not to let the door hit your good eye," she said with a smile while Mick frowned and got up to leave.

6

A Meeting with the Mediocre Man

Mick walked from the office to his car in an absolute daze. Along the way, he passed the department trophy case. He took a second to glance at all of them. He looked up at the wall and saw the endless parade of pictures of ex and current chiefs of the department. All of them are wearing the same ensemble to show respect to the chiefs who have retired or passed on. He started at the frames reflecting light from the ceiling wondering to himself how many of these chiefs had to go on medical leave due to psych issues. God knows how many had their own demons, but how many had to sit on the sidelines to deal with their own demons and watch as the others thrived. Surely there had to be one, but thinking to himself that he'd be sitting on the sideline and not growing as a person goes to show how long he has to go to get better.

He made it back to his car, put his seatbelt on, started the engine, but did not put the car in drive. He sat for a few seconds and stared at a yield sign on the side of the road, relating to the word with how he was feeling. He took a deep breath, then let out a throat curdling scream while he repetitively punched and slapped the steering wheel. If anyone was around, they'd of thought a murder took place. But the scream went unheard by anyone but himself. He finished his scream but went straight into an ugly cry that produced tears and snot bubbles. He hadn't been this upset in years. He had no idea how to handle this, but he knew he had plans to get to after work. He pulled himself together and took his phone out to call his friend Doug, the musician and teacher extraordinaire.

The phone rang only once. "Hey, you still coming over? Ang and I just got back from the movies." Mick thought it would be nice to have someone to take to the movies. "Yeah, is that cool?" he asked.

"Hence, why I just asked if you're coming—ya know what, just get over here will ya? I'm dying to talk about this movie." Mick giggled at the notion. "Yeah, I'm on my way." Mick hung up the phone, put his car in drive, and took off. Doug only lived 10 minutes away, but Mick made the trip stretch out a bit by driving the speed limit or slower. He looked at all the buildings a little differently. Trying to see if there was anything new in his town he could explore now that he had time to kill. Having a sudden abundance of time after having almost none at all can be an overwhelming experience. You think of what to do with yourself or count down until you have something to do again. Now that Mick could afford it, he'd spend the time doing things he always wanted to try—this he promised this to himself as he pulled into Doug's new home.

Doug was always a card-carrying mama's boy so he bought the house behind his childhood home in case his parents needed help in their old age. Angie has his back no matter what so she erected a new fence along the perimeter to have a gate for emergency use only. It was a ranch-style home that looked straight out of *Better Homes and Gardens*. The only exception was that since Doug was a fanatic about keeping things as an extension of himself, he put up a sign that said "Manning Manner; the Mediocre Estate. Keep off the Dirigible Plums." Noting his friend's craving for having a Harry Potter reference on his property made him roll his eyes as Ang has done countless times since their wedding. He opened the gate to walk in, and Ang was already at the door readily with a drink and a hug waiting for Mick. "Hi! How was work?" She said as Mick gave her a hug.

"I'll explain later," he said before taking a sip of his drink. "Is this a Long Island or a regular iced tea?"

"You're not working tomorrow so you should unwind with us a bit," Ang said with a smile. Ang's new thing in the home is to be sure everyone feels welcome to stay as long as they want to be as happy as they are. Doug came in wearing a t-shirt and gym shorts holding a guitar, his usual attire.

"Okay, so we just got back from Brooklyn right?" Doug didn't even say hello. Doug and Mick have been friends since elementary school, so hello's have become arbitrary at this point. "So we went to the Alamo Drafthouse in Brooklyn to see the movie Ang wanted to see, right?"

"What movie did you want to see, Ang?" Ang came back from popping the top off her beer, "'Won't You Be My Neighbor,' Mister Rogers documentary, but we were about a year too late so we decided to see 'Spiderman Far From Home' instead." Mick's interest peaked. "How was it!"

"Fucking excellent dude, not as good as the Civil War, but still." Mick stopped taking a drink to say "say that again?" in an accusatory way.

"Civil War was way better, it's just a fact, dude," Doug said stating the obvious. Mick put his drink on a table. "State your case," Mick said as though he were judge, jury, and executioner.

"Civil War was the best-told story in the Marvel Cinematic Universe. It had love, politics, and betrayal. It was almost Shakespearean. It had Ant-Man becoming a giant, the introduction of Spiderman to the universe, and Vision wore a sweater. Tell me I'm wrong."

Mick took a big gulp of his drink. "Civil War was a good movie, but the sides they were on were completely the wrong choices for the main characters. Ask any die-hard comic book fan and they'll tell you Captain America, a man from the '40s, a man who seeks to do right by the world and to push for a greater future, is most likely an old school democrat-FDR new deal type of guy. He'd lean in hard for government intervention. Tony Stark is a multi-billionaire, who wants to do right, too, but is really a libertarian. He is more likely to want this to maintain a private organization and run with as little government involvement as possible. Yes, they changed it from the comic drastically to suit the MCU, but realistically the biggest plot hole is sitting right in front of you." Doug rotated his neck as though he heard someone talking shit about how KISS isn't the most successful rock band of the 20th century.

Doug stood and started clapping his hands to make his point with passion. "How are you going to tell me that finding out Bucky killed the Starks isn't one of the best cinema moments since finding out Darth Vader is Luke's father."

"Because if you read the book, they forget the biggest point of the story. After Captain America is about to waste Iron Man for good, he gets bombarded by police officers, firemen, and EMT's who try to tell him 'none of this is about you. It's about the job you signed on for and the people you help along the way.' Throwing his point down the toilet. Civil War is good, but Endgame is a masterpiece of cinema." Ang ran in the middle of them screaming "I still like Iron Man 3!" clearly making a joke. Mick and Ang laughed while Doug took a drink to swallow some booze along with his pride. "So why'd you sound weird on the phone?" he said trying to change the subject after losing an argument.

Mick's mood went from delighted to dower. "I got put on medical leave at work." Ang, the nurse, peeked her head up to do some work out of the office. "Did you pull a muscle at work lifting a patient?"

"No, it's for my psychiatric well being." Doug and Ang were flabbergasted and ran to sit down next to him. "Do you feel like hurting yourself?" Ang said while stroking his arm to be sure he's okay.

"No Ang, I'm fine. I got in a fight at work."

"You can't fight for shit, are you okay?" Doug said, keeping it real.

"Yes, and it's not like you're Mike Tyson either singer-boy." Doug looked at Ang and shrugged his shoulders in agreement with Mick. "So what exactly happened?" Ang asked.

"So I came back from a shift with an attitude and the crew coming on was drunk. So when I confronted them, the crew chief punched me, then I was sent to the office, where he attacked me again in the hallway." Doug and Ang were confused about how the circumstances had come to surface.

"So why are you out on medical for psych?"

"Because I confessed to the Chief that I'm unhappy with my life and I feel like everything I do is the wrong step, and that was the reason why I started screaming at the crew."

Ang got up and hugged Mick from the back. He reciprocated by putting a hand on one of her arms while Doug was dumbfounded by his friends' feelings.

"Dude, you know you could always come to us if you feel unhappy," Doug said in support.

"I know, but I just feel like I need to make myself happy. Not rely on others to be there for me. Sometimes nobody will be there for me, so I have to learn to pick myself up. But I kind of just feel alone in my world some days." Ang sniffled as though she were about to cry. "So what do you do now?"

"I have to see a social worker a couple of times over the next two weeks so I can get signed off to come back."

"So that's not too bad!" Ang said patting him on the shoulder.

"Yeah, I guess not."

"And think about how much you can do in the meantime!" she continued. "Think of this as a blessing, not a curse. You have a whole world of opportunity waiting for you to grab it."

This pep talk did make Mick feel better. But what made him really feel better, was a match he was about to get on the dating app.

Mick's phone sat on the table vibrating with a notification on his dating app. "Hey you're phone is going off from some dating app," Doug said hinting at something.

"Eh, it's probably a notification for an ad to swipe more or upgrade an account and pay money for it," Mick said with a sense of hopelessness in his voice.

"Nah I think you should take a look," Doug said hinting at something.

"What is it? A fake account that asks me for money?" Doug rolled his eyes and said, "look at your phone, dick."

Mick grabbed his phone in annoyance and looked at the notification. It turned out to be a young woman, his age, with brown hair, blue eyes, and a welcoming smile, named Lindsay. The profile read "25, food enthusiasts, mom's love me, and yes I will pick you up when you're drunk as long as you buy me potato skins." Mick scrolled through her profile and he was elated to see she was the same girl in all 4 photos, none of them was a group photo. "She seems awesome! What do I say?" Angela slapped Doug's hand to signify her tagging in to take over from here. "Don't say anything about her looks or her description. Just say something nice, or funny," she said like she was a teacher. Mick and Angela sat and debated over what to say to the girl first while Doug sat there as useless as a bum hand. He realized he was not necessary, so he went to the bathroom. He was there for about 25 minutes while he did his business, scrolled through his phone, and read the back of cleaning products. He came out and they were still debating on what to say first. He was confused to see these two debates over a simple "hello." He had enough of it and went over to take the phone out of their hands. He snatched it, typed "hi, you seem sweet, hope you have a good day."

He put the phone back in Mick's hands and they both read it. They were both pleased with the simplicity of not trying to sound macho or impressive. "Let your personality come naturally and she'll love you. If you need to borrow mine I'll understand." Mick rolled his eyes, but Ang stood up and went "what's so great about your personality?" Doug looked at her baffled. "I don't know Mrs. Manning, I think I came up with some stuff once upon a time to charm a girl I met who hit me in the head with a book." Angela blushed at Doug mentioning her clumsiness when they met. "Point taken," she said sitting back down.

7

Mick's First Session

ick slept over Doug and Angela's house that night.
They stopped drinking and chatting to go to sleep at
around 3:30 that morning. They laughed and drank all night
while trying to make Mick feel okay about his situation. And
when he woke up at 8 am, he still felt okay. He got up, went to
the kitchen to see if anyone was awake, but nobody was home.
The only thing that was in the home was Mick and a note on
the refrigerator. "Mick—went to visit my parents for brunch.
Feel free to stick around as long as you want, but we won't be
home until after your meeting. Keep your head up, it'll all
work out. Love always, Ang." He smiled at the note, looked
around the house, and realized he'd much rather be in his
apartment. He had until 5 pm that day to go to the social
worker, so he'd much rather be in his own environment than
someone else's. So he decided to take a shower, then go home.

He went to the bathroom, got undressed and turned the water
on. He put his hands out to feel the water temperature and
adjusted it. He got inside and closed the glass shower door. He
started sudsing himself up with the soap when he felt a rush

of depression. He looked down at the drain and saw the water rushing down, relating to it as waves of emotion were crashing over his life that he couldn't comprehend. The overwhelming feeling was so much larger than life that he started to cry. A lot of people who face depression feel that their current situation was so overwhelming that they'd never recover. It isn't true of course, but when your brain is giving you such a feeling, it's hard to ignore.

He went to reach for the shampoo but grabbed a shelf instead to hold himself upon. He grabbed the top of the shower door for support of his other arms, but his knees buckled and he crashed to the floor. He wasn't physically hurt, but he felt so defeated that his emotional core seemed to be broken or at least bruised. He thought about returning to his apartment and having nothing to do but wait to see a social worker, and it felt like he had lost. He felt that he had lost all sense of control in his life and he would never recover. He was a broken-down car of a man, and he'd never be able to get into drive and feel the sense of movement. He sat at the bottom of the shower and cried for what felt like an eternity. He looked out the shower door and saw his clothes scattered around the floor and thought "Ang wouldn't want to see that." He stopped the shower, dried off and picked them up. It occurred to him that his breakdown in the shower was so unlike his character. He had to pick himself up and take these social work sessions seriously for his benefit. He put his clothes on with a sense of determination, grabbed his keys and took off to go home.

He arrived home and ran straight up the stairs. His hair was still wet from the shower from before, so he decided to take one in his apartment. He shut his shower curtain and took a shower like he normally did, and he felt better. He thought to himself how that could have possibly happened. He never had a mental breakdown before, so why did it happen now? He made a mental note of it to talk with the social worker about why that could have happened. After he finished, he dried off and lay in bed without getting dressed. He awoke at 4 pm in a panic. He rushed to his wallet to find the card the Chief gave him to look for the social worker's address. He panicked, even more, when he realized it was a half-hour drive in a direction that's littered with traffic. He had no time to make coffee or dress properly. He put on jeans and a t-shirt and ran to his car. He put the car in drive and took off as he was typing in the address for the office with one hand and keeping the other on the wheel. He sped off toward this office like it was the end of a race he could win. And he, like anyone else with his problems or symptoms, can win.

He was dodging cars left and right while he fixed his hair in the rearview mirror. He took the main highway all the way there, got off at the correct exit, and the office was in a development surrounded by a flower nursery and a hardware store. There were multiple social workers and licensed mental health counselors who shared this office with him. He parked his car, ran inside and approached the assistant. "Hi, I'm Mick Thomlinson, I'm here for an appointment with Christopher Lazlo," he said panting his breath.

"Hello sir, yes he's with another client at the moment he'll come out to get you when he's done," she said in a voice that sounded like a voice from an automated system from a large corporation.

"Thank you," Mick said, and he walked over to the chairs in the lobby and took a seat.

He was waiting for about 5 minutes when his phone vibrated. He took it out and it was a response from the girl from the dating app, Lindsay. His heart was surfing on his chest and it was beating so fast. He opened his phone and saw what she wrote back to him. He prepared himself for a letdown, but she responded saying "Hi! Sorry for the late response, but you seem sweet! How is your day going?" His stomach was overloaded with butterflies. She seemed like a normal person. He started to respond back saying "Very well thank you! I'm just going into a doctor's appointment actually." He saw the app saying "typing," showing that she's starting to respond back. "Kind of late for a doctor's appointment. Hope all goes well!" He smiled at his phone and responded back saying "Thank you!"

At that moment, Christopher Lazlo LMSW comes out of his office. "Is there a Mick Thomlinson here?" Mick put his phone away and raised his hand. "Come on in, sir," Lazlo said motioning his hand into the hallway as a welcoming gesture. Mick got up, nodded his head to Lazlo, and walked into the hallway. "My office is the last on the left, I'm going to grab a cup of coffee, would you like one?"

"No thank you," Mick said.

"Okay, I'll be back in a minute. Make yourself comfortable."

"Thanks," Mick said already striding toward the door. He opened the door to see an office with an elegant chair for Lazlo with folders and a laptop beside it, a large couch for a client, and air conditioner, a lamp, and prints of art on the wall that Mick recognized immediately. They were prints from Jean-Michel Basquiat. Mick knew at once he'd probably like this guy.

Mick was still looking around the office when Lazlo walked in. "Sorry about that," Lazlo expressed.

"'The Basquiat Skull', right?" Mick said pointing at the painting.

"Yes, it is, good eye, sir."

"Oh, you don't have to call me sir, just call me Mick." Lazlo gave a friendly smile, and said "Sounds good, have a seat, stay awhile." Mick sat on the couch. He analyzed Lazlo as Lazlo looked at his computer to remind himself about Mick's case. Lazlo didn't look that much older than Mick, maybe just a few years, but he seemed more comfortable and confident with himself. Lazlo put the laptop down. "So I see what your Chief wrote about what happened and why you're here, but why don't you tell me in your own words about what happened."

Mick took a deep breath. "Well, I was coming back from a rough day at work and the next crew was drunk coming in on shift. So I lost my temper and tried to discipline them the best I could, but I guess my anger got away from me and one of them punched me in the face. And when we were sent to the Chief's office he attacked me again. So the Chief fired him and sent me here so I can at least return to work."

"Well, there's obviously more to it than that. Can you explain in a little more detail?" Lazlo said, clicking his pen. Mick made a face of embarrassment, he hated this story even though it was a day old. "So my day started with a patient who was an agitated diabetic. He made crude remarks to me, my partner, and a female police officer. We had to restrain him, actually."

"Mhmm, keep going," Lazlo said jotting down what he was saying.

"Then I had a geriatric patient, that means someone whose—"

"I know what it means, keep going."

Mick made another embarrassed face. "So the geriatric patient pressed her life alert by accident and was not at all happy we had to break into her house to help her. And then we had a patient who overdosed on heroin in an alley next to a liquor store."

"The liquor store on Elm St?"

"Yeah, the same one."

"They sell heroin out the store, I've been campaigning with other substance counselors to get it shut down for months. But please, continue."

"So we get back from all of these wretched calls, and while I was venting to my partner, the next crew comes in, clearly inebriated, and starts ranting and raving about how I'm a shitty captain and poking the bear. So after the Ex-Chief started talking poorly about my father, I insulted him, then he punched me in the face." Lazlo looked up from his pad.

"The whole crew was drunk?"

"Well, one person wasn't. She was a newbie and is the daughter of someone in authority. She actually was apologizing for her earlier bad attitude."

"So, before we continue, you had a bad day, and people weren't showing you respect as their captain, so you grew angrier, and insulted them."

"Well, it's a bit more complicated than that."

"How so?" Lazlo said clicking his pen once more.

"Well, earlier they were poking fun at us for being a man down on the crew so we worked the entire shift more than we should have."

"It seems like to me, you were working harder than you should, and when it went unnoticed you grew impatient. Would that be fair to say?"

"Yes, I think so," Mick said with a serious tone to his voice.

"Why do you think that is?" Lazlo said crossing his legs.

"I worked my ass off to become a captain. I didn't get the treatment that the girl did."

"What kind of treatment did she get that's different from yours?" Lazlo said looking at him and speaking with an inquisitive yet sympathetic tone.

"When she came in, we were corralled by the Chief to hear her talk about how we have to behave and not pull any funny business. Normally, new members are put straight to work cleaning up the kitchen, cleaning the bathroom, landscaping and upkeeping the trucks. She didn't have to do any of it. She walked in as the kid of a Fire Marshall who had good connections with City Hall. When I showed up, the son of one of the best members, I was given the worst kind of hell. They subjected me to worse hazing than usual."

"What would they do?" Lazlo said keeping his tone sympathetic.

"They would throw food at me if it wasn't cooked right, then tell me to do it again after I washed all the dishes, they'd put me in a corner and tell me to drink a whole 12-pack of beer then sit on my head until I threw up, they'd jump on me and give me a beating. I had to go to the Chief at the time and explain my black eye was because I walked into a door. I had no place else to learn to be a good EMT so I had to suck it up, be a man, and take it. But I have to show respect to someone who got none of the treatment? Fuck that."

Lazlo took a sip of his coffee before he spoke again. "Does anyone else but the perpetrators know about the abuse?"

"It was just hazing, it wasn't abuse or anything that bad."

Lazlo dropped his tone and spoke clearly. "Mick, if someone lays their hand on you without your permission, and you tell them to stop and they don't, it's abuse. You ought to talk about it with your current Chief and be sure it doesn't happen to anyone again."

"She was a new person around the same time as me and she knew. She cracked down on it long ago. But thank you for the concern. We're really the only people who knew what went on back in the day."

"Well, at least it stopped." Lazlo took another sip of his coffee.

"So, about how you spoke to the other crew."

"I know, it was deplorable, inept, and outright stupid of me to speak that way to them," Mick said hanging his head.

"Well, your feelings toward it are completely valid, in my opinion. But how you went about it wasn't up to par with your capabilities as a captain and paramedic. The Chief sent over your file, it's quite impressive. Especially for someone your age."

Mick couldn't help but smile. "You're very kind," he replied.

"My pleasure. But anyway, I'm not going to do the whole 'if you were in their shoes' scenario because we know you aren't the same people. I think the lesson to take here is that you know how good of a captain you are and how great you are in the field. If someone is obviously being insubordinate towards you, you should go to your Chief, explain the situation, then talk it over with them. If they still act in an insubordinate way, the Chief will handle it. You're better than how you acted, so always remember where you came from, and clear your head of what you feel like you should do, and do what you know is right."

Mick had the feeling of an anvil being lifted off his chest. This talk had made him feel better than he had in months. "You're right, and I'll try to remember that."

"You're damn right I'm right. You're not the only one here who's good in their field," Lazlo said pointing back at his diploma on the wall. Mick chuckled and kept a smile throughout the rest of the session.

8

Lovely Lindsay

The next few days following Mick's first meeting with Lazlo were filled with doing things he's always wanted to do but never had the time with work. One day he went to Manhattan to see a few museums he'd been dying to check out, another he went to a few new restaurants he'd wanted to dine in all in a single day, and other days he stayed in. All the time while enjoying his medical leave, he checked in with Richie, Doug and Ang, and the Chief on his progress. All were supportive and trying to make him laugh about his scenario. Richie went as far as to drop off a straight jacket in a box. Mick laughed until he thought about how Richie could have possibly got his hands on a straight jacket. While his friends were checking in on him, he was messaging Lindsay every day on the app. Their conversations were filled with humor and compliments with growing anticipation of the one asking the other out. Until one day, Lindsay took a stand and did something about it.

She messaged him saying "I've been really enjoying our talks, and I was wondering if you would like to meet up and grab a drink soon." Mick had never been asked out before. He was excited and nervous. He quickly responded with "only if I can pick up the bill. You took the risk, and I'll be sure it isn't all for nothing." "Deal :)," she messaged back. They decided to meet at a bar called "Noekerbrau," a bar that doubles as a library. A place where you can read about Sam Adams, and drink a cold Sam Adams.

Mick and Lindsay set up a date at 7 pm. Mick got there at 06:30 to have a drink to calm his nerves, and see if they have a copy of the new Keith Buckley book. He arrived in a button-down shirt and skinny jeans. He walked in and took up a seat at the bar. The bartender/librarian took notice of him and couldn't help but comment. "First date huh?"

Mick was rattled by it. "Is it that obvious?" he asked, rethinking his outfit.

"Little bit, I'd get a drink and kill it before she comes in. What'll it be?"

Mick looked at the specialty drink menu and saw the eccentric drinks they made. They had the 'Ernest Hemingway,' a drink that makes the bells toll, the 'Stephen King,' a drink that makes you see two twins in the hallway and scared for your life, and the 'J.K Rowling,' the drink that makes you feel like the chosen one. He chose none of those, but went with the 'J.D Salinger,' when you have one and you're done.

Mick finished his drink and sat waiting for Lindsay to show up. The clock showed the time of 07:30. "She is coming boss?" the bartender said.

"I hope so, she seems really cool."

"You ever talk to her on the phone?"

Mick thought about it and couldn't help but think about it. "Well, no not really."

"Okay, she ever sent you a picture that wasn't on her profile?"

Mick thought of that again. "No, not necessarily."

"Uh-huh," the bartender replied. Mick knew what he was getting at. "You ever ask to facetime her and she says she can't because her camera is broken?"

"Well, wait just a minute. Are you saying she could have been catfishing me this whole time?"

"Maybe, maybe not?" the bartender said, cleaning a glass then checking the computer to see if a book is in for a customer. "She could have been one of the guys who came in and is just staring at you hoping you'll be cool with her Adam's Apple."

"I doubt it highly, sir." Mick looked over his shoulder to see if there were any suspicious characters staring at him in the bar. But he was elated to find someone familiar entering the bar. It was Lindsay. She was dressed beautifully, had the kind smile he had seen in her pictures and had no Adam's Apple of any kind.

She came over and stuck out her hand. "You look familiar, I'm waiting for a date but you seem just as sweet. Hi, I'm Lindsay." Mick chuckled and said, "Nice to see you, I'm Mick." They shook hands and she sat in the seat next to him.

"Sorry I'm late, I'm a perfectionist and this is all hard work."

"Well, you make it seem easy." Lindsay's cheeks went red from the compliment. She diverted attention by checking out the drink menu. "I'll have the 'Edgar Allan Poe,' the drink that'll make you hear the beating of the hideous heart. I'd also like a book on how to properly arrange daisies." She handed back the drink menu and looked at Mick. "What? I like a variety." Mick looked at the bartender and said, "Make it two."

The drinks were served and they came out darker than Poe's work. They were served with a candy eye to represent the Black Cat from his short story. While they drank they read the book on how to arrange daisies and acted very silly from then on. After they read up on how to arrange them from tallest to smallest, Mick asked Lindsay a little more about her life. "So where are you from exactly? I don't know if I really asked." Lindsay put her napkin in the book as a bookmark. "Well, I was born in Paris actually, but my family moved to the states for job opportunities."

"Oh! Do you speak French?"

"Not at all, but we have family who's over there so we go every couple of years."

"So, where did they move to?"

"They moved to Sayville to continue the family business over in the states. They ran a French restaurant that's going pretty strong."

"Well, whatever makes them happy."

Mick and Lindsay continued talking and found out they had a mutual friend. "Wait, you're telling me your friend dated Schneider?" Mick said about a person he always couldn't stand. "Ugh, yes. He was the absolute worst. He broke up with my friend because she wanted him to move in with her and out of his parents' basement. When they broke up, I saw him in a bar and when he asked me out I said no because I didn't think his mother's umbilical cord could stretch to my apartment. Mick slapped his knee and he was laughing so hard.

"That's amazing. He used to work at my friend's hospital and fucked up so bad they fired him mid-shift."

"Oh my god, what did he do?"

Mick put his drink down. "Alright, well he used to do house cleaning, but he always wanted a little more. So from time to time, he'd help people do the jobs that were outside his scope of practice. So one day a patient passes away on one of the floors. The laboratory brought up this special stretcher they have for bringing bodies. So since he was trying so hard to get in with good people, he stops what he's doing and helps pulls over the body. He does it, no incident there. However, an hour or so after he needed to call in for checking where he's supposed to be. They are running around like maniacs trying to find his phone. They can't find it anywhere. It took 2 departments to try and find it but nobody can. That is until a guy in a suit that smells like fluid comes up and hands it to him. It turns out the dumbass pulled the body over, had dropped the phone onto the body, they slid the body into the morgue and it sat with the other bodies for a good hour and a half."

Lindsay put her head to the bar she was laughing so hard. "That's the best thing I have ever heard! What an idiot!"

"I know right? At one point he—" Mick stopped talking when he noticed Lindsay bobbing her head to a song on the radio. She was bobbing her head to one of Nick Basquiet's songs "Bite My Tongue" that Doug wrote.

"You like Nick Basquiet?" he asked.

"I love him, he's so good."

"My friend Doug found him and helps write his songs."

Lindsay perked up. "You're kidding? I love this song!"

"Yeah, Doug's awesome and Nick is the humblest dude you'd ever meet."

"I'll tell you what, let's discuss this more over ice cream. Sounds like a plan?"

"Sounds great," Mick said getting out of his chair and paying the bar tab. Lindsay walked to the bathroom before they left. So she didn't get to see the bartender reach across the bar, grab Mick by the shirt and pull him in and say "Marry her, study her, and clone her. We need more of her, like yesterday, man." He put Mick down and he was so taken aback, he did nothing. Lindsay came out and grabbed his hand to escort him out. He looked back at the bartender who pointed at his ring finger mouthing "clone her."

Mick and Lindsay were walking on the sidewalk, which was lit only by street lamps, and they popped in to an ice cream parlor. "So yeah, Doug played one last show and walked away from it all," he said putting his spoon back into what was left of his ice cream.

"That's incredible. That's good of his wife to have his back as much as she does too," Lindsay said with ice cream in her mouth and dripping down her chin. Mick handed her a napkin. "Yeah, Ang is the best. She really pushes people to be the best version of themselves."

"We need more people like that."

"Yeah, we really do. Although more people like you would be pretty great too." Lindsay looked back at him and said "I'm often imitated, but never duplicated. I'm a bad bitch and I like it, so nobody can be like me but me." Mick quickly got turned on by her confidence in herself. "I have to tell you, this is one of the better first dates I've been on."

"I was thinking the same thing," she replied smiling with chocolate sauce on her teeth to be funny. Mick chuckled again.

"So let me ask you something," Mick asked.

"No, just kidding what's up," she replied.

"What're you looking for on the dating app?"

"I'd like to be with someone, not necessarily a relationship off the bat, but to develop something good over time. Let it grow gradually and make something beautiful from the time we spend together." Mick was thinking the same thing except he wanted an absolute relationship and he was willing to do anything to make sure this girl was it. "I was thinking the same thing myself. And if you're up to it, a second date."

Lindsay paused and thought about it for a moment. "I'll do it on one condition."

"Name it."

"Well, I'm not someone who likes to be told what to do, bossed around, or even be spoiled. So how about we split the difference with most things. Be good to each other, instead of one being good to the other while the other reaps the benefits."

"Did you have an experience that was like that?"

Lindsay looked down at her ice cream and said "another time."

"For what it's worth, I'm more than happy to do what it takes for a girl I'm seeing to be happy. If it's not good for both of us, it's good for none of us. We're the Yankee's, not a golfer and his caddy." Lindsay smiled at this and thought more highly of him than she already did. "So, do we have a deal? She said sticking out her hand again.

"We got a deal."

Mick looked down at the handshake and couldn't help but say something stupid. "Oh look, our first physical connection." But Lindsay looked back at him and said: "Follow through on our deal and it won't be your last," as she turned around and kept walking. She walked backward and twitched her finger at him and said "come on," and he followed like a dog.

9

Mick's Parents

M ick's first date with Lindsay went better than he could have hoped for. The days after he spent laying in his bed looking up at the ceiling and smiling thinking about plans for future dates. He'd love to take her to museums, walks on the various Long Island beaches, or maybe dates where they stayed in and cooked for each other. The possibilities were endless. He thought about how he could provide for her in the future despite her wanting to be her own entity. And wanting to be with her more and more as time went on. It's something that kept coming up in his sessions. And at that moment, he looked at the clock and saw he had to start leaving for Lazlo's soon. He picked up a jacket off the floor, dusted it off, brushed his teeth, and even gave himself a smile in the mirror.

He made his way to his car, started it up, but sat for a minute looking up at the sky. He looked at the rolling clouds and noticed a few black ones. Noticing it will probably rain later, he shrugged and put the car in the drive and took off. "Can't be worried over a few black clouds. They'll roll past and a nice day will come soon," he thought to himself as he continued driving. He drove over to a coffee shop and got his usual order while texting Lindsay. Mick decided to fill Lindsay in on his situation and to his surprise, she was very supportive. She asked him to message her after he got out of his appointment to be sure it all went okay.

He made his way to the office parking lot and checked in. As soon as he sat down, Lazlo was at the door saying "come in." Mick and Lazlo we're becoming as close as a mental health professional and client can by law. They went into Lazlo's office and closed the door.

"So how are you, Mick?" Lazlo said sitting in his chair.

"I'm doing a lot better. I went out with that girl I was telling you about."

"We'll talk about her later. But for now, how are you feeling the more we meet and you continue with our sessions?"

"I've been feeling a lot more optimistic and I've been smiling more and more as we go on. I feel like I'm not fighting with everyone every second of every day and I haven't felt that way in years."

"So your anger precedes the incident at your job?" Lazlo said with a puzzled expression.

"Oh yeah," Mick said. "I got it from my mother. When we were speaking she would initiate fights over such minuscule incidents it would make us all puzzled as to what she was mad over. She made such mountains out of molehills that she could make Everest out of crumbs on the floor."

Lazlo giggled at Mick's misfortune. "So you and your Mom are not on speaking terms?"

"No, I have not spoken to her in two years."

"What caused you two not to speak?"

Mick adjusted himself on the couch. "Well, we would always disagree about little things here or there, But after I applied for FDNY, she lost her cool and said I would be dead in a week."

Lazlo looked flabbergasted at what Mick just said. "Why would she say that?"

"Because my father passed away on 911. He was last seen entering a stairwell and minutes later the tower came down."

"Is that the reason you decided to become a paramedic?"

"I can't say that's not a part of it, but the reason I became a paramedic is that I just want to help people. It's as simple as that. Even if I didn't get paid for it I'd volunteer in a heartbeat. I know that being a paramedic is what I was put on this earth to do." Lazlo sat there and smiled. He waited a moment before he spoke again.

Lazlo took off his glasses and pinched the sides of his nose before he put them back on. "Do you think the reason your mom doesn't want you to be a paramedic is that she doesn't want the same thing that happened to her husband to happen to her son?"

"Obviously, but it's still what I want to do. You couldn't keep me away from an ambulance with a shotgun."

"I can see that. But now that you say that, I have another question for you." Mick nodded his head as a gesture to show he's ready to listen. "I'm getting the feeling that the reason you're lashing out at people is that you want to lash out at your mother but you don't have the chance. And knowing that your dad passed away in such a horrible way made you swell up with anger to the point that you lost control. So where we go from here, is resolving your issues and finding ways to avoid similar things to happen. How does that sound?" Mick had a tear roll down his face. It was like someone was pulling emotions out of him he did not know he had. He nodded his head silently.

"Great, now in your first session we talked about ways to quell your anger and how to control yourself, and the last session we talked about how your low self-esteem can bring you down in life. Do you remember that?"

"Yes, I do."

"So I'd like to combine the two to help you realize how to maintain a good relationship with people in your life. When a relationship is affected, albeit a romantic, family, or platonic one; a rift can happen by something happening. It could be caused by a domestic or foreign source. Regardless, you need to know how to seek a resolution to the problem. There's nothing better for your self-esteem or coping with anger than to finish what you start and to find a resolution to appease everyone involved. If nobody is satisfied with the resolution, then at least you did something about it. Even that is finishing what you started. Leaving a problem unresolved, will make your self-esteem atrophy and leave you exposed to a new source of anger," Lazlo said as though he's said this to dozens of other clients.

Mick sat for a few minutes in silence. He was taking in all the information that seemed so simple but was hitting him like a truck. Mick was as breathless as a marathon runner. Lazlo said nothing along with him. He was there to help Mick when he was ready to take action, not go in front of him and drag him alongside. Mick thought over ways that he could communicate with his mother that could be beneficial, but all of them seemed like a foreign language to him and a result that could only happen to an alien. So instead of asking for positive forms of communication, he said the first joke he could think of. "If I can't tell my mother to get off my back, life ain't worth living." Lazlo saw right through it but laughed anyway. It was clear Mick wasn't ready to meet that trauma, so they had to take a step back.

"Do you always use humor as a defense mechanism?" Lazlo said.

"If Chandler can, then so can I," Mick said jokingly.

"Did the girl you went out with find these jokes funny too?"

"She found my stories funnier than my jokes, but she got them."

"So tell me, how is it going with her?"

"She is really something great. I finally found someone that I can communicate with."

"That's great. I remember you telling me that she can speak French. Is the language barrier a problem?"

"Oh no, she's from France but she can't speak it. At best she can say what's on the menu at her parents' restaurant, but that's it. She always gets asked 'Voulez-vous coucher avec moi ce soir,' though. By the way that means—"

"I heard the song—I know what it means."

"So is she your girlfriend now?"

"No, we have a way to go for that. We hung out again the other day and it was fantastic. I'm really falling quite hard for her. But, she still wants to be Miss Independent though."

"What do you mean?" Lazlo said lowering his glasses.

"She's always bothered when I pay for things and don't let her contribute. She wants everything to be split 50-50 and I'm just not okay with that."

"Well, did you communicate that to her?"

"No, but she'll get used to it."

"Well, if that is her boundary then you have to respect that." Mick rolled his eyes because he was told something he didn't want to hear. "Don't roll your eyes at me," Lazlo said not taking an inch off Mick. Mick sat himself up like he had actually been yelled at by his dad.

"Let me explain something to you, Mick," Lazlo said firmly. "Relationships only work if the give and take are equal. If one is providing so much that the other doesn't contribute anything, resentment and laziness build up. So if she's saying she wants to be an equal partner and provide as much as you do, you have to accept what her conditions are, or there is no relationship to build on."

"It just goes against everything my dad taught me. He always taught me to be a gentleman regardless of what people say or do. That's one of the few ways I can connect with him now that he's gone," Mick said. Lazlo reclined his chair back slightly.

"I see what you're getting at here. You want to be the man he wanted you to be. Regardless if he can see it or not." Mick nodded his head like a child. Lazlo smiled. "I think it's great you're trying to live up to his legacy. And he sounded like a top-notch dad, but I don't think he'd want you to make the girl uncomfortable by not giving her the conditions she needs to feel secure in the relationship. Maybe you'd be honoring him by being there for her in the way she needs you to be."

Mick sat back flabbergasted by Lazlo's analysis. He always followed the example his father set. He had never thought of his father's mentality or life lessons as something that could be called into question. He sat with a profound look on his face. The only thing he could say to Lazlo was, "damn, you're good."

"I know," Lazlo said without taking his eyes off his notepad. "Times up."

Mick and Lazlo got up and shook hands. Mick said nothing as Lazlo escorted him out of his office, down the hallway, and opening the door to the lobby. Before Mick left for the night, Lazlo grabbed him on the shoulder, in a friendly way, and said: "Have a good night, don't be stressing too much." Mick looked back and nodded silently. Mick went out the door and opened the door to his car. Before he got in, he looked back at the office and shed a tear. He was realizing the progress he was making and couldn't wait to come back. He couldn't wait to go back to work with a newfound optimism. He got in the car, took a deep breath, and took his phone out to call Lindsay. He called her and she picked up on the first ring. "How'd it go? All okay?"

"Yeah," he said in a somber but happy voice. "I was just thinking about how good life is and I wanted to thank you for being so good to me."

"It's what I do," she said smiling through the phone. "Want to go to the movies tomorrow? I'm tired of doing new things, I want something comfortable."

"I'll pick you up this time, I'm tired of you picking me up."

Mick laughed and said, "I thought you'd never ask."

You Just Don't Get it Do You?

After Mick got home from his last appointment he went straight to sleep. Once his head hit the pillow, he was out cold. He awoke the next morning without an alarm and the sun shining through his windows. He had nowhere to be until later in the evening when Lindsay picked him up for their date, so he decided to go for a run again. But once he stepped outside, he decided to take a walk instead. He also decided to take an alternate route to Main Street to see what he could have missed on his normal routine. While he walked, he noticed very little that was new or exciting. He made it to Main Street, went to his favorite deli, sat inside and had a bagel with coffee. He went his usual route home with a humble grin. He made a mental note to bring up to Lazlo that the alternate route made him realize he's happy with the choices he made in his life. Taking a look at what he could have done is making him realize how good he has it and he's more appreciative of what he has.

He got home and lay around watching Netflix and chilling by himself. All day, Lindsay and Mick texted back and forth between what movie they wanted to see. Mick wanted to see the new Spiderman to catch up with Doug and Ang, but Lindsay wanted to see an indie film she's been dying to see. They settled on a dark comedy that was playing in a theater on the other side of Long Island. "Wear something slutty so I got something to look at," Lindsay messaged Mick in a clearly joking manner.

"If I do, you have to buy me something cute after. I'm not cheap," he sent back.

"Ugh you're so needy," she sent back. "By the way, I'll be picking you up around 6 okay?"

"You got it," Mick sent back, actually feeling bizarre about the inevitable date. He had never been picked up by a date before, and he was actually nervous. He actually considered going out and getting a new dress and his nails done. All joking aside, he couldn't help but think of Lazlo talking about having to respect what she wants, and if it violates your morals, you have to walk away. So he told himself to suck it up, pull himself together, and go with the flow.

Lindsay message Mick at 5:30 PM. "On my way. Do you want flowers?" Mick laughed at his phone. "No, I'm quite fine. However, I could use some coffee."

"Ten steps ahead of you," she said, sending him a picture of two iced coffees." Mick was impressed. He didn't even have to ask and she picked up his order. He was excited to see what the rest of the night had in store.

Lindsay arrived and he ran out the door. He made it down his path to her car when she rolled her window down and went "Woah Woah Woah." He stopped in his tracks and looked back thinking he left the door open. Instead, she swirled her finger and whistled suggesting he "twirl" for her. Obviously, she was joking, so he waved her down, got in the car and said "very funny." She giggled to herself and said, "you know I'm funny." They arrived at the movie theater and trotted up the curb to enter.

They walked into the theater and stood in line to get their tickets. Mick looked at the showtimes to be sure the movie wasn't sold out and to his relief, it wasn't. He took his wallet out while he was waiting in line and Lindsay immediately put her hand on the wallet and pushed it down. "Uh-uh, nope nope nope," Mick said. "What?" Lindsay said with a giggle. "I'm not going to be subjected to this treatment. I want to pay," Lindsay said. "I picked you up so I get to pay."

"Wait a minute, what happened to 'you fly, I buy?'"

"What are you talking about?"

"The 'you fly, I buy' arrangement is a societal cornerstone. You drove so I treat you."

"Societal cornerstone? It's okay, Charles Dickens I can pay for the movie."

"I'll cut you a deal, I buy tickets, you buy snacks."

"You got yourself a deal," Lindsay said as they walked up to the box office.

"Two for 'Falling Forward' please?" The ticket taker processed their transaction and they made their way to the snack counter. "A large popcorn and two cokes please," Lindsay said rifling through her purse. She stopped and showed a look of horror. "I left my wallet in the car," she said trying to take off to the car. Mick grabbed her wrist and made a face. He took his wallet out and paid for the food.

Lindsay immediately was furious and embarrassed. "I know you wanted to pay, but I figured it was easier than holding up a line while you maintained your pride." Lindsay knew it would be silly to make a whole line wait while she got money from her car, so she got over it by the time they sat down and put their feet up in the reclining theater chairs. They watched the indie film they came to see while teasing the other's hands as a sign they wanted to hold each other while watching the movie. Lindsay leaned next to him and whispered, "you're not fifteen, you can hold my hand," then pecked him on the cheek. Mick blushed in the dark theater like he was fifteen. He leaned next to him to whisper something in her ear when she turned and kissed him. He quickly pulled away and was almost as loud as the movie saying "I'm so sorry! I didn't mean to! I was going to whisper something in your ear, I swear!" She looked at him and made a face. "I know what you were doing, I wanted to kiss you, jackass." Mick slapped himself on the head because he was getting tired of screwing up. She pulled him in and kissed him passionately.

Mick barely watched the movie because he was replaying a better scene in his head. The site of Lindsay kissing him and feeling the fireworks between them. The movie ended and they got up holding hands. "Your hands are sweaty," she said then took his hand away to wipe the sweat off her hands onto her pants.

"You're a charming woman," he said, giving her a look like she was a madwoman. She showed a mile-wide grin dripping with sarcasm. They loaded into the car and Mick dropped his seat back to soak in the rapture of his newfound happiness.

"Hey, I want to make a pit stop," Lindsay said.

"You need gas?"

"No, I'm still hungry I want snacks."

"Okay, there's a 7/11 on the way to my place." They pull over to the 7/11 and Mick pulls his seat up. They walk in and go up and down the isles picking out snack food. Mick has nothing but a water bottle in his hands, Lindsay had an armful. "So let me get this straight, we go to the movies, get popcorn and soda, and you still have to come here to get snacks?"

Lindsay faced him with an armful of food and a Twizzler already in her mouth. "I have the munchies. Do you like me? Do you want to be with me? It's what you do!"

"Who said I like you again?" Lindsay came closer to him and swallowed the rest of the Twizzler.

"So you don't want to be with me tonight?"

Mick went scarlet but kept his cool. "Well if it's not all night, I don't want any part of it."

"Is that so?" she said leaning in an inch away from him.

"Do you mind if I grab condoms while we're here?"

"Go for it," she said chuckling at Mick.

They went to the register and put everything down on the counter. "That'll be $15.75," the cashier said.

"Can I grab a pack of the magnums, bro?"

The cashier looked back at the condoms then back at Mick. "Really? You?" the cashier said patronizingly.

"Yes, the magnums," Mick said quietly but getting his frustration across. The cashier turned around to grab the pack when Lindsay realized she grabbed the wrong bag of chips. "Oh crap, I don't like this kind. I'm gonna go grab the sour cream and onion ones," she said, making a motion to go back. "No worries I got it," Mick said grabbing the bag then walking halfway across the store.

Mick made it to the shelf that carried the chips when Lindsay let out "Mick!" Mick turned around and saw that she had a look of panic on her face.

"What?" he said at full volume.

"You can't leave me like this!"

"What are you, in a bear trap?" Both of them were speaking at full volume across the store.

"No," Lindsay said stamping her foot. "But I don't want to be the one holding the condoms."

"I'm coming back you know. I'm not stuck on a deserted island you know."

"But it's supposed to be a secret when you buy them," she retorted.

"Well, speaking at full volume, I'd say you blew your cover." Lindsay stomped her foot one more time and screamed like she was at a metal concert

"I'M NOT GONNA BLOW YOUR COVER IF YOU DON'T COME OVER HERE."

Mick admitted defeat, grabbed the proper bag, and sauntered back to the counter. He took out his wallet while Lindsay made a motion to take hers out. Without thinking about it, he made an "I got this" motion and put her hand down that carried her wallet. Her face was down, but she was looking up at him with beaming eyes of hatred. The cashier put the food in the bag and Mick took it and walked back to the car. Lindsay took a deep breath at the counter when the cashier whispered to her "don't worry, I gave him the small pack." Lindsay smiled and walked back to the car in a better mood.

Lindsay came out and unlocked the car for Mick to get in. Lindsay was obviously in an irritable mood and Mick was quick to address the elephant in the room. "Hey, I'm sorry if I was a jerk in there."

"A jerk for what?" Mick was puzzled, he thought it was obvious, but they were clearly thinking about different things.

"Well, for shouting across the store and embarrassing you."

"Mick, all that was funny, what I'm annoyed with is you pushing my hand down when I was trying to pay for my food."

"I was just trying to speed things up like at the movie theater."

"I didn't know me paying for things would delay you so much. Mick, I adore you, but you're clearly not listening to me and you just don't get it. I don't want to have a dynamic of one being better than the other. You paid for everything at the theater because I forgot my wallet, which I'm very grateful for, but I wanted to carry my own weight and pay for my food after."

"Why is this such a big deal to you? You drove me around all night and I'm just trying to be good by you."

"You just don't get it, Mick. Whatever, it's fine." It clearly was not fine. Lindsay pulled up to Mick's apartment and parked the car.

"Let's just go in and relax," Mick said.

"No, I'm going home," Lindsay said. Sensing Lindsay would go home then end things tomorrow, he went for broke with her.

"Look, I'm sorry. Can I at least explain myself?" Lindsay groaned but nodded her head to hear him out. "At my sessions, we've been talking about my dad. And not just a little bit, but a lot. He was my everything. Not just in my lord and savior kind of way. But really my lock, stock, and barrel. That's even something he'd say leaving the house. I idolized him and showed him the utmost respect for him. So after he passed, his life lessons became commandments to me. One of those lessons wasn't just "treat someone the way you want to be treated," but "treat your partner as though you never have before." I always want to be sure that you are shown the utmost respect and dedication. So this whole treat me as your equal thing can sometimes clash. I really like where it's going with us, so if you could please have some patience when it comes to that. I'm breaking a talisman to be with you your way. I just need to adjust a little bit."

Lindsay never realized he was trying so hard. She put her hand on top of his. "Thank you for sharing that with me. I understand and am willing to accommodate. He sounds like a real man, I'm glad he showed you how to be one. I'm sure your parents would be thrilled to see you benefiting yourself with this therapist because not many have the courage to do so. I know I am." She kissed Mick again before she opened her door and said, "come on, let's go to bed."

11

You Screwed Up, Mick

Mick woke up and faced his bedside table. He had a smile from ear to ear and he couldn't wait to wake Lindsay up for morning shenanigans, but he let her sleep a little more. It was 7 in the morning after all. "A weekend is no time to wake up early if you didn't have to," he thought to himself. He then scrolled through his phone and various social media platforms and learned about the inevitable split between Sony and Marvel, ending Spiderman's involvement in the Marvel Cinematic Universe. This got him so irked he had the urge to lean over and wake Lindsay up. But he fought his impulse and walked into the kitchen without looking at her to make a cup of coffee for her.

He made his way to his coffee machine when Doug called. He picked up the phone and all he had to say was "hello," and Doug was already involved in a rant with Angela. "Can you believe this shit? They make all the money on the planet and it's not enough for these billion-dollar companies to come to a peaceful negotiation between the outcome of a teenager who has superpowers. This just proves there is no god and—hold on Ang wants to talk to you, "Hello to you too, Doug."

The phone was passed to Angela and all she said was "I'm going to need you to take him off my hands regarding this so I can have a day to myself. Can I drop him off?"

"No can do Ang, I got a girl over."

"Oh, how exciting! How much did she cost?"

Mick rolled his eyes and stirred Lindsay's coffee. "Very funny, no it's the girl from the dating app."

"How is it going?"

"She's really great," Mick said starting to walk into the bedroom. "We had a great night and I'm thinking of what to do this-—" Mick stopped talking when he realized Lindsay was not in bed after all. "I'll call you back," he said then hung up the phone.

He looked in the bathroom, living room, and checked for her car outside. She wasn't in the apartment and had left it entirely. He called Angela back, "Yo, she spent the night and left without saying goodbye. Who does that?"

"I don't know what you're calling me for, call her, dumbass."

"Oh, yeah that would be good. I'll call you back." Mick scrolled to her name in his phone book and called her up.

The phone rang and rang as Mick's anger started coming to the surface. She picked up and said, "Can you believe this about Spiderman?" Although he was relieved to find out she liked Marvel movies too, he had an agenda. "Yeah it sucks, why did you leave?"

"Well my bed was lonely and I thought it would be good if I spent the night with it after we were done. I didn't want to wake you up so I thought I'd explain in the morning."

He was baffled at how she didn't think it was a big deal. "You know you could have left a note or something right?"

"Beds empty, no note, car gone!" she said imitating Molly Weasely in the second Harry Potter book.

"I'm serious Lindsay, I feel a little hurt by this."

She was now really confused. "What are you so upset about? We had a great date, had some fun after, cuddled for a little while, then I went home."

"Well, I'd of thought my girlfriend would communicate to me she wanted to go home." There was silence on the other side of the line.

"I'm sorry, what?" Lindsay said in disbelief.

"I said I would have thought my girlfriend would of—" Mick said before Lindsay interrupted. "That's what I thought you said. Okay so let me break something down for you. I'm not your girlfriend because you never asked me to be, and if you did right now, I'd say no because I'm not ready. If we progress past this, I want you to know you're lovely and sweet, but we move at the pace of two people, not just one." Mick's anger had reached his Adam's Apple.

"How can you do this to me?" Mick said in utter disbelief.

"What're you in a bear trap?" Lindsay said mocking him from yesterday.

"I thought we had something special."

"We do," Lindsay said. "And I'm not ending things with you, I'm just not going to tolerate being dragged into a relationship without having my say in it. You didn't ask and I'm not ready. Accept it, and we'll move past it," Lindsay said as she hung up the phone.

"What the actual fuck," Mick said out loud on his phone.

He called Lazlo immediately. The phone rang and rang as he paced his apartment in frustration. "Hello, Christopher Lazlo LMSW, how may I help you?" Lazlo's secretary said.

"Hi, it's Mick, I need to speak to Lazlo immediately."

"I'm sorry who is this?"

"It's Mick, he sees me today at 05:00."

"Well, he's with a client at the moment so I'm sorry he's unavailable."

"But I need to speak to him now," Mick said yelling into the phone.

"Sir, do not talk to me that way, I'm not the problem you're facing. If you would like to see him earlier, he has an open appointment at 11:30."

"Yeah sure, fit me in." "Okay, he'll see you then. Goodbye," she said and slammed the phone down.

"I fucking hate people," Mick said as he got into the shower. His phone was going off the hook from Angela and Doug calling to check in on him. He got out soaking wet and answered the phone. "What?" he said to Angela.

"Don't you 'what' me, young man," she replied.

"Sorry Ang, I'm just furious right now."

"Well, what happened?"

"Lindsay left in the middle of the night and didn't bother to tell me."

"That's a little odd."

"Right? Like I'm not delusional when I think it's annoying right?"

"I mean, it'd be better if she let you know, but she didn't stab you in your sleep so I don't know why you're getting so upset."

"Well, Lazlo's office wouldn't put him through so I could only get an earlier appointment either." Angela took a deep breath before she said anything else.

"So listen, I know you're having a hard time, but the other person he's with right now probably is too. You're not the center of his universe, you're one person. He's not going to cut one person off just because you think you're the more important client. Calm down before I come down to your apartment myself." Mick just hung up without responding. His tolerance was gone and he'd rather be alone than be lectured.

He waited around until 10:45 then took off towards Lazlo's office. He stopped and got a coffee, then resumed his commute. Lazlo's office has a view of the parking lot so he saw Lazlo in his office reading while he walked up to the lobby. He walked in, waved at the receptionist, then walked through the door without a care if she signed him in. He walked into Lazlo's office, sat on the chair and went off about what happened. "I cannot believe this. I bust my ass to give her what she wants out of this relationship and she drops this bomb on me. She could've at least left me a note or something. Or at least tell me last night before we finished our date. I'm not some guy who's in and out before breakfast but apparently she is, what am I in some role reversal exercise? Am I some punk who she takes for granted for a couple days and then I'm off to the scraps? I have never in my life had treated a woman like this and I don't see why even if she has, I should be treated like this. I know she's had shit before but she shouldn't be this mean to me." Lazlo did not look up from his book once. Once Mick had finished, he put a bookmark in his spot, took off his glasses, breathed on them, cleaned them with his sweater, put them back on, and leaned forward. "Mick! So good to see you. Man, I almost didn't hear you come in with the sound of an invitation being so loud. Hooooo man you seem like you're so happy. Why don't you tell me about it?"

Mick gave him a look and said, "are you serious?"

Lazlo raised his voice to him and said, "Are you serious?" Mick jumped a little bit in his chair. "Before we get to what happened this morning, let me give you a little rule on house-keeping around here," he said with his voice still raised. "First off, you do not talk like that to Christine. She may be my secretary, but she works for me and you will treat her with the utmost respect. I thought maybe you realized your error and bought her that coffee as an apology, but now that you come in here with an entitled attitude as though you've done nothing wrong, it shows me how much of your anger we still have to work on. I'm not afraid to call your Chief up and tell her you're not ready to come back to work and I'm not afraid to drop you as a client altogether. If you want to continue coming, after we're done, you will go out and apologize and you will never act like that to my staff again. Do you under-stand that?" Mick didn't even speak, he just nodded vigorously as a child would for getting caught taking a cookie out of the jar when he wasn't supposed to. "Thank you. I refuse to let you treat my staff like an entitled soccer mom who asks to see the manager when they don't let her use an expired coupon. Don't do it again. You're a good dude, but knock this behavior off."

Lazlo finished and Mick was almost shaking. "Calm down dude, you're acting like you've never been yelled at before," Lazlo said sitting back. Mick started to tear up and Lazlo pointed at the tissues next to him. Mick reached for two and dabbed his eyes and blew his nose. "So what happened today?" Mick went into detail about his date with Lindsay and the aftermath of this morning.

"So you jumped the gun and you screwed up," Lazlo said.

"I mean, I guess I did, but I listened to everything she said and—"

"First off, no you didn't," Lazlo interrupted. "If you listened she wouldn't have been giving you the business in the car. Second, you called her your girlfriend when you didn't have the talk. Yes, the talk sucks, but it's what you need to define the relationship. That being anywhere from bedroom buddies or boyfriend and girlfriend. I've never babied you before and I'm not going to now. You jumped the gun and screwed up." Mick winced at the aspect of making an error.

"Wanna go a little easier on me?" Mick said trying to lighten the mood.

"No, I don't. Truth hurts, the only way to get better at taking it is through repetition. Now, could she have been a little more upfront with you on what she wanted, you bet? Could she have left a note when deciding to go back home? Absolutely, and it probably wouldn't have killed her to tell you before you went asleep I will agree with you on that. But you can't just assume things are going to work out for you every time. Hate to bring up work, but when do things go as planned when you're on the rig?"

"Not worth looking into because it just doesn't."

"Right, so why should the rest of life prove otherwise? It can be going just as planned and as soon as you think life is going your way, it throws you a curveball when you least expect it. I know it seems like I'm going pretty hard on you here, but I just want it stressed that as the father of a baby girl, she owes you nothing just by staying the night and going out with you.

Would a little bit of communication benefit her? Absolutely. But you can't change her. If she does things you don't like, move on. Take that to heart. Have a better rest of your day. And don't forget to apologize to Christine."

Mick was shaky getting up. "Relax, we're cool, sometimes you just need to get told you screwed up and you have to deal with it." Mick apologized to Christine and got in the car when he felt his phone ring in his pocket. It was Doug, and he's sure he's going to yell his ear off about how he spoke to Ang. "Here comes my second apology today," he thought to himself.

12

Have Some Fun For Once

M ick's phone vibrated in his hand, but he was also trembling slightly at the verbal ass-kicking he was about to get for mouthing off to Angela earlier. "Might as well get it over with," he thought to himself. He slid his finger across his phone slowly, put it to his ear, and just started talking. "Hi, I know I mouthed off to Angela before, but I'm going to call her after and apologize. I had misplaced anger about Lindsay this morning and I took it out on Ang and my therapist's office assistant. I'm sorry, and I fucked up," he said while nobody spoke on the other line. "Hello? Hello?" he said, hearing nobody.

"I'm here, I'm just soaking in your apology," Angela said while using Doug's phone.

"Very funny. What're you guys doing?"

"We're shopping because we're having a little hootenanny at the house later."

"Oh, family party?"

"No, Basquiat just mastered his new album and we're throwing a party for him. And because you apologized, this is turning from a 'you're not invited call' to a 'you're invited' call."

"You were going to call me to be petty?"

"Yup, and I'm not ashamed about it. Make sure you bring your happy face and party pants because it's gonna be lit. And come by when you're done to help set up, we'll be home in 10. Good byeeeee!" she said as she hung up the phone while also being obnoxious.

Mick looked at his phone and shook his head. He put his car in reverse and backed out of the parking lot. He got on the main highway and realized his errors of the day, so he went and got Angela her favorite bottle of wine, and Nick Basquiat his favorite whiskey. His hit "Whiskey Eyes" talks about his favorite time drinking Jack Daniels and staring up at the stars while he was homeless. He was leaving the liquor store when someone cut him off leaving the parking lot. He laid on his horn and yelled "Get off your phone!"

The person driving promptly stomped on the breaks, put his car in park, and got out and approached Mick's car. "You got a problem bro?" the driver yelled. Looking at the driver, he seemed to be 18 years old, with a Juul behind his ear and probably driving his parents' car. Mick felt no need to engage him, but he did reply. "Look where you're going, man, you almost hit me." The driver then spat on the hood of Mick's car and said, "I'll look where I'm spitting, bitch." He then got in his car, and drove off into traffic and narrowingly cut off another person's car, causing them to weave into another lane and honk their horn and yell the same thing Mick did.

Mick was, for the second time today, absolutely furious. He carefully took his car out of the parking lot and made his way to Doug's. He thought back to a session with Lazlo when they discussed his anger. "If someone is giving you anger, it's okay to let it out when nobody is there to take the hit for it. As long as it doesn't hurt you, let it out." So he lowered his window and let out a blood-curdling scream. He yelled so loud that someone across the street heard him and yelled "me too, buddy. Let em all know they ain't shit." And oddly enough, the anger left.

He continued on to Doug's house, parked in the street in front of the house, opened the car, got a box full of booze and made his way to the house. He started to open the gate when Doug came outside and helped him. "How you doing grouch?" he asked with a tone of sarcasm, but also shot him a look that said, "Never treat my wife like that again."

"Doug, I apologized to Ang, I want to apologize to you."

"As long as you apologized to her, you apologized to me."

"Deal," Mick said as he walked into the house lugging his box.

"So I heard your therapist read you the riot act too huh?"

"Yeah, but I deserved it. Honestly, I don't know why I acted that way."

"Well, I do," Doug said completely flustered that Mick doesn't know he has a temper.

"What do you mean you know?"

"So you don't remember in high school the number of times you've been to the principal's office for your temper with a teacher on any given day?"

Mick made a face as though anyone dared to defy him. "Well, if they were incorrect, I'd correct them."

"It's because you have no sense of how to read a room or know a social cue when it hits you right in the face. It's not the time or place, and just because you think you're right, it doesn't mean you get to embarrass someone for it. Stop acting like your mother and respect other people."

Mick sat with a sense of horror. He realized he was becoming his mother. "If I ever turn into a slight resemblance of my mother slap me so hard that I can see—" Doug took no time in winding up and smacking him in the face. "Ow dog dammit!"

Doug doubled over and he was laughing so hard. "You've acted like your mother since you tried to tell me how to organize my amp wires. If it doesn't involve you, back off, bud." Doug walked away laughing his ass off while Mick rolled around his floor clutching his cheek in agony.

Mick stopped rolling around to look up at Nicholas Basquiat himself looking down at him. "Doug slap you huh? Been there." Nick put his guitar down to help Mick up off the floor. "You lose a bet or something?"

"No, just used the wrong words."

"That's a tough brother."

Doug shouts from his basement: "Basquiat, quit fraternizing with the enemy. You help his ass up, he can carry your shit down."

Basquiat shook his head. "This guy thinks he's my manager. I can't wait to not use his songs on the next record."

Mick's eyes grew wider. "Wait really?"

Basquiat looked over his shoulder and shook his head. "I'm just playing, they're too good not to use. You're staying for the party?"

"Yeah, I just bought booze."

"Dope, you gonna play too?"

Mick shook his head vigorously. "I can't play shit bro, I'm a groupie at best."

"Been there too, man, but happy to have you here."

Mick smiled and followed Basquiat down the stairs to help set up. Before he reached Doug's basement, Basquiat had opened a beer. "Didn't I tell you not to drink before a set?" Doug yelled from across the basement.

"Mother fucker, you ain't my manager so chill out. Does this look like a garden to you? Have some fun for once," Basquiat called back at him. A simple message, but it made Mick relax and have a wide smile.

"Sorry Baq, Doug takes everything Sammy Hagar tells him to heart." Basquiat started to laugh too. Doug had a scowl at his two friends ganging up on him.

"I don't care if it's a bar or a garden. If there's one guy in that crowd, you play for that fucker," both Mick and Basquait said at the same time to mimic the words Sammy Hagar once told Doug. "It's your basement. Unless Jimmy Iovine wanders down here looking to produce a record like 'Damn the Torpedoes' again, we're gonna get drunk and have a fun night," Basquiat said to Doug. Doug rolled his eyes then wandered off to another part of the basement.

Mick and Basquiat each took a beer and took out their keys. "Shotgun this mother fucker," Basquiat called out. And that's exactly what Mick did. He popped a hole with the key to his mother's house, put it to his face, and popped the top. He shotgunned a beer for the first time since his graduation party. "Ah, that felt good," he said chucking it at the wall.

Some time went by as they continued to set up the equipment in the basement and people started arriving upstairs as Ang entertained them all. "Basquait did you ever hear about the last time Doug was allowed to have an orange soda?"

"Mick I swear to god!" Doug shouted from behind the drum set.

"Do tell," Basquiat said.

"Well Doug and I went to the store to buy some snacks and shit before we played video games, and I went to his parents' front yard to go bring his dog in the house, all of a sudden I hear 'shit! Shit! Shit!' I run back in and he's nowhere to be found. I looked around and I saw orange soda all over the windows and ceiling and a pack of mentos on the table. This dumbass decided he wanted to see if that urban legend of mentos in soda worked on orange soda. He booked it from his parents living room across the house, past the dining room, kitchen, and tried to put it in the shower so it wouldn't leave a mess. Forgetting the fact that there was a bathroom next to him, and a door to the outside."

Basquiat was doubled over in laughter and pointed and laughed at Doug. Doug was red in the face and furious. "Mick thought that L-M-N-O-P in the alphabet was pronounced "elemeno" until he was 12!" Doug shouted and pointed with a drum stick. Basquiat turned and started laughing at Mick. "Doug still has a stuffed animal from his crib as a baby and cuddles it when he has writer's block!" Mick shouted back "You leave Pinky out of this!" Ang came running down the stairs shouting "I want to go live with Dad!" Everyone looked at her with a face of confusion. "What? I thought we were yelling things. By the way, Maggie's here," she said as Maggie stumbled down the stairs. "Mag, you gotta put one foot in front of the other, babe."

"I'm okay!" she said jumping to her feet. Mick looked at her with drunken lust and thought in his head, "I'm making out with her before I go home."

"Thank god your bass is here or you'd probably lose a limb," Doug said, tightening his ride cymbal to the stand. Maggie checked her head and said "nope, still on. Let's let them down!"

"You head her Ang, let them all down. Mick, can you chill with Doug behind the kit in case he can't reach Pinky?"

Mick laughed and moved behind the kit. "See what you do?" Doug said through gritted teeth.

"Shut up, you love attention," Mick said poking him in the side. Doug shrugged his shoulders and said, "Yeah, you're right."

The crowd assembled down into the basement all dying to see international recording artist Nicholas Basquiat. He was swarmed with people trying to take selfies and get a hold of him. It didn't matter if they were friends and family, he was a star now. The crowd backed up and stood at a mic stands length while Doug counted off to start the new song. The song sounded like early Taking Back Sunday with a new emo feel. There was nothing Basquiat couldn't make his own. He laid into his Fender Telecaster Hollow Body Deluxe and kept the emotion on the surface. Mick was completely shit faced and couldn't help but be moved. Basquiat got to the chorus and Mick started to well up when he heard the lyrics *"Maybe I'm homesick, no you never led me on, told you that I'm here now, knew I missed you all along, told you that I'd hold you, even when I'm dead and gone. I know you think I'm acting crazy, but I just want to come back home tonight."*

Mick felt an overwhelming feeling of missing something that's been absent from his life. He looked back down at his keys and promised himself that before the week is out, he's going to have to call mom. "Later, not now," he thought to himself. He took a chug from another beer and let the song finish out. He came out from behind the drum set and fell after tripping on a guitar cable. "Ow, that hurt," he thought as he saw Maggie hover over to check if he was okay. "That's a new method," he thought as his eyes shut.

13

Ghosts of the Past

M aggie picked Mick off the floor and took him to Doug's bedroom to let him relax. "You sure know how to have fun!"

"Yeah, I guess so," Mick says trying hard to pick his head up. Maggie put Mick in Doug and Angela's bed. She took his phone out of his pocket and put it on the bedside table. Maggie looked over Mick and rotated him on his side. But before she did that, she put her phone next to him. She rolled him over, and after he was stationary on his side, he said, "Thank you, Maggie."

"It's okay! Do you need anything?" she asked genuinely.

"A good dating life if you have one laying around," he said sarcastically.

"Haha, I can't seem to find my own, but if I find one I'll split it with you," she said jokingly.

"What's wrong with yours? A gorgeous girl who can play music like you shouldn't have any problem finding someone," Mick replied back.

"Well, when you play music, most people want to just have you for a night. And being bi-sexual, most people only seem to want you in a group or for one night. Or sometimes both."

"I'm sorry to hear that, dear. My gender kind of sucks."

"Eh, girls suck too. In fact, all people suck. Doesn't matter who you are, you suck. You just have to see if someone doesn't suck enough that you'll keep them around for a while or for eternity."

"You can say that again," Mick replied.

"Are you sure you're okay? You seem sad. I don't mind sitting with you and talking if that's what you need," Maggie said sweetly.

"I feel like all I do is talk, I need some excitement in my life besides work, a mental health counselor, and a shitty personal life," Mick said.

Maggie flipped him on his back and gave Mick a kiss on the lips. "There, a sense of excitement. Now lay down and maybe go to sleep."

Maggie got up to walk out when the phone started going off. "Oh that's my phone," Maggie said.

"That's funny, my phone has the same ringtone," Mick replied.

Maggie picked up her phone and said "Hello?" She had a look of confusion on her face since she had a contact name for this person, but had no idea who was calling. "I'm sorry, who is this?" she said into the phone again. "Why are you asking for Mick when you called my phone?" she said as Mick started to panic.

"Maggie, I think you answered my phone," Mick said with a sense of impending doom. "Whose on the phone?" he asked.

"Some girl named Lindsay."

Mick dropped his head back down and said "Fuck my life. Can you hand me the phone dear?"

Mick looks at the phone and looks at Maggie. Maggie has a face on that says "you're in trouble." She excuses herself so Mick can get yelled at. He put the phone to his ear and said "Hello?" Lindsay exhaled and said "so who's the girl?"

"It's my buddies bass player. I got too drunk so she escorted me to his bed to sleep it off. She has the same phone so she thought it was hers."

"Oh, that's all? You guys didn't sleep together?"

"No, we didn't sleep together. She just kissed me when I was feeling—"

"Woah woah, you guys kissed?"

Mick realized he just destroyed the future with Lindsay for sure now. "I mean I didn't lean in for one or want one, but she did kiss me out of nowhere."

Lindsay was seething now. "I don't talk to you for one day and you go and kiss another girl? I thought you were different Mick. I thought we had something special and you just jumped the gun because you got excited. Thinking about it today, I was thinking maybe it could have led to something, but now I forget it. Fuck you and the horse you rode in on."

"Lindsay, just listen to me before you—-" But it was too late. Lindsay hung up the phone and wasn't interested in talking anymore. Mick ended his side of the call and put his head back to look up at the ceiling. He stared at all the bumps in the ceiling and thought about all the things he might have to do to make things right. If he can make them right at all. He also realized while he didn't do anything wrong, it is assumed that he is the perpetrator. So since she won't talk to him anyway, he might as well go back down to the party and have fun. So he picked himself up, realized his stomach was feeling better, looked into the mirror, smiled, and let it go. If there's nothing you can do to fix the situation at the moment, you might as well have a good time.

Mick started walking back down the stairs and met Maggie's eyes across the room. He smiled as he reached the bottom of the stairs, but was dragged away by Doug pulling on his left ear. Doug forced him down the hall and pushed him up against the wall. "Did you fuck my bass player?" Doug said in a whisper.

"No, she kissed me to make me feel better and—" he said before Doug put a finger to his lips and said "shhh." Mick was very confused.

"I'm going to ask you one more time Mickie and whatever you say I'll believe you. Did you fuck my bass player?"

"No, stupid. I didn't fuck your—"

"You little liar! You're actually smiling at her and the only woman you've smiled at in your life is my wife because you're buddies. Now tell me you didn't fuck Maggie. And while we're at it tell me you didn't fuck Ang either."

Mick was boiling over angry. "Doug, if I have to say it again I'm going to slap the shit out of you." Doug took his hands off him and said "great! Just for that, you're allowed to help me with the beer run."

"I don't want to help you on the beer run."

"Tough shit, you're my best friend, therefore you get to carry shit. Let's move cupcake." Mick scuffled over to his shoes, put them on, and started walking down the street with Doug.

The convenience store was only a two-block walk for the boys. However, after having about 5 beers each, they were stumbling and moving pretty slow. And at the same time, Mick was scrolling through his phone looking through the old and new text messages from Lindsay and his missed calls to see if she called back. While he was drunk he looked down at his pinky. He looked at it confusingly since he was inebriated, but it seemed as though there was a dip in his finger. "Hey man, something is wrong with my pinky," Mick said to Doug.

"Oh yeah, Angela told me about that. It turns out that it's a new deformity started in millennials. It's from people leaving their phones on their pinky. It has left a permanent indent," Doug said as though he was teaching Mick something in his class.

Mick stood with his mouth hung open. "I can't believe it I'm deformed!" Mick said slurring every word.

"Yeah, we knew that for a while now Mickie," Doug said as he opened the door to the convenient store. "It's a literal scar we left ourselves because of our dependability on technology." Doug made a "give me a break" face.

Mick continued. "No seriously! It could be real or an optical illusion Or maybe I'm drunk, but my god what are we coming to. It starts with a small deformity on our fingers but then it goes to our brains. This could bring about the rise of the moles and have me working in mines collecting salt, and I have a cut on my finger so it stings! And not just any finger, it's on my pinky!" Doug exited the convenience store. He grabs Mick's phone, puts it in his pocket, looks at him, and slaps him in the face. Doug doesn't say a word to Mick, and Mick realized he was being ridiculous. Mick walks in under Doug's arms and Doug pats him on the back to calm him down.

Doug carried Mick under his arms until they reached the beer cooler. However, once he saw a 12 pack of his favorite beer, he dropped him straight on the floor. "You'll pick yourself off the floor at some point right?" Doug said to Mick.

"At some point. Feels like I've been hearing that a lot lately though," Mick said staring at the space under the shelves.

"Right, well if you can't I'll pick you up before we leave."

"Good on you, Doug." Doug walked away and picked up a couple of snacks off the shelves and other various party supplies. Mick lay on the floor until he saw a person on the other side of the shelves. He recognized the person's boots and recognized them as the one he wears to work. "Ay, you there. I got the same boots at home for work."

"At least you got work, bro." The voice said. The voice was recognizable to Mick.

"Who's that you're talking to?" said a second familiar voice.

"Some guy who likes my shoes," said the first. Mick recognizing both of the voices made him realize he needs to pull himself together and get up. In a moment of his losing his beer buzz entirely, he jumped to his feet as the second familiar voice came around the aisle. "Oh, it's you," said the man revealing himself to be Ex-Chief Fauler.

The Ex-Chief looked at Mick with absolute disdain and a vehement dislike. The first voice came around and revealed himself to be Diaz. Diaz, however, looked nothing like himself. He was sloppy, unkempt, and utterly grotesque.

"Diaz? Is that you?" Mick said in disbelief.

"Oh, so you remember me."

"It's been almost two weeks, not twenty-years since I last saw you."

Yeah, but I've been drunk and high ever since," Diaz said.

"I've got nowhere to go, nothing to live for, and I'm on the streets. Thanks to you!"

Mick was in absolute disbelief. "You lose your job and you're on your ass in two weeks? How does that happen?" Mick said getting louder and more confused. "And how is it thanks to me? I didn't force booze in your throat. And I didn't even know you got high."

"Well, my girl threw me out when I lost my job and I just bumped into the Chief on the sidewalk."

"Then it's thanks to you, moron. Boy, being out on the streets sure hasn't gotten you any brighter." Doug heard Mick causing trouble and came over quickly.

"Can everyone de-escalate?" Ex-Chief Fauler said.

"Oh now you want to de-escalate? Not when you decked me across the jaw, but now. Well, that's just great."

"It seems, Thomlinson, that I learned a thing or two about calming down. Your therapy seems to be doing very well for you though," Fauler said sarcastically.

Doug got in between the argument and got in Mick's face. "Knock it off. Let's go back to the party, you'll regret anything you say or do here. Just walk away." Doug getting in Mick's face calmed him down and Mick agreed.

"Fine, yeah let's go."

"Oh, now you want to walk away? You fucking pussy, your dad must have been just a big a pussy as you," Diaz said.

Whatever Doug said before made no difference now. Mick was out for blood. So much so that he started to charge at Diaz but Doug grabbed his shoulders so quick that Mick's legs hung in the air as Doug pulled him back. Ex-Chief Fauler had Diaz in a headlock to keep him back.

Now what none of them knew, is that the store clerk had called the police once the shouting started. And by the time Mick's legs hit the floor, the police lights were visible throughout the whole store. Mick realized he needed to get his act together quickly cooled down and acted normal as the police came in. "What's going on?" the first officer said to the clerk.

"Those men are yelling and causing a disturbance, I want them out of my store." The officer quickly came over and Mick and Doug put their hands up and said: "We'll go, we're out of here."

Diaz, however, was still trying to break free of Faulers grip screaming "let me go, I want to die. I don't want to live anymore." Doug and Mick were outside looking into the store as the police officer was putting the cuffs on Diaz.

"We need to go, now," Doug said. They both took off down the street in a sprint and didn't stop until they reached Doug's block. They both caught their breath and were doubled over on the sidewalk.

"Jeez, that was crazy huh?" Mick said trying to relieve the tension.

"What the fuck is the matter with you?" Doug screamed at full volume.

Mick jumped back from the yelling. "Look, I'm sorry I didn't expect that to happen."

"I don't care that they were in the store and they started with you. That would have happened if I were there or not. What I'm pissed at is how you handled it."

Mick realized what Doug was getting at. "Between Ang and I being there for you, this Lindsay girl, and your fucking therapist, it's like you've had both ears shut and not listening to a word we say. Life is going to throw you a curveball when you least expect it. You need to know how to handle it. And so far, you've done a shit job at hitting any of them. Grow up, start acting like a man, and get your fucking temper under control. Because you aren't just affecting yourself anymore, you're affecting the people around you." Mick started to tear up. This was the second time in twenty-four hours he's been yelled at. "If you're not going to grow up and take responsibility for who you are and what you've done, then forget having me as a friend because I've fucking had it. Go home, you're done for the night and you're not staying in my house." Doug walked away and left Mick on the corner. Alone, again.

14

Mick's Final Session

Mick stood on the corner and felt as empty as a human being can feel. He took out his phone and tried to call Doug. The phone rang and went to voicemail on the third ring. He tried again. "Come on, Doug. Pick up. I'm sorry," he said to the phone like that would make a difference. The phone went to voicemail again. Mick didn't just tear up at this point. He was full-blown crying. "Doug, come on man. I know I fucked up. Please don't leave me," he said to the phone while he started calling again. The phone only rang once and went to voicemail. Clearly Doug was not in the mood to talk. He then tried to call Angela. She picked up immediately. "Doug told me what happened, I'll talk to you tomorrow. He's pissed and I can't talk. Goodbye," and hung up before Mick could say anything. Doug may have been his best friend, but Angela was close to it. They had gotten close since Doug met Angela 3 years ago. The only thing he could think of now was to get an Uber and go home. He opened the app and ordered a car.

The car picked him up on the corner and he sulked his way in. The driver was a man from India who was middle-aged. "Sir, if you feel sick, let me know and I'll pull over."

"Thank you, sir," Mick said in the back seat. Mick sank in the seat, knowing he wouldn't get sick and throw up in the car. But he glanced at the passing scenery. Seeing the branches from trees that hung above the street made him think that hanging from a rope from those branches would be fitting. He'd thought of suicide many times in his life, but never really considered it until now. "Sir, have you ever considered what happens after we die?" he said very straightforwardly to the driver. The driver was very nervous now. "Um, not really sir."

"I'm thinking of dying right now. What do you think would be a good way to go?"

"Sir, do you need me to call the police?" the driver said back while starting to slow down.

"If you do, can you ask for that hot officer from the park my buddy tried to pick up? Just mention a hypoglycemic patient in Hunters Park. They'll look it up."

The driver pulled over to the side of the road. "Sir, you are scaring me. I'd like for you to get out."

Mick scoffed and opened the door. He only opened it slightly then kicked it open the rest of the way. "Fine, nobody wants to help me? I'll just fuck off," Mick said as he pulled himself up by the car handle on the ceiling.

"You have a negative way of looking at life. You need help," the driver said as Mick got out. Mick chuckled. "Life is not so bad you know. Look at it as being half full instead of half empty. You crazy man," the driver shouted as Mick was walking away.

stopped and turned around. He looked at the driver intensely. "My father is dead, I have no relationship with my mother, my girlfriend thinks I'm crazy, my best friend and his wife don't want anything to do with me anymore, I'm in intensive therapy, and I'll probably be out of work soon." The driver was getting very frightened. "You say life is half full instead of empty? If life is measured by a glass, then there is absolutely nothing in my glass. I'm empty and I don't give a fuck anymore." Mick flipped the driver the finger and started walking backward. The driver started his car muttering under his breath and drove away quickly.

Mick took his phone out and opened his maps app. He was only a ten-minute walk from his house. "That ain't so bad," Mick said out loud. He walked the best way a drunk man could home from the side of the road. He realized he was on a side street around the block from his house. He looked to his left and realized the house he was looking at was the house behind him. If he cut through the yard, he'd be home in seconds. "Tempting," he said. He thought about it for a few seconds and said what all drunk people usually say before they enter an ambulance. "Fuck it, what's the worst that can happen." It was 2 am, so he doubted the people in the house would be awake. He grabbed ahold of the first fence and hopped over it clumsily. He hit several things on his way down, and pulled himself up quickly. He started to get up to sprint toward the next fence when he slipped on the grass and face planted into the ground again. Luckily his inebriation was strong enough that he wouldn't feel it. He got up again and made a stride for the fence the two yards shared. He sprinted at it and jumped. He made it over body first but got his leg caught in between two fence posts. He hung by the fence by his foot. The rest of his body was in his backyard. "Shit shit shit shit shit," he whispered.

Realistically, all Mick had to do was slip out of his shoe and he'd be free. But his drunken state of mind wasn't thinking rationally. He decided to undo his pants because he figured that's what was keeping him held. So Mick is now with his pants around his knees, in his own backyard, hanging by his fence. Mick rolled himself around to try and break free. He ended up on his back looking up at the stars. All he had to do now was lift his leg up and he'd be free. But he just stared up at the stars. He looked into the heavens above and didn't think of Linsday. He didn't think about Doug or Angela. The ex-chief and ex-co-worker couldn't be farther from his mind. He looked up and thought of his dad. He took a deep breath and said "Dad, I hope you're proud of me." He started to drift to sleep as he rolled and got his leg free. He woke up from his foot hitting the ground and laid in his backyard thinking about the mess of a man he became. But he picked himself up, went around the side to the front door, and went to his bed and fell asleep in his dirty clothes.

He awoke the next morning to his alarm. He had an hour to get to Lazlo's office. He rolled out of bed, took two Tylenol for his aching back, and took a shower. He rubbed soap into a washcloth and wiped the grime from the night before off. He got out, got dressed and took off. Today was his last day with Lazlo, so he was ready to have another end to a relationship today. Hopefully Lazlo will tell him if he believes it's in Mick's best interest to return to work. Mick parked his car, waited in the waiting room, and started clambering his hands together. Lazlo came out to get him by waving his hand without saying a word. Mick got up still clambering his hands. "Calm down, they're going to think I'm doing something to you," Lazlo said trying to be funny.

They walked into the office and Mick started talking before even hitting the couch. "So last night was awful," as Lazlo sat on the couch. "This is gonna be a long day." Mick launched into detail about everything that went down since leaving his office. From his rage driving, his fuck up on the phone with Lindsay, the encounter with his old co-worker, the fight with Doug, the Uber drive home, and the drunken walk home. He went into detail taking up half his time with Lazlo before

Lazlo got a chance to speak again. When he finished, Lazlo reached into his jacket and got out a flask. "Excuse me, I just have to take this," Lazlo said, taking a quick swig.

"Alright, so let's start with the phone call. Doug seemed to handle that business with the car rage so I'm skipping over it," Lazlo started.

"Did you really just take a swig of a flask in the middle of a session?" Mick asked.

"Stay on target," Lazlo said immediately. "So, what happened is an honest mistake, but it just goes to show you're not ready for a relationship as much as Lindsay isn't." Mick had nothing to say. He nodded along since he realized Lazlo was right all along.

"Second of all, what happened in the convenience store is showing me that what we've been working on with conflict resolution is both working and not working. Yes, your old co-worked crossed the line, and you did just walk away before that happened, but just because someone is an asshole doesn't mean you need to be one back."

Mick repositioned himself and asked, "what would you have done?"

Lazlo tilted his head. "You know that's the first time you've asked me that. Maybe you are making strides." Mick snickered. "I would have said 'I'm sorry you're in this situation. I hope you get back on your feet soon,' then walk away and realize that whatever he said after that is him trying to get to me. Although he crossed a line, I know I won't be like that and I know he's in pain." Mick nodded his head quietly.

"And lastly," Lazlo started saying as Mick rolled his eyes. "Roll your eyes at me again, and I'll be sure that you don't go back to work for another month," Lazlo said sternly. Mick straightened himself out and gave Lazlo his full attention. "Now, I don't blame Doug for being very angry with you. You were being inappropriate and undermining all the work we've done. What I'm really concerned with though, is your questioning of your own mortality in the Uber. You're lucky that man didn't call the police and have you brought to a psychiatric ward. Tell me what was going through your mind when you decided to torture the poor man while he was driving you home."

Mick cleared his throat. "I was taking a mental stock of all the things that I have and it was coming up pretty empty. I don't have my father or my mother in my life for different reasons, my best friends won't talk to me, the girl I'm seeing is pissed off at me, and my self-esteem is pretty low. I got drunk and got really sad about the situation I was just in so it all started swirling and making me think the worst thoughts."

"Why would you think the worst thoughts instead of positive ways to earn the trust back but you lost? Yes, making mistakes is a bummer, but every time you get knocked down you have to pick yourself back up. It's like that Uber driver said, you can be half empty or half full. Your perception seems to be your downfall. You need to turn your perception around in order to progress. I'm also seeing that you don't have a lot of closure. Your dad died without you saying a proper goodbye, your mom won't speak to you because of your choices, and this girl situation is still in limbo. You have a lot of work to do and you can't just sit around waiting for it to be fixed magically. By the way, times up." Mick had his hands on his head taking in all this information. "Take your hands off your head, you can think this all over while you're back at work."

Mick picked his head up with a big smile. "I'm allowed to go back to work?"

"I am allowing you to go back to work, but I'm telling your supervisor to put you on probation in case you need to come back for more. We know how good you are listening." Mick dropped his jaw. "Don't worry it's only for two weeks. Now get going, you have work to do."

15

Let's Take a Drive

Mick got up out of the couch and shook Lazlo's hand. Never has one person done so much for Mick in such little time. "Listen," Lazlo started saying.

"I know," Mick finished.

"You don't even know what I was going to say," Lazlo replied.

"Take one day at a time, realize when to be the bigger person, and although you have a right to be angry, being aggressive and screaming does not solve the problem at hand," Mick replied.

"Wow, so you have been listening. So who're you going to start with when it comes to finding a sense of closure?" Lazlo asked.

"I guess I'll call up Doug and Ang. They're the easiest to get a hold of right now. Then maybe I'll hit up Lindsay if I have anything left with her, and then I'll wait till hell freezes over to talk to mom, and by that time comes, I can talk with Dad in heaven."

Lazlo chuckled and said, "I have a feeling you'll try to get it all done in a short amount of time and try to have as much fun with it as you can."

Mick snarled at him and said "wise ass." He walked out of the office waving goodbye to Lazlo, walking down the hall, waving goodbye to his receptionist, and got in his car to plug his aux cord into his phone. He called Angela hoping she'd pick up. And she did.

"Hey, I'm not sure if he's up yet, I'm at my parents while he's asleep," Angela said.

"Are you okay if I stop over and wake him up?"

"If you do, whatever he does is on you."

Is the spare key still under the third brick in the walkway?"

"Yes, godspeed, and I hope my husband doesn't murder you, or at least gets acquitted at the trial."

"Fuck you too, Ang." Angela giggled and hung up the phone. Mick made his way over to get Doug his coffee order so he at least has something pleasant to wake up to. He then parked the car, retrieved the spare key, and let himself in. He made his way to Doug's room where he was asleep. He slowly opened the door and crept his way in.

"If you think my wife wouldn't tell me you're on your way over to make up what happened last night you're out of your mind," Doug said.

"I still brought your coffee," Mick said as if it made up for his behavior.

"Well, it's a start," Doug said back. Doug set up and put his back to his headboard. "So what do you have to say."

"First, I'd like to apologize for the last few weeks. I've been leaning on you a lot and taking advantage of your good kindness. You and Angela have been putting up with me for a long time, and I never told you 'thank you'. Not even once."

Doug took a sip of the coffee. "Keep going, you're not done yet."

"Last night was inexcusable, and it completely undone any progress I made at my sessions. I'm allowed back at work so I won't be bothering you too much."

"Mick, you're my friend and I love you. I could never cut you out of my life, but last night just pissed me off more than anything you've ever done. I'll help you through anything, and I'm sorry last night was so bad for you, but what I was really annoyed with was that you put me in danger with the law, and if I didn't hold you back who knows what you would've done to that dude. That's what I'm really mad about."

"If it helps I don't think I would've killed him," Mick said.

"Well there is some good news."

"But I do think I would've beat him senseless."

"Everybody has skeletons in the closet, ghosts of their past, and other things they aren't proud of. Do you think I'm proud of my dating history before Angela? No, I'm ashamed of it. But if I saw a girl I was with in public while I was with Angela, I'd behave myself and if she approached me, I'd be kind and courteous. Having something bad in your life doesn't give you an excuse to be an asshole."

"And I get that now. I'm sorry for everything."

Doug got out of bed and gave Mack a hug, and just to show him he wasn't mad at him anymore, he squeezed his butt in a playful way and said: "All right, get in bed, we'll make it up the old fashion way." Mick laughed and pushed him off.

Doug and Mick went to the basement so Doug could show him the new riffs he was working on for Basquiat. Then they got lunch, brought it home, and laughed and talked all day. Mick stayed so late to wait for Angela to come home. Angela walked up the driveway and was greeted by Mick in the doorway. "At least let me walk inside before you slobber my doorstep with apologies, Jesus," she said playfully. She gave Mick a hug and was quick to forgive him. "Don't think you're off the hook yet," she whispered in his ear. Mick was slightly scared as to what Angela would ask of him. She let go and said "I want a grilled cheese with tomato soup with an iced tea, make it snappy," she said patting him on the arm, "All while you apologize. I want to see you work for it."

Mick giggled and got to work. "So Ang—" Mick started, getting butter and cheese out of the refrigerator.

"Oh Mick, make it two of each. I'm making sure my husband gets in on the deal." Doug got behind her and kissed the top of her head.

"Right, so anyway, I've been mooching off you and Doug for the better part of the last few weeks. Off of your kindness and good nature," he said while turning on the stove to low and dropping a small portion of butter.

"Blah blah blah, get to the good stuff," Angela said putting her feet up on her counter.

"Anyway, I'm sorry for the way I was last night and I'm sorry you two had to put up with those shenanigans and anything else I've done recently. You're better than that and deserve to be treated as such."

"Very good Mickie, not too dark on mine, and put a little extra pepper in my soup." Doug finished prepping their meals and sat with them. He made his own and explained what Lazlo told him he ought to do from now on.

"So basically, Lazlo wants you to do everything we've been talking to you about, but try and seek closure with everyone?" Doug said before eating a spoonful of soup.

"Basically, although he advised me to just stay away from the ex-coworkers," Mick said back.

"No, really? I'm so shocked," Angela said sarcastically. "So when are you going to talk to Mom or Lindsay?" she continued.

Well, Lindsay I guess in the next day or two, I've been texting her throughout the day and she won't answer. I guess she's thinking of ending it too."

"So if we know that's over, and we're settled already, what are you going to do about mom and dad?" Doug asked.

"I have no idea. I don't think dad is going to say much, and knowing mom, probably even less."

"I thought your dad was, oh, now I get it," Angela said coming to the realization of the joke. "How about we go talk to him today?" she asked.

"Ang, the cemetery is already closed, I don't think I can do that today.

"I don't think they'll kick up much of a fuss in the cemetery. I'm pretty sure they'll be quiet," Doug said.

"Douglas! That's not nice!," Angela yelled.

"What? He already hopped a fence last night, let's do it tonight and get his closure. He'll probably be the only one there, I doubt there'll be security," Doug replied.

"You know what, start the car. Let's go," Mick said.

"You two can do that on your own, I will not be an accessory to this," Angela said.

"Great, let's go," Doug said. Doug auto started his car, they finished their meals and went on their way.

The sky was pitch black and there wasn't an ounce of wind. It was warm and humid. The boys took off towards Mick's apartment. His father's burial site was only a mile away from there. "When was the last time you visited him?" Doug asked.

"Probably when I graduated high school."

"It's been that long?"

"Well, a lot has been going on Doug. It's not exactly a happy place to visit, and anything that had to do with mom and dad has been out of my mind since I was , so this wasn't exactly on my radar."

"So you just happened to pick the apartment around the block from your father's grave and just never plucked up the courage to go visit?"

"Shut up, it's sad. I just wanted to be close to him."

They pulled up next to the cemetery and parked the car. "So where is he in relation to here?" Doug asked.

"I think he's just over the fence."

"You think so? How do you not know?"

"The place is huge dude, I don't exactly have the schematics of the place in my back pocket now do I?" Doug shrugged his shoulders and admitted defeat on reasoning with Mick.

"Alright, I think two people wandering the place is a bad idea so I'm gonna go alone."

"What do you mean? I loved seeing him too, so I want to go."

"Doug, I need to do this alone, if you don't mind."

Doug put his hands up and said "If you insist. But I'm gonna come tomorrow and say 'hi'. Now that you mention it, I haven't visited in a while either so I'd like Ang to come see him."

Mick opened the door, walked over to the chain-link fence, and hopped it like he was getting a kickball out of a neighbor's yard. He took a brisk stride and remembered his father was buried in section T. The cemetery went from A-Z and saw a small sign for the section he hopped into. He hopped into section A. He rolled his eyes and realized he had some walking to do. He took the brace of a quick jog like he did every morning before work. He passed section G and H while thinking of what he could possibly say to an unanswering grave. He passed section L and M thinking about how guilty he felt for not visiting over the past few years. As he passed section Q, the section changed quickly to Z. He was confused but realized he had to go inward more. Doug was only parked a half-mile away on the same side. He rolled his eyes again and took up running further inward. He heard something drop and looked to his left. Some maintenance workers dropped a wheelbarrow. He kept his head low but sneaked further inward as though he were the pink panther. He made his way into section R then S and stopped dead.

Ahead of him was section T. He walked toward it and there, immediately on the roadside, was the site of his father. Carl

Thomlinson. Mick couldn't help himself when he said "It was a bit of a pain to find you, you know that right?" He felt his phone vibrate. It was Doug calling him. He answered. "Hey, you find him?" Doug asked. Mick was exhausted and wasn't in the mood to talk to anyone at the moment. "Yup, found him. Oh, yeah here he is. He's waving right at me. Oh my it seems like he lost some weight too, how nice," he said sarcastically.

"Shut up and hurry up, some landscapers just asked what I'm doing here and I told them I was lost. I pulled away for a sec but I'll be back in 5."

"Okay cool, bye," Mick said hanging up. He looked back at his father's grave. He sat down to avoid being seen, but also to get at level with his dad. "So look, life's been pretty crazy and I'm pretty fucked up. I've stopped talking to mom and I had to take a break at work because I have her anger. Guess we're more alike than I thought. I always thought you'd be with me but lately, I feel so little a connection from you that it scares me. I know I can't get you back, but I don't know how to keep you alive in my soul." Mick started to tear up.

"I really wish you were here to help guide me, Dad. I just want to know if you're proud of me and if you think I'll be alright," he said through tears. Although the night was still and quiet, a wide gust of wind blew across Mick's face and filled him with such joy it was beyond measure. He started giggling. "I'll take that as a good sign." He got up to his feet while still looking at the site. "I'll come back next week, but Doug and his new wife are going to come by tomorrow. Be good to them will you?" The site laid still. "I love you, Dad," he said sweetly. Mick made his way back toward the fence and hopped it just in time for Doug to pull up. He got in and Doug was smiling.

"How is he?" Doug asked.

"He's Dad. So he's the best," Mick replied. They pulled away for Doug to drop Mick off back home.

"Thanks for today, I needed it," Mick said to Doug. Doug said nothing but put his hand up for Mick to grip it and give him a pat on the shoulder. He went inside and Doug pulled away.

16

The Last Time

Mick was allowed back to work but had to wait until he was told by the chief when his first shift was. He awoke the following morning to her phone call and he answered it quickly. "Hello?" he said in his tired sounding morning voice.

"Captain Thomlinson, it's good to hear your voice. How are you feeling?" she said with a tone that was stern yet friendly.

"Good morning chief, I feel great and like a new man."

"Not too new I hope. I like my captain regardless of how coarse he is."

"You're very kind, Chief. But I took this seriously. I wanted to do right by your name and do the work I love best."

"Oh, stop kissing ass, Thomlinson. If you weren't allowed back at first I would have kept your position until you returned."

Mick's heart fluttered. "You mean that Chief?" he replied.

"Sure, if that makes you happy."

Mick giggled. "Due to the vacancy of the position of Lieutenant, your partner Richie has been promoted. He now has directly answer to you."

Mick's eyebrows raised. "Oh dear god."

"I felt the same way at first, but he's been a vast improvement over Diaz, and has shown himself worthy. Sarcastic and a prankster still, but worthy nonetheless. Since he is now Lieutenant, he will be riding with Violet and a new member. You will have a new member to ride with. I expect you to come back this coming Friday to teach him the ropes."

Mick's heart leaped. "Thank you, Chief, but I think I have a date on Friday. Mind if we reschedule?"

The Chief took a moment to take a deep breath. "You make jokes now? This Lazlo sure did a number on you."

"You can say that again," Mick said with a chuckle.

"Get some rest Thomlinson and study up, you'll be needed this Friday. I'll see you in three days, goodbye," and she hung up the phone. Mick hung up and rolled over to fall asleep.

Before Mick could close his eyes, his phone rang again. The number was not one the phone, or one he recognized. Although he usually would not respond to the number, he picked up the call. "Hello? He said in a confused tone."

"Mick Thomlinson?" the caller said in an exhausted tone as though they were calling an absurd amount of people that day.

"Yes, who may I ask is calling?"

"Resident of Riverside, paramedic to the Riverside Ambulance Corp?" they said in another exhausted tone.

"Yes ma'am, how can I help you?" he felt his anger creep up, but he remembered Lazlo and pushed it back down.

"This is Linda Himbledon of FDNY recruiting center, you put in an application 2 years ago, your class is being called to go in for training, do you accept?"

Mick's stomach did a backflip in his body. The only words he could come up with was "oh my god."

"Fantastic, you'll be getting a letter in the mail in the next week to come in for your physical. Have a good day, good-bye." The phone call ended and Mick jumped on his bed letting out a "woo-hoo" at full volume.

Mick hopped in the shower again but quickly after called to tell Doug and Angela the good news. "Yeah, apparently my life is beginning to turn for the better. Who'd of thought huh?" he said to Doug.

"Sure as hell not me," Doug replied. "Mick, I'm so proud of you. You've learned a lot these last few weeks. It was no easy task and you did a good job," he finished saying.

"Mickie, if you need anything just call us. Just keep it in a good tone," Angela said leaning into the phone.

"I'd like grilled cheese, tomato soup, and iced tea. Does that count?" he replied with sarcasm.

"Sure, but I'll make it since you suck at it," she snickered back.

"What're you going to do about work now?" Doug asked inquisitively.

"Well, I'll tell them I'll finish up my time as Captain, which is only another few months. Then, I guess I'll drop down to per diem. It's a good way to make extra money but not have to go to the city to make it."

"Good thinking, man. I'll talk to you later, we're about to go visit your dad."

"Tell him I said I love him," Mick said.

"Will do, talk to you later." They hung up. But as soon as he hung the phone up, it rang yet again. "Jesus, I'm popular today," he said to himself. It was Lindsay who was calling.

He answered inquisitively, "Hello?"

"Can I come over?" she asked.

"Yeah sure, I'm home all day. He then heard his doorbell ring. He had a look of suspicion on his face. "Are you here already?" he asked.

"I'm not going to dignify that with a response," she replied. He kept her on the phone as he went down the stairs to answer the phone. He kept his phone to his ear as he opened the door to see her in his doorway. "But yes, I am," she said while also on the phone.

"What're you doing—" he said realizing he still had her on the phone. He ended the call and continued. "What're you doing driving over here?"

She still had her phone to her ear. "Don't you hang up on me," she said seriously. He made a gesture to get inside with slight irritability. They walked upstairs and closed the door.

Lindsay walked over and sat on his bed. "Look I'm sorry for how I spoke to you," he started saying. "And I shouldn't have inferred on a relationship being official when it wasn't. And also the girl you spoke to and I didn't do anything. She helped me up Doug's stairs and put my drunk ass in his bed."

"Duly noted," she said back to him.

"But, I still don't want to be together anymore. Now, before you say anything," but Mick interrupted.

"It's fine, I understand."

Lindsay looked puzzled. "You're okay with this?"

"Why wouldn't I be? I can't be mad at you for being honest." Lindsay grabs her heart, falls back on the bed and bellows "be still my heart!" Mick laughed. "First amicable break up huh?"

Lindsay sits back up and crosses her legs. "Yeah, I could get used to that."

"Can I ask one question?" Mick asked.

"The last one you get to ask as two people dating each other," she said.

Mick giggled. "That bad experience you had with someone taking everything from you? Did you and he have a bad breakup?"

Lindsay took a beat before answering. "Yeah, I took everything from him. Not in the literal sense like possessions, but he paid for everything, I broke his heart because we were so mismatched, and he called me a slut and tried to post my nudes on the internet."

Mick was disgusted. "Wait, seriously?"

"Mick, thank god you aren't a girl. It really can suck sometimes. That was such a bad experience, I carried it with me into every relationship I've ever tried since. This is why you and I are just never going to work, and I mean that in the most wonderful way. When you date someone, you like to take them to their absolute best and be sure they live up to their most potential. You're amazing, but I'm looking for someone to be my teammate, not my coach."

Mick understood fully. "I'm so sorry that happened to you. I sincerely hope you find what you're looking for. I only wish I could help."

Lindsay looked at him with bedroom eyes. "Well, there is one thing you could help me with," and she uncrossed her legs. She was wearing a skirt with no underwear.

Mick was thunderstruck. "Ah, hell, why not?" Mick kissed her passionately, but she quickly threw him onto the bed. They made passionate love since it was the last time they would be together. It was passionate, glorious, but quick.

Mick and Lindsay laid next to each other and glanced over to the other. "Are we sure about this?" Lindsay asked.

Mick's heart said no, but his head and mouth said, "it was great, but we aren't good for each other. I still have my shit to work through, and shouldn't be with anyone until I'm ready."

Lindsay had a look of amusement. "Clearly it wasn't enough to keep you," Mick tapped her on the shoulder and said "come on, stop that. One session of sex doesn't make up for toxic behavior we have on each other."

Lindsay came to her senses. "Yeah, you're right," she said.

"So where do we go from here?" Mick asked. "Well, I go back to my life before you came into it. I go to work. I come home scrounge the internet for dates and once in a while find someone who is possibly a good match. It'll be unlikely that I find someone good on the internet but that's a choice I'm willing to take to not be lonely." Lindsay said.

"Well, we don't have to be total strangers. But, I don't think dating is a good idea," Mick replied.

"So how about this,every once in a while we check in on each other. Maybe go for lunch or a movie, but we don't have sex and we keep it friendly. We keep things strictly platonic."

"So we'll actually be friends?"

"Yup," Lindsay said. "I haven't had a real friend in a while so it would be a nice change of pace. I know you have two already but I'd like one."

"I think that sounds nice," Mick said.

"So what about you? What lies ahead for Mick, my new friend?"

Mick giggled at the thought. "Well, before you came up here I finally got the call from FDNY to go and be a paramedic. I'll be doing the job my father had when he was alive and the one that got him killed. So I'll be on edge for a little bit and probably busy for a while, but after a while I'd like to see you too. I'll probably be doing the same thing you are with going to work coming home and scrounging the internet, but maybe once or twice a week I'll go see Doug and Angela and have dinner. They'll probably have a kid that takes up all their time, And I won't see them as much so I guess I'll have to find myself a wife to settle down with. But before any of that, I'll have to patch things up with my mom to be sure I stick to Lazlo's plan, but ultimately before that I'm going to take a shower so I don't have your perfume smiling on me when I go visit my mother. I'm sure she'll inevitably ask about my dating life which will be an absolute let down for her."

"Well, you've been let down from the getgo so I don't think she'll be that upset."

"You've got that right, so I think it'll just be a relief to see me alive, and she'll probably go back to nagging me as much as she used to."

Lindsay got up to put her clothes on. After she finished, she made her way toward the door, but before she left, she turned around to look at Mick. "Take care of yourself Mick. You have people who care about you, me included. I know life is pretty crazy and it will throw you a curveball when you least expect it, but I'm sure you'll hit it out of the park from now on."

"Thanks Lindsay," he said with a smile on his face. "I'll see you around."

17

Mama, I'm Coming Home

M ick took another shower and got dressed. He looked himself in the mirror and could feel his heart race fast. He thought of taking that drive to the other side of town where his mom lived. The thought of going to see her for the first time in years was giving him anxiety. He washed his face in the sink and then washed his hands. He was panting. He made his way down the stairs to get in the car. He sat in the driver seat without turning the key to start. He panted at his wheel and slapped it repeatedly. His breaths grew shallower and shallower each second. "I don't know if I can do this," he said to himself. "Yeah I definitely can't do this," he said opening the car door and starting to walk out.

He got halfway up his walkway and stopped dead in his tracks. Lazlo's voice ran through his head. "You need closure and you need to change your ways," echoed through his head. He stammered his feet and grabbed his hair while grunting. He calmed himself down and got back in his car. He turned the key and took off. He started driving toward the house he hasn't been to in years, as he has not been to his childhood home since he was 21. He had not even driven the route anywhere near his home at that time. He drove past the various places he visited as a kid and had fond memories growing up with Doug, his father, and times his mom when they were speaking. He took a left down the street where he grew up and parked his car in the spot where his father would park so he wouldn't wake anyone up on the way home from work. He sat in his car and called up Doug. Doug didn't answer. He had no one to talk to distract him from going inside. It was now or never. He took a deep breath, opened the door, and walked up the driveway. He opened the gate and saw his mother eating at her countertop. She looked up and saw him, and she was as scared as he was. They hadn't spoken in 4 years, but that time was up.

Mick pointed at the door to confirm that it was okay to come in. His mother nodded with her mouth wide open as wide as a codfish. Mick approached the door, took a deep breath and walked in. They looked at each other and Mick said "Mom, I am home." She put her food down and said "I can see that. Although I'm not sure why."

"I know it's kind of weird to see me home, but I have an explanation."

"Well, let's hear it."

"I had an incident at work."

"What happened?" She said interrupting.

"One of the ex-chiefs and the lieutenant were drunk on the job and I got in a fight with the ex-chief."

"As in a verbal argument or a fistfight?"

Mick chose his words wisely. "A little bit of both," he said.

"As you do at work. But I don't blame you. Who shows up to an ambulance job drunk?" His mother replied.

Mick opened his arms and made a face saying "I know right?" without saying anything. "But anyway, the current chief sent me to the mandatory therapy."

Mick's mom put her hands on her head. "Alright, how bad of a mother am I?" she asked.

"I never said you were a bad mother in the sessions"

She looked at him confused. "I'm not following you. Were you living here the whole time without me knowing and on a 4-year long milk run?"

"I'm lactose intolerant, Mom."

She giggled. "Go on," she said, continuing eating.

"We discussed the last few years without you."

"What've you been up to then?"

"I've been going to work, Doug's parents, Doug's new house with his wife."

She picked her head up and said, "Dougie got married?"

"It's a long story mom, read the first book." She shrugged and continued eating. "All that time I thought life was better without you, but I've been missing a big part of my life without you."

Mick's mother didn't pick her head up. "Keep going, Mick."

Mick got annoyed at this. "Well, what've you been up to these last few years?"

Mick's mother put her food aside. "I've been working two jobs and taking care of you."

Mick looked at her with confusion. "You haven't been taking care of me," he said.

"Your garbage goes out to the curb on its own then? Your packages get put on your stairs on its huh? Does your mail get delivered from my house by walking? Dumbass," she said while eating more of her food. Mick had never realized half of the things that go on around him wasn't because of his awesome downstairs neighbor, who he now remembers was actually a prick.

"You did all of that for four years without telling me?"

"You really didn't think that someone was helping you the whole time? Do you think all the stuff happens without you doing something? Grow up, Mick." Mick shook his head and thought he'd relax later and thank her before he left.

"Look," he started saying.

"Look at what?"

"I just wanted to let you know I got the call from the city and I'm taking it." Mick's mom took a deep breath as though she's about to start a rant. "I know you're not happy, but I want to do it and you can't stop me."

"I know I can't stop you, jackass."

"That's right, you can't."

"I think you have the paperwork here from them. You'll need it when you go for your physical."

"Oh, thanks." Mick sat at the table with her.

"Look, I know you went to this therapist. I want to have a relationship with you, too. But don't expect me to be happy about this. I understand that you do what you want to do, but just because I disagree with something doesn't mean you have to not do it."

"How did you get so wise?" he asked.

"I went to a therapist after you left. She said you have to come back to me in your own time. Any connection I try to make with you you'll reject. You'll have to come back in your own way and on your terms."

"She seems pretty smart."

"Yeah, she was kind of a bitch though."

"Mine was an ass too." And following that, Doug and his mother regained their relationship by talking about a mutual hate for their therapists. Whatever makes it work right?

18

Half-Empty or Half-Full

The following Friday, Mick pulled up to his job early. He showed up so early that he beat the new recruit he was supposed to train. The new recruit showed up about a half-hour early, so Mick couldn't have slept longer if he wanted. But he was done with resting. He wanted to get to work on his ambulance. He had been working on himself for the last two weeks. It was time to work for someone else and help heal those in need. He opened his door and made his way to the Chief's office. He passed a mural he rarely stopped at. The mural was for those in the ambulance corp. that perished on 9/11. His father's face had been there all this time, and he never stopped to appreciate it. He stopped and stared at his father's face with a newfound appreciation. He realized his father was looking over him all this time even if he didn't remember it. "In light of recent events," Mick said, "I'm going to start taking what you would do into consideration. Not just do my own thing anymore. You were pretty great, even if I didn't appreciate it."

"Thomlimson," The chief said walking toward him. She was dressed in her business casual attire but also had a Riverview ambulance badge on her sleeve.

"Hey Chief, just taking a look at Dad."

She approached him and put her hand on his shoulder as she leaned in to take a look. "Every day I pass this, and get a little annoyed I never met him," the Chief said without looking at him.

"He was really kind and had a witty sense of humor. You probably would have loved and looked up to him."

"Mick, I'm sorry we put you through all of this," she said in a whisper.

"Chief, it was the best thing for me. Is there anything else you need before I get started for the day?"

"Well, now that you mention it, we need to do a debriefing on everything."

"Let's do it," Mick said. They walked to the Chief's office and sat in their respective seats.

The chief opened her briefcase and took out Mick's file. She clicked her pen and started asking the follow-up questions. "Are you Mr. Mick Thomlinson."

"Yes Chief, I am."

"You were out on medical leave following the incident with Ex-Chief Lawson?"

"Yes, I was."

"You have gone to all forms of rehabilitation recommended by your Chief?"

"Yes, and it was an eye-opening experience."

"Very good. Do you think you are able to return to work, full-duty, no restriction?"

"I'm willing to do all my old duties and more, Chief."

The Chief gave him a confused look. "Did he give you some happy meds or perform some voodoo to give you someone else's personality?"

Mick giggled. "No Chief, I'm just very happy to return and I can't wait to get back out there." The Chief was happy to hear this.

"Mick, what do you think would have happened if we didn't send you to therapy? What would have happened if all we did was send you to the hospital for getting your face checked, then put you back on the rig?" the Chief asked. Mick had never thought of it. The prospect of not having the knowledge he knows now scared him.

"Chief, I don't have the faintest idea. The only thing that comes to mind is that I'd end up like Lawson. Probably bitter, angry, probably kicked out of FDNY for a bad attitude, and most likely never would of gotten the new relationship I have now with my mother. I probably wouldn't of visited my father and have a newfound respect for him, or worst of all, been burnt out and probably looking for a way out. I'm beyond grateful for everything you've done for me in the last few weeks."

The Chief smiled and closed his folder. "And just like that, you're back to work. Your lieutenant is finishing a call so I think you should go see him." Doug rolled his eyes and smiled. He got up and shook the Chief's hands.

"Thanks, Chief. For everything." The Chief smiled and said "it's what we do for those we care about, Mick."

RICHIE STEPPED out of the ambulance while on the phone with central asking for the times he was on scene and for when they arrived at the hospital. "Yeah central, can I have the on-scene times for the—" he stopped when he saw Mick lacing up his boots. He couldn't help himself, he smiled from ear to ear and yelled "Return of the King!" Central was trying to speak over the radio but Richie couldn't have cared less. "Riverview please —" Richie cut off the transmission and began running in a circle yelling "Wooo!!!! He's fresh out the nuthouse and into the friar. Here he is, CAPTAIN THOMLINSON!" Mick showed his teeth to smile while still lacing up. "So what goes on man you less angry than when you left?"

Mick giggled and said "I feel way better. Although I am concerned you're my new lieutenant."

"Hey man, we gotta fill them vacancies." Richie takes a moment to notice Mick looked visibly uncomfortable. "Listen, I know you. I'm sure you're a little upset we had to force Diaz to quit but—" Mick stood up and realized Richie said 'forced to quit' instead of 'fired. "He wasn't fired?" Mick asked.

Richie didn't realize Mick wasn't told the whole truth. "The Chief felt pity on the poor bastard. Only did that so if he cleans up his act he can come back.

Mick was overjoyed. "You mean when he cleans up."

Richie was shocked Mick was so optimistic. "Since when are you looking on the bright side?" Richie stops Mick from fixing his uniform. "By God, you got laid and didn't tell me! Oh, tell me, tell me, tell me!" Richie is hopping up and down at the prospect. Mick walks away, but he is still hopping next to him. "Tell me, tell me, tell me, tell me, tell me." Mick stops in his tracks and Richie continues. "Tell me, tell me, tell me, tell me."

Mick got annoyed. "Alright!" Richie stops hopping and takes deep breaths doubled over. He grabs Mick's hand to put it to his carotid pulse. "How am I doing?" Mick takes 15 seconds to count the beats. "120 strong and regular and you're 100% full of shit." Richie springs back up. "Hoooo who needs cardio. So, go!"

Mick rolled his eyes and told Richie the quick version of what happened with Lindsay. "I met her online, didn't work, so we moved on."

Richie put his hands to his forehead as though he was in 'A Streetcar Named Desire.' Oh my god, you gave me so much detail I can't deal with it.

Mick rolled his eyes again. "Look, man, she was nice, she thought I was nice, but ultimately wanted to be her own entity with a co-pilot. Not some dingy skipper who answers to a captain.

Richie nodded his head. "I can respect that. Ultimately though how'd the sessions go though? Do you feel better?"

"Oh, loads. I learned a lot too. It made me realize what I'm worth and what I've got going for me."

"Did you have those Rorschach tests too?"

"No," Mick said laughing.

"Come on—you didn't see 'some nice flowers?'" Richie said in the voice of Rorschach from "Watchmen"

"Great, now Alan Moore is going to kick my ass."

"What?"

"Nothing, no, none of that" They walked through the door to the kitchen. "He did bring up that thing whether you're a glass half full or half empty guy. It's really been puzzling me." The two sit down.

"And which would you be sir?" Richie asked.

Mick cocked his head back. " I got to tell you, I don't know. All I know is that if life is measured by being half empty or full, I'm just happy to have half. Some got it all, some have none; I'm cool with just half" The alarm sounds off. "Another day in paradise, I'll drive." The door behind them closes.

Shots With Mom
And Dad

Part I

1

Jack Daniels Urn

D aniel stood on the curb of the airport drop-off section
waiting for his brother Wade to arrive. He hadn't seen
Wade in a while, and his nerves showed every time he fumbled
the keys in his pocket. They lived on opposite sides of town
and barely spoke to one another unless it regarded urgent
family matters. However, Wade often made attempts to see
Daniel by leaving messages for him to come for dinner. Daniel
never returned a call. He didn't see why he should; they had
nothing in common besides being brothers. But that was
enough for Wade to try and made an attempt.

Daniel looked at his watch in anticipation of Wade's arrival.
The flight was at 10:30 p.m., and it was currently 8:28 p.m.
Daniel was getting anxious at the time since you're supposed
to arrive two hours before your flight departs in order to get
through security efficiently and have time to catch the flight.
Wade's car service dropped him off at 8:35. He stepped out of
the car with his luggage bag and two carry-on bags. He was a
tall man with the common stomach length of most active
parents and wearing a plain white T-shirt that had a small
brown stain over his shoulder that was a mystery even to him.

Daniel was repulsed by his appearance, going as far as to show him by fake vomiting in his mouth. Wade came over to Daniel with a warm smile and a hug. It was not reciprocated.

"Danny! Buddy, how are you?" Wade asked as he lifted his brother into the air with a hug, unabashed by the possible opinions others might have.

"I'm fine, Wade. Seems like you're taking care of yourself," Daniel said, pointing out the stain on his shoulder.

"Oh yeah. Little Danny had an upset stomach before I left. Mel thinks maybe it's nerves because he'll miss me. But I think that was her way of saying she'll be upset while we're over in Europe."

"Charming sentiment," Daniel said, looking at his suit to be sure none of the stain got on him. "Why do you have two carry-on bags?" Daniel inquired.

"Oh, well, one's a real carry-on and the other contains mom and dad," Wade said, spinning the bag humorously.

The bag Wade regarded cheekily as "carrying mom and dad," contained the urns of their departed parents. The purpose of the trip to Europe was to follow the trail of their honeymoon and spread their ashes in the rivers, lakes, or waterfalls in each location. However, they were about to find out about the slight policy change regarding carry-on luggage. They brought their bags to the curbside baggage check-in kiosk.

'I'm sorry, Mr. Fontaine, but you're only allowed one carry-on bag.'

"Oh, my. Well, then may I step inside and see if I can move a few things around?"

"Absolutely, sir. Sorry for the inconvenience."

"Not a problem, dear. May my ward here check in his bag or does he need to also get in the bag?" The kiosk woman giggled; however, Daniel had a look of disdain on his face.

"No, I can check him in as well."

Daniel sent his bag in and followed Wade soon after. "So what're you going to do?" Daniel asked, genuinely asking regarding the bag containing the remains of their parents.

"Well, first let's go to the bar. I could use a stiff one." The two brothers walked through the airport looking for a bar. "So what's new Danny?"

"Nothing really. Work is booming but nothing much else."

"No kidding! What's been happening at work?" Wade knew all too well this was the only thing Daniel was comfortable being open about. Daniel was the head of his division in the Suffolk County Police Department in the drug trafficking division. A very intense job that included long hours, sleepless nights, and a career of thankless individuals.

"Well, we had a bust over the weekend in a heroin house over on the south shore," Daniel stated.

"Yeah? Then what?" Wade responded, genuinely trying to make a connection with his brother.

"We found out from a hospital patient that she bought a bag from the location we've been keeping an eye on. She admitted that she's bought from there on multiple occasions, confirmed the suspect in question, and also that there is a missing girl in the basement who we've been trying to find for three weeks."

"Get out of here! Then what happened?" Wade's eyes opened up and his mouth was agape as they found a kiosk that sold liquor.

"After we got the ID on everyone, we sent in an undercover to go in and buy a few bars, that's heroin laced with alprazolam, otherwise known as Xanax."

Wade purchased a Jack Daniels bottle and two Coca-Cola bottles. "That sounds intense Danny, then what?"

Daniel continued, although his tone was of confusion as to why Wade made his purchase. "Then the dealer sold it to my guy. My officers broke in and all is well. What the hell is this? I thought you wanted to go to a bar?"

"Nah, just needed to get this," Wade said, holding up his purchase in a bag.

"You know Europe has all this, right? You don't need your own supply."

"Shhh follow me into the bathroom."

The two went into the bathroom. Wade put his purchase on the counter along with his bags. "Take out mom and dad while I do this." Wade proceeded to take out a roll of large, clear, plastic garbage bags.

"Why the hell do you have a garbage bag in there?" Daniel inquired.

"It was for the bus tour. In case we or anyone else needed to throw out snacks. Being a dad always has me prepared for eating and throwing away snacks." Daniel took the two urns out carefully. Wade then proceeded to pour out the Jack Daniels bottle entirely.

"Why the hell are you—" Daniel said before he was cut off by Wade quickly pouring half of mom and dad into the garbage bag." "You're not serious," Daniel said in defiance.

"I'm gonna put them in the bag together, then pour the coke into the bottle to make it look like it's full, then we'll empty it in London and keep them in the bottle and take them around Europe that way. Simple!" Wade said without a care in the world. Daniel was mortified but proceeded to go along with it.

"Between the two urns, we'll only have enough of half of each quantity," Daniel said, getting ashes on his suit jacket and the entire countertop and floor of the bathroom.

"We'll flush what's leftover. It all leads to the ocean anyway, so technically it's kind of like a prequel to the trip." Daniel looked up at Wade, disheveled, but agreed. They stood over the toilet, Wade holding the finished product of their experiment, and Daniel holding the remainder of their parents in each urn. "Mom and Dad, we're sorry for the inconvenience, but I didn't want to start a fight with a TSA agent and I can't control the rules of the sky. I love and miss you both."

Daniel looked over at him dourly and full of disdain, but merely replied, "Ditto." They poured the remainder of what was left in the toilet and flushed while Wade played "Taps" from his nostrils. Wade put the Jack Daniels bottle into his carry-on, threw his other bag in the garbage, then walked out while Daniel threw his washcloth from cleaning his suit jacket in the trash.

They walked out in time to see the custodian walk into the bathroom and hear him proclaim, "I quit!"

Wade and Daniel stood in line at the security desk. Wade was there without a care in the world while Daniel looked as though he'd seen a ghost. "What's wrong, Danny?"

Daniel looked up and grunted, "What the hell do you mean, 'what's wrong?'"

"Do you need a tums? I got some in my bag if you—"

Wade picked his bag up and started rifling through it until Daniel cut him off. "You just poured our parents' ashes into a Jack Daniels bottle, and you're asking me what's wrong."

"Well, technically, since mom and dad were Jack and Delilah, respectively, I think it ought to be referred to as the Jack Delilah bottle."

"I think I should beat you over the head with it, respectfully."

"Calm down, dad practically lived in a Jack Daniels bottle anyway. Now they can be together where no mom has ever gone before," Wade said in a voice similar to a voice-over of a science fiction film.

"I cannot wait until this backfires on you," Daniel said with sincerity.

"Oh yeah? We'll see." Wade was next in line to go through security. He put his bag on the moving belt and sent it through to the other side. He stepped through to the security guard with the metal detecting wand, was cleared, and he was let through.

The third TSA agent looking at the bag through the screen noted to him, "Enjoy your drink on the flight, sir."

Wade smiled and said, "Oh, thank you very much, sir." Wade walked several feet away and made a "touchdown" motion to Daniel as he stepped up to put his bag through. Although Daniel's bag was secure, he was not secure when the second TSA agent waved his wand and it stopped at his left armpit. Panic flitted across his face when he realized he forgot to check his gun and badge.

"You got a reason for that gun, sir?" The second TSA agent asked in a serious voice.

"If you allow me to put my arms at my waist, I can show you my badge and credentials," Daniel quickly explained and revealed his identification, showing him to be well within his rights to carry a weapon. He then went to the security desk to make a phone call to one of his team members to come and claim his gun from the airport. After all the drama, they finally arrived at the gate.

Before boarding, Wade cheekily made a remark to Daniel, "Talk about backfire back there, huh, Serpico?" Daniel just lowered his head in embarrassment and they boarded their flight.

The flight from JFK airport in New York to Heathrow airport in London was about eight hours, so Daniel arranged for them to take an overnight flight so he could work all day and sleep on the plane. Wade had other ideas.

"So how's dating life?" Wade asked shortly after takeoff.

"Dating is something I don't have time for, Wade," Daniel said, lowering an eye mask.

"Oh, that's a shame. You deserve a nice girl. Or guy, whatever it is. You know I love you, right?"

"Yes Wade, I know. But no, the last girl I dated was seven years ago. Work takes up all my precious time."

"You should really take more time for yourself, you know. I worry about you. You never return my calls so I worry something's happened. But then I see your name in the paper for a big bust and I get so excited to see you're okay," Wade said as he opened a jar of peanuts.

"Thank you, Wade. May I please sleep?" Daniel had never been one for sentiment, although he did feel a sense of guilt.

"Yeah sure, I'll let you sleep. But before you do, what do you want to do in London? We got two days there before we catch the tour."

"Whatever you want to do, Wade."

"Awesome! How about we go see Abbey Road before we go to Parliament and all that to do the first shot of ashes."

"Shot of ashes?" Daniel asked, lifting his blindfold.

"Yeah, we can get shot glasses and pour them out at each location from the bottle," Wade said, without batting an eyelash.

"Terrific, Wade."

Wade shoved a handful of peanuts in his mouth. "Yeah, and we can get fish and chips and get drunk while taunting those guards at the palace."

"Wade, I'm not going to be uncivilized and get drunk. If this is what you want to do in London, I'm scared for my safety in Amsterdam."

"No, we won't get crazy in Amsterdam. I figured we can do some classy stuff there, too, like go to the Van Gogh museum like you always wanted. See if maybe they got his piano, a couple wigs, some old sheet music."

"Wade, what're you talking about piano and wigs for?"

"You know, Van Gogh, the deaf piano player who made all those big symphonies they use on car commercials and everything."

"The deaf piano player is Beethoven."

Wade looked confused. "What's the difference?"

Daniel took off his blindfold in annoyance. "Van Gogh is a famous artist. He cut off his ear to give to the woman he loved."

"Yeah, the deaf guy," Wade said, completely convinced they were talking about the same person.

Daniel rolled his eyes and said, "Yeah, him." He took melatonin out of his bag, took it with some water, and put his blindfold back on while muttering to himself in frustration. However, Wade shrugged his shoulders, put headphones in, and listened to a playlist he made of his wife's favorite songs while looking at the photos of his son in his photo album. They both eventually fell asleep together, yet separate.

2

Take Me Back to London

The flight landed and shook both the brothers awake. They gathered their belongings and set off to disembark the plane. They came out and went to the English TSA agents. Upon entering England, you have to tell the TSA agents why you were in the country, be it for vacation, work, or returning home. Daniel went first being very straightforward as usual with the TSA agents. Wade came forward and bragged about the vacation they were on and spoke at great length about his brother's accomplishments while holding up the line.

"Must you always have more to say than the average person?" Daniel asked in frustration.

"I like talking to people. Mel works all day so the most I get to say is to online bill pay, my vacuum, and whatever little Danny can understand. He looks just like you, by the way. He's got a beam of confusion in his eye every time I talk."

"Smart boy," Daniel said. "We have to take the tube to Kings Cross station, then walk two blocks from the hotel."

"Kings Cross!" Wade yelled with excitement. "You get to see platform 9 ¾ like in Harry Potter. I remember you inhaling those books. They're still a bit too thick for me to read, though. Maybe I can start in the summer. Mind if I borrow them? I can read them to little Danny, too."

"Sure, Wade," Daniel said with a tone that sounded slightly less irritated.

They boarded the train from the airport and traveled toward Kings Cross station. Looking out the window, Wade was elated to see the passing by landscapes and homes of those in a country foreign to him. Daniel had a look of confusion. "Where is the ticket taker?" Daniel said, looking around.

"Huh?" Wade said, not taking his eyes away from the window.

"The staff was supposed to take our tickets. I paid 50 pounds each for these tickets. I think someone ought to take them."

"Couldn't tell you, Danny," Wade said, not losing his positivity.

"Jesus, I wish the LIRR was this cavalier with rules. I had to pay 25 extra dollars because I once got a one-way instead of a roundtrip."

"Must be their tea break," Wade said in a voice imitating Ringo from the movie *Help!*

"Jesus, I haven't seen that movie in a while," Daniel said, recognizing Wade's movie quote.

"I'm just happy you remembered it," Wade said with a subtle smile.

"How could I forget? That was your favorite stay-at-home-sick movie. You'd play it on a continuous loop. If I hear "The Night Before" one more time, I think I'll puke." Daniel had love and affection for his brother, but he had no idea how to show it without being slightly insulting. Wade, however, was ecstatic that Daniel remembered his favorite movie.

The train pulled into Kings Cross station. After many different escalators, they arrived on the main floor. "Danny, don't forget your—"

"I have my bags, Wade. I'm not an imbecile."

The boys took their luggage down the halls of the train station, passing various platforms. They passed platform 13, 12, "Danny don't they have a—"

"I don't know Wade." They walked further down seeing platforms 11 and 10.

"Look! I see a 9. Oh, look, a sign that says to platform 9 ¾." Daniel couldn't help himself. He let out a smile that couldn't go unnoticed. They followed the sign to the main lobby of Kings Cross station where there stood a display for platform 9 ¾ from the Harry Potter series. There also stood a line that went out the door. "Do you want a picture?" Wade asked, taking out his phone.

"No, I'm fine. I think seeing it is enough."

"But Danny, it's your favorite."

"Wade, I'll always remember it. I don't need a picture every time I see something I enjoy. Let's go, we need to check into the hotel." Wade had an expression of slight disappointment, but he put his phone away. The brothers took their bags out to the street.

"Look around, Danny. London, England. Can you believe it?"

"Yes, it's quite overwhelming. Now come on, we have to get to the National Royal Hotel. It's a few blocks from here." The brothers strolled along, passing the beautiful British architecture sights, humble pubs, and a gelato shop, arriving at the

National Royal Hotel at 7:00 a.m. EST; however, being in a new time zone, it was about 5:00 p.m. BST (British Summer Time.)

"I know it's evening here, but I'm wide awake. Want to take a quick trip somewhere?" Wade asked, unloading their bags in their room that looked more like a college dorm.

"Yeah, sure. We'll do Abbey Road and then grab dinner."

"Sounds like a plan, Dan." Daniel moaned in annoyance.

"We're going to need two adapters, by the way. Our plugs are different from the English plugs."

"Great, let's shower and go." Daniel showered first while Wade tried to FaceTime his family. He called once and his wife, Melony, answered immediately.

"Honey, I miss you already!" Melony said sincerely, holding their baby.

"Oh, baby, I miss you, too. Both of my babies, actually. How's my baby boy?"

"He misses his daddy. How was the flight?"

"The flight wasn't too bad. Had a snafu in the airport, but I'll tell you about that later."

"Is Danny being, well, Danny?"

"A little, but nothing I can't handle. I missed him a lot, so I think I'm overwhelming him."

Melony put the phone down to put the baby in a crib. "Oh gimme one second, hun." She picked the phone up again. "Sweetheart, and you know I love you, but you know how you get when you get excited."

"Oh, I know. I'll chill out, but I'm just so excited to catch up and visit all the sights mom and dad talked about. Well, the sights dad talked about."

"Mom never talked about it that much?"

"Mel, mom never really talked about much without it involving criticism or her job. Sound familiar?"

"It's odd how you both look nothing alike but act like your parents."

"Yeah, but what're you gonna do?" Wade shrugged his shoulders, making the best of a sometimes uncomfortable situation.

"I'll FaceTime you again in Amsterdam, sweetheart. Hopefully, I don't fall in love with a prostitute and come home."

"Oh, honey, you know I'm far more expensive than a prostitute but will always love you more than one."

The shower stopped and Daniel came out. After Wade got in, Daniel changed and checked to see if he had any messages. There was one from his co-worker busting his chops about the gun. Wade came out, and they took the tube from Russell Square five stops, transferred to Green Park, and went three more stops to St. John Wood. From there, they came out and walked straight to Abbey Road studios. There, they walked across the famous crosswalk where Paul, John, George, and Ringo took their famous walk for their album cover. However, the studio was still active, so nobody could explore the studio which went over very well for Daniel. Just kidding.

"What a waste of a train ride! Can you believe they don't do tours? What a pile of shit."

"Oh, look! A Beatles shop right down the street!" said Wade. The key to dealing with certain people was just to listen. They didn't necessarily need problems solved, they just needed to complain. Wade found himself putting on various costumes from the Sergeant Pepper era, while Daniel looked at his watch wondering when Wade would be done being silly. After the brothers were finished, they took off to the hotel and had a good night's rest.

The following morning, they awoke to Daniel's alarm clock. Rising promptly at 7:00 in the morning, Daniel woke up sharply and was ready for the day by 7:30 in a button-down shirt and nice khakis. His mantra had always been to be prompt and ready for the day no matter where you were. Wade was still in bed after the third alarm. Daniel went over and dropped his luggage next to Wade's bed. It fell with a thud while Wade woke up in a panic saying "I'm up! Where's the baby, is he clean?"

"Your son is miles away. Time to start for the day, Wade."

"Sorry, Danny, must have slept in."

"You don't say. Now get ready, Wade. We have things to see."

"You got it, Danny." Wade got out of bed, dropped his pants, put on a pair of jeans, brushed his teeth, and said, "Alright, let's go." Daniel took a look at Wade and made a face like he just farted.

"You're really going out like that?" Daniel asked.

"What? Who do I have to impress? I'm married with a kid." Daniel rolled his eyes. "You'll see, Danny. Everyone loves to be relaxed on vacation." Wade followed behind Daniel while grabbing the carry-on full of Jack and Delilah. "So Danny, I was thinking maybe we can walk from here to the Mall and spread the first shot of ashes in the River Thames." Daniel nodded in agreement and they proceeded to head south.

"Danny, we're on vacation. Why don't you try to relax for a minute? You're not on the job."

Daniel swung his head back in annoyance. "Wade, not all of us have the privilege of being a stay-at-home dad. Yes, being a stay-at-home parent is stressful; but with what I do, it carries a weight of responsibility that some just can't grasp." Wade proceeded to cartoonishly act like a police officer, crouching on his knees with his hand in the air imitating a gun. He walked in a circle as Daniel stood still, annoyed. Wade came up behind Daniel and said into his hand to imitate a walkie-talkie, "This is Wade 1 to officer asshole. The perimeter is secure, no job is in sight." Wade put his hands on Daniel's shoulders. "Come on, brother! I'm sure there are drugs here somewhere, but maybe you should let the London police worry about them. It's not your problem. Let's go grab a crepe and Nutella and try to relax. I know you still have that sweet tooth."

Daniel lowered his shoulders and opened his eyes wide. "I could go for a crepe and Nutella."

Wade clapped his hands in the air. "That's what I'm talking about. Come on, I'm buying." The brothers found the closest crepe cart and made their purchase.

They proceed to walk further toward the river. "Very good idea, Wade."

"I have to tell you, we need more crepe stands in Manhattan. Enough of this hot dog cart crap. Crepes is where it's at."

"Wade, Manhattan hot dogs are a staple of the city. You might as well throw out all the pizza joints while you're at it."

"And then what, huh? Kick out all the pigeons? Not on my watch." Wade put his hand on Daniel's chest and said, "Whoa." They stood on the sidewalk that proceeded to the River Thames and Parliament Bridge. They continued to walk until they stood in front of Big Ben and the Parliament build-ing. They stared up at Big Ben together in silence, saying no words but feeling the same thing. They really were on the other side of the world.

"Pretty amazing, isn't it?" Daniel said.

"Pretty incredible," Wade said in agreement. They then went over to another crepe cart; but instead of getting more crepes, they asked for two empty cups. They went down the stairs to the river and opened the bottle.

"I didn't know it would feel like this," Daniel said nervously.

"Like what?" Wade asked, genuinely confused.

"We're really here doing this. I know I can be hard to deal with sometimes, and I'm sorry. You just are going to have to wait for me to really uncork."

"Danny, I never wanted you to be anything but yourself. You're perfect as you are. I know mom rode you pretty hard, but she was proud of you and so was dad. I'm proud of you, too." Daniel nodded as Wade poured out a small amount of their parents' ashes into both cups. They held them up to cheer them on.

"Mom, dad, sorry about what happened at the airport. You deserved better than that. We're on the trip and we're already off to a great start," Daniel said.

Wade looked over at him and said, "Ditto."

They poured out their respective cups and a gust of wind caught the ashes and spread them all over the people passing by. Without even thinking, they both booked it up the stairs and didn't stop until they reached the Churchill War room.

They stopped to catch their breath. "Jesus that went bad," Wade said as he hunched over panting his breath.

"You got to get back in shape, Wade. I'm not even sweating," Daniel said, not even slouched over.

"Well, not all of us are around catching bad guys. I usually run from the crib to the oven. Where do we go from here?"

"Let's cut through this park and go see the mall," Daniel said, pointing toward a nearby park. They walked all the way through the park to the other side to see Buckingham Palace. To which, there were no guards around for Wade to mock. He showed his disappointment by kicking the dust in the street.

"Wade, stand in front I'll take a picture." This did not disappoint Wade in the least.

"Danny, give it to someone so we can take one—alright, nevermind." Daniel hated pictures and showed Wade by moving his mouth like a dog who didn't want you to take his bone.

"Let's keep walking," Daniel said as they strolled around London. They stopped in a pub for lunch, then continued to sightsee before returning to their room to nap before meeting up with the tour group with whom they'll be shown the rest of Europe.

3

ITourEurope

The brothers woke from their nap and headed down to the lobby where they found the transportation company they would be using for their tour around Europe. To say this caravan was full of characters would be an understatement. They met the tour guide, Sean, a young man in his mid-to-late 20's who was visibly growing tired of his job. Like many people in this age group, he was searching for his passion and a deeper meaning in his life. Something about showing people the same sights he'd been to dozens of times got boring after a while, no matter how fun the tourists were. And these tourists were no exception. On this tour were Zhang Wei, the husband, and Chenguang, his wife. They were English teachers in China on a vacation away from the kids. No matter what culture you're in, sometimes your kids can drive you up the wall and you need a break. There was also Maria from Newark, New Jersey, who would be known as the drag of the trip. There were also several groups from Australia; numerous groups of 4-5 people together who came for the fun of exploring new territory. However, there was one member from New Zealand, the "class clown" named Bill. Bill spoke at great lengths, whether you wanted him to or not. But trust me, you really wanted him to.

When the group gathered around to do a meet and greet of sorts, Bill opened with the following. "Oi yeah, my name's Bill. I'm from New Zealand." He then nudged Daniel's arm and said, "They call us sheep shaggers, aye!" The group, including Daniel, laughed. Bill continued with a joke. "A New Zealand man walks into his house, drunk, with a sheep under his arm. He walks into his bedroom where his wife was sleeping. She woke up and he said, 'This is the dog I've been fucking. His wife says, 'That's a sheep, you idiot.' The man turned to his wife and said, 'I was talking to the sheep.'" The group howled with laughter. The group was then treated to an all-you-can-eat buffet and an open bar.

Daniel, Wade, Bill, Zhang Wei, and Chenguang were all at the bar having the first of many drinks on this trip, all while they were eating heartily and having a good time.

Chenguang spoke to Wade. "Oh, sir, why did you bring a bottle of Jack Daniels to the bar?"

"Wade, why the hell did you bring that down?" Daniel asked while putting his palm to his face.

"I thought mom and dad would like to meet the group!"

"Oh? Your parents are here, too? I don't remember them speaking before," Chenguang said.

"Oh no, Cheng. This is mom and dad," Wade said while holding up the Jack Delilah bottle.

"I don't understand," Chenguang said like any normal person.

"Both our parents passed away last year, and their dying wish was to be spread along their honeymoon trail. So we're here to honor their wishes."

Chenguang started to tear up. "That's beautiful," she said, overlooking the fact that no urn was in sight.

"Yeah, they couldn't accommodate the urns on the plane, so we had to make do," Wade said.

"Wade, to be fair, we didn't really ask if there was anything we could do." Wade opened his eyes, realizing Daniel was right.

"Oi, mate, but this is more fun!" Bill said, overhearing the conversation. Bill took the bottle and held it up. "I vow that I'll help you boys on this trip to protect this bottle at all costs. Er, what were your names again?"

4

Checkpoint Blues

After the meet and greet was finished, the groups went back to their rooms. The tour group had to meet downstairs at 6:00 a.m. Naturally, Daniel was ready to go by 5:00 a.m. while Wade arrived at the bus at 6:30.

"Wade, I'm getting you an alarm clock for this trip."

"Why didn't you wake me up, Danny?"

"I can only shake you so much before you fall back asleep."

Wade and Daniel sat next to each other on the bus after putting their luggage down below. The bus pulled off and they were on their way. They were off to explore uncharted territory and to see if their parents really took the trip of a lifetime or if they were just in love. Admittedly, it was a big concern for both Daniel and Wade. To live up to that kind of hype was a nerve-wracking thing. But now it was time to see.

As the bus moved along, Sean took the microphone from the front of the bus and started his opening monologue. "Hello, everyone, and welcome to the ItourEurope experience. I know we all are up and it's early, but now it's time to hear what we have planned for the day. We arrive in Amsterdam at approximately 3:00 p.m., this is after we depart from the ferry that gets us from Britain to Holland. Until that time, we're going to play a game so we can get to know each other. We're going to pass around a bowl with questions in it; and whichever you pull out, you have to answer it honestly. We're going to start in the front and work our way back. Let's get started!" The bus roared with applause. The bowl started in the front and worked its way back.

The first people to get the bowl were Zhang Wei and Chenguang. Zhang Wei's question was "What destination are you looking forward to most on the trip?"

Zhang Wei said, "Anywhere away from my job and children is fine with me. I don't care if we end up on the side of the road for three days, it's in Europe." The bus clapped in agreement.

Chenguang pulled her question out of the bowl, which read, "What destination do you wish was on the trip that isn't?"

She replied "I wish we went to Helsinki, Finland. Something about it just seems appealing to me and I'd like to go." The bus clapped in agreement.

The bowl went down the rows of people with questions like, "What is your most embarrassing childhood memory, what is your favorite meal, what do you wish you could do that you cannot do?" Some answers were interesting, like someone wished they had no gag reflex (someone's trying to get laid on this trip...fucking Maria), some were not so interesting like one person had his pants pulled down in front of the class and someone else told that his favorite meal was spaghetti.

Bill got his turn. Naturally, his question was, "Do you have a crush on anyone on the tour?" His retort was, "Ladies and gentlemen, as a bisexual, I'd like to remind everyone that I sleep with the door unlocked and naked. Do with that information as you like." Maria licked her lips. However, one girl from the group of Australians, named Zoey, had this question from the bowl. "What is your hidden talent?" She stood up from her seat, revealing herself to be a tall, skinny blonde girl with bright blue eyes, did a cartwheel in the aisle, and then a full split. Landing at eye level with Daniel, and smiled. Then said, "I'm also a police officer in Sydney's drug enforcement division," while making eyes at Daniel and making him slightly blush.

"Danny, if you don't have sex with her before the trip ends, don't even come home."

"Wade, will you have some decency?"

Wade put down his copy of *How to Be Mediocre.* "Danny if she didn't give you the 'fuck me' eyes then, she must have a sight disorder."

"Wade, she looks to be half my age."

"Danny, you're only 40. Have some fun. I'm sure she's a little older than 20, maybe 25 or 26."

"I'm here to honor our parents' wishes, not end up with a foreign STD."

"Danny, will you have some fun for once in your life? You have fun on vacation then never see her again. Just don't fall in love with her, although it would be a nice change of pace from your grouchy, self-righteous, malodorous ways, you little sh— oh, look, the bowl!" Wade's excitement peaked as he pulled out a question. "What about home are you missing the most?" Wade suddenly sounded a bit sad. "Oh, that's an easy one, I miss my wife and baby boy so much it hurts to breathe some moments." The crowd took a collective "aw" and applauded.

Wade passed the bowl to Danny, who pushed the bowl back at him. They pushed the bowl back at each other until Wade slammed it in his lap and three questions came out the side. Daniel exhaled in annoyance, then pulled out a question. "How do you think your job is doing without you?" He crumpled it up and said "It's fine without me, but I miss it so much it hurts to breathe at times," in a monotone voice. The bus gave a collective "boo" and threw their crumpled-up pieces of paper at him.

Wade shrugged his shoulders and said, "Maybe it's because you stole someone's answer."

After the game finished, the passengers took out their books to read, listened to music, and talked amongst each other. Once the bus got to the ferry, all the passengers departed to grab something to eat from the ferry's cafe.

"Oi, mates, let's go have a couple of drinks, I'm buying," Bill said to Daniel and Wade.

"Sounds good to us," they said simultaneously.

The boys sat at the bar having a good time, when over the intercom they heard, "Wade Fontaine to the bus, Wade Fontaine to the bus." Wade and Daniel looked at each other in confusion, but both of them went down.

"What could it be, Danny?"

"I don't know, Wade. I didn't make the call."

They walked down to the bus to see the two security guards and a German Shepherd police dog with Wade's carry-on. The security guard looked impatient and angry immediately. "Mr. Fontaine, we went through the bus with the dog, and he seemed to be sneezing uncontrollably with your bag. Can you explain this?" The security guard held up the Jack and Delilah bottle.

"Oh my goodness, officers, I can explain that."

"Mr. Fontaine, are you aware this is a drug-sniffing dog? And he told us this bottle contains American drugs brought into this country."

Wade's eyes opened wide. "The dog can speak?"

The security guards and Daniel rolled their eyes. "No, Mr. Fontaine, the dog communicated in his way that there are drugs in this bottle."

"Oh my god, can I see?' Wade said, forgetting the severity of the situation.

"Gentleman, my name is Detective Daniel Fontaine. I'm a drug enforcement officer back in the States. There is a reason the bottle is filled, but it is not any form of drugs."

"Then why did the dog tell us this, officer?"

"I can't speak for the dog, but I can say he's sneezing because our parents' ashes are in that Jack Daniels bottle."

"The Jack Delilah bottle, Dan—" Daniel thumped Wade on the back of the head.

The security guard started getting visibly upset, "Gentlemen, what idiot would make a Jack Daniels bottle an urn to transport their parents to a foreign country?"

"Well, there was a change in policy at the airport and—"

"It was a rhetorical question, sir!" The security guard raised his voice. "It is a ludicrous idea, and I don't believe it."

"You don't have to believe anything, however, it is the truth," Daniel said patronizingly.

"Are you getting smart with me, sir?" chided the security guard.

"Well, you're saying stupid shit so someone had to be smart."

"Danny, I don't think this is a good idea."

"Wade, please. Who would be stupid enough to smuggle drugs into Amsterdam, where pot is legal?" Daniel said.

"It's not legal, it's tolerated," the security guard said through his teeth."

"Oh, I'm sorry. Is it illegal on the boat?" Daniel asked, putting the officer down.

The security guard had enough of this. He opened the bottle and filled the cap with ashes. "Listen, I've been guarding this boat for nine months. Don't tell me what is and isn't drugs."

Out of nowhere, Bill came over and said, "Did someone say drugs?" He took the cap out of the security guard's hand and brought it to his face.

"Bill, no!" Daniel and Wade said simultaneously. Bill inhaled the ashes and started sneezing and coughing uncontrollably.

"Ow, fuck! Oh shit, that's not drugs! That fucking hurts, mate! Goddammit, it burns, someone get me water."

"Someone get the first aid kit!" Daniel yelled at the security officer. The security guard rushed and brought it back. Daniel took the saline that was in the kit and flushed out Bill's sinuses. While this scene was going on, Wade talked it over with the security guard, closed the bottle, and put it back safely under the bus.

"Something tells me you know your drugs, Bill."

"Danny, I've done all the drugs you can think of; but your parents just snorted me under the table." Daniel and Wade chuckled. While Daniel and Wade took care of Bill, the rest of the tour boarded the buses, and Bill earned the nickname "Wild Bill" for the remainder of the trip.

"Wade, Danny, I've never met your parents, but somehow I feel like they're with me right now. There's just this feeling like they're in my head." The brothers were laughing uncontrollably.

"Are they saying anything to you now, Bill?" Wade asked, setting him up for a bit.

"Oh yeah! I can hear your mum racking around saying, 'This all looks well and comfortable, doesn't it, darling?' And pop is trying out the furniture in my brain doing, 'Oi, this seems a bit soft, and the lights aren't all on in here. Is there something dim about this brain?' 'Well, I don't know, darling, we've only just arrived. Make me a cup of tea, will you?'" Wild Bill was making the entire bus laugh for 10 straight minutes of banter about Jack and Delilah on vacation in Bill's brain. A bit that made Daniel, the uptight, un-humorous working stiff, laugh until tears came out of his eyes.

5

Wham Bam New Amsterdam

The bus continued on until they reached the hotel in Amsterdam. The hotel, however, was actually a hostel. It was listed on the brochure as a hotel, so obviously Daniel was pleased to see it. And by pleased, I mean irritated beyond measure. He would rather stay in a tin can in the alley that was currently being used to light up a joint by two other Americans who decided to start their own business.

"Let's open a dispensary in Colorado!" the first tourist said.

"That sounds dope, but let's also sell comics and coffee in it, too," the second said. And thus, the most successful dispensary in Aspen, "Cannabis, Coffee, and Comics," was formed.

But anyway, Daniel, Wade, and a gentleman who turned out to be Zoey's brother Oliver, found their room in the hostel to be what can only be referred to, by Daniel, as squalid conditions. "I wouldn't let any perp I arrested stay in this for a night," Daniel said to Wade.

"Danny, calm down. It kind of looks like your college dorm. It's clean, it's got bunk beds, and it has a phone charging station!" Daniel looked at Wade with his usual "are you stupid" look and marched down to the desk to demand someone explain themselves. On the way down, he noted in his head that he wished he could look on the bright side of things like Wade, when all of a sudden, he stopped and noticed Zoey having trouble with her luggage. She was trying to take the elevator, but it was so small it could only transport her or her luggage, but not both.

"Need help with that?" Daniel stated the obvious. Zoey turned and saw Daniel and slightly blushed.

"I'm not sure if both of us can fit," also stating the obvious. Daniel went over and noticed that his palms were sweating. This hadn't happened since his first day as a police officer, so clearly he was nervous, or he had a sudden onset of fever. His red ears could also be a symptom, but let's just say he was nervous.

"Here, I'll take it up for you," Daniel said, offering his hand to the bag.

"Are you sure? I'm up two more floors," Zoey said, hoping he'd say yes anyway. Luckily for her, he did.

"Nonsense, I like stairs," Daniel said. And the two made off for the stairwell.

"Thank you so much. I feel rather silly having you do this. I pull my own weight at my job and this just seems foolish of me."

"Oh, I get it. I have officers on my unit who can break in a door time after time but can't open a jar of pickles in the break room. Some things just happen," Daniel said, trying to be sincere.

Zoey noticed it and smiled a little more. "So if you worked in Sydney, you'd be like my boss."

Daniel fumbled the luggage for a slight second. "Yes, it uh, would appear so, yes."

Zoey giggled and made Daniel's heart beat faster. They reached the first of the two floors they needed to ascend. "Daniel, you don't have a girlfriend, do you?"

"No dear, I'm single."

"That's a shame."

"Is it?" Daniel said in an elevated nervous voice.

"Yes, you work hard for what you do and you save people's lives. Hopefully, your division isn't too busy or you'd work yourself to death."

"Oh, we're working harder than ever. The opioid crisis in New York is at epidemic proportions. We're working overtime, off the clock, training officers to do EMS work–" Zoey cut Daniel off, and nobody cut Daniel off without him replying louder.

"Hey, hey, hey, you're on vacation. You can't stress yourself out this much or you'll fall apart. You already worked harder than you should by carrying my bag for me. So I'm going to return the favor by making sure you're having fun this whole trip."

"Zoey, I'm grateful, but that isn't at all necessary."

"It is necessary, it's time someone noticed you for your hard work." They reached Zoey's floor and she took the luggage from him. "When we go out tonight, I'm going to make sure you have fun and do something outside your comfort zone."

Daniel went pale. He spent years developing a comfort zone and had already gone to the end of it by leaving his office and home. This scared him more than anything. "Please, it isn't necess–" he was cut off again.

338 • SHOTS WITH MOM AND DAD

"Shhhh, you're having fun tonight. You and Wade meet me and my brother in the lobby when we all assemble. It's time someone helped take care of you." She disappeared down a hallway to go to her room, leaving Daniel the most confused and scared he'd ever been. Then all of a sudden he heard a slow clap behind him only to find Wade clapping his hands with a shit-eating grin on his face.

"How do you do it, Danny?" Daniel's color returned when he pictured himself drop-kicking Wade down a flight of stairs.

"Shut up, Wade," Daniel said, passing him to go down the stairs.

"No time for shutting up, brother. Time to get you looking dapper."

They returned to the room where they tried to dress Daniel up for a night out in Amsterdam. Wade and Bill insisted he dress more casually than he usually did. Something about a suit and tie spelled out disaster in Amsterdam. Oliver, however, insisted he dress how he wants.

"I know my sister, mate. Dress how you want, she'll float to you because of your personality anyway," Oliver said, cracking open a small bottle of Jack Daniels. No, not Jack and Delilah.

"Oliver, not to get too personal, but is she normally this, how do I put it, friendly?" Wade asked, trying hard not to insult him.

"Not like this, sir. She only gets like this with people she thinks could be a good relationship, friend or otherwise."

"Oliver, I don't know if I'm comfortable with this conversation," Daniel said, trying to be honest.

"Nonsense, Danny. I'm protective of her, and I'd rather have a well-educated, dapper, and serious gent like you instead of some asshole her age who just wants to fuck. I know you ain't out to get in her pants, you want to get to know her. That's an A in my book," Oliver said, lifting Daniel out of his doubts.

"Well, thank you."

"Not to mention he probably hasn't gotten his rocks off in a few years, eh Danny boy?" Wild Bill said from the top bunk on the opposite side of him.

"Thank you, Bill. I was feeling self-conscious."

"You wanna have a go with me and remember what it's like?" Bill jokingly asked, trying to sound more like a friend helping another with a roofing job than someone offering themselves for sex.

"I'm good, Bill, thank you."

The tour group was to assemble in the lobby by 6:00 p.m. that evening to catch the bus to go into Amsterdam. Since this excursion was time-sensitive, Daniel was dragging Wade by the ear to be sure he came down on time. Since Daniel refused to be late to the first person who had been interested in him for many years, he was a good two paces ahead of Wade while dragging him along. Wade's ears looked as wide as an elephant as he was trying to put his shoes on while screaming, "Danny, let go! Ow! Ow! Ow!" Nevertheless, Daniel kept stride and would deal with Wade's whining afterward. "Danny, I swear to God let go. Danny! The stairs!" Wade mustered the courage to accept the possibility of falling down them but kept surprisingly nimble while dodging the banister. They reached the lobby of the hostel to listen to Sean talk about the evening's schedule.

"Hello everyone, I hope you all rested well. We'll be heading out into Amsterdam tonight." The party gave a collective roar of applause, much to Sean's disdain. "Tonight, we will be headed to a boat ride that will take us down the canals of the city. This ride will include bread, cheese, and wine tasting. Then we will disembark and take a walk and give you the true Amsterdam experience with a–" Sean saw Wade raise his hand. "Ugh, yes sir."

"By the Amsterdam experience, will we be going to the Anne Frank House, the Heineken brewery, or the Van Gogh museum?"

"Something like that, sir." Wade will find out that "something like that," meant no. "The tour will disembark from the gondola ride and head straight to the red-light district. Keep in mind, ladies and gentlemen, if there's something we don't do tonight that you're interested in, we don't leave for the Rhine Valley of Germany until 1:00 p.m. tomorrow. So you can do as you want in the morning."

Wade tapped Daniel on the arm and whispered, "Van Gogh," while tapping an imaginary piano. Daniel slapped his hands down and they boarded the bus.

The bus took to its route and arrived at its destination without incident. When the tour arrived at the docks to board, everyone was stunned by the sites of Amsterdam. The rustic yet artistic look of the city had overcome a history of terror. They took it in like it was a spliff with coffee. They boarded the gondola and felt like they were a million bucks each. There was not a worry in the world, nothing outside this gondola mattered at all. All was at ease in the world and there were no problems to be had. Daniel and Wade had a seat across from Zhang Wei and Chenguang. The conversations rolled out like fresh-made Holland rolls. Daniel and Chen-guang discussed the lives they live when they're at home and any troubles they may be experiencing, while Zhang Wei and Wade talked about a mutual love for their favorite band 'Alexisonfire.' All of a sudden, Zoey walked up behind Daniel and just rested her hands on his shoulders, as though they were husband and wife for many years and taking a getaway from their own children. Daniel turned around and saw Zoey with her blonde hair flowing in the light breeze that made the hairs stand up on the back of his neck. Her bright blue eyes looked at him with admiration and respect. Standing in a white crop top with a long white skirt that covered her belly button, the adulation between them was palpable. She looked, as Daniel would put it, as perfect as one can be. Wade, however, had eyes popping out of his head like a cartoon hunter looking at a cross-dressing rabbit.

"Am I going to be sure you're having a good trip or are you getting along without me?" Zoey said in a tender voice, hoping Daniel would still be interested in seeing what became of them.

"I thought you'd never ask," Daniel said, not knowing how he'd be able to go home without her.

They found a section of the gondola unoccupied while Wade slipped a waitress some euros to be sure she didn't wait on anyone else for the ride. "There's more where this came from. Make sure they fall in love before we reach the docks," he said while the waitress hauled ass over to the table.

"So tell me a little more about you," Daniel said.

"Well, besides being a police officer in Sydney, I'm into yoga. I'm very passionate about art, and I love a good night out with my friends," Zoey said happily,

"What's having friends like?" Daniel asked in an attempt to make a joke.

Zoey looked at him perplexedly. "You don't have friends back home?"

"I have associates who I talk to every once in a while; but ultimately, I keep to myself. I live a quiet life while I'm home."

Zoey reached out and held his clenched hand. "Whatever happens here happens, but just know you'll always have a friend in me."

Daniel was sincerely touched by this gesture but said plainly, but meaning sincerely, "Thank you, Zoey." Wade sat at the next table, eavesdropping, and cried into a napkin.

As the sun was setting on the horizon, the gondola pulled up to the dock. Both Zoey and Daniel had to be tapped on the shoulder to stop talking and step off. They walked together next to Wade, Bill, and Oliver down the streets of Amsterdam. They were guided by Sean but walking at their own pace. They walked all the way to the red light district, where Wild Bill stepped away after telling them he'd meet up with them after the show.

"Bill, where are you going?" Wade asked, but Bill said nothing as he went to a coffee house. Not so much walking, but more floating toward it to see about some local and legal herbs. Sean guided the rest of the tour to a theatre that had 3 X's on it with a woman in the window.

Later, everyone came out as though they'd seen a ghost. "I need to call my wife," Wade said.

"I don't know if I'll ever be able to have sex the same way after that show," Daniel said.

"I need a drink, with many more lined up after," Zoey said.

Later, Bill met up with them at a bar next door. "There he is!" Wade said, welcoming his red-eyed friend.

"Oi mate, you guys see the spider on my arms?" Bill said, making scratches on his arms.

"I think you've had enough, Bill," Daniel said, sitting on a couch with Zoey laying on his chest.

"How are you not freaking out?" Zoey inquired.

"Dear, I live in New Zealand. I can deal with a spider or two."

"Well, we missed you during the show. You didn't want to come in?"

"Wade, I could teach those dancers a thing or two. I've run the gamut, and it's also run by me."

"I think this man needs a drink." Oliver came up beside Bill patting him on the back.

"I think you need one, too," Zoey said.

"Oh, no, thank you, Zoey," Bill said, pushing the drink away from his face.

Zoey then proceeded to sit in Daniel's lap facing him. "Do you not remember our deal?" she said, holding his shirt collar so she had his full attention.

"Yes, I remember," Daniel said, with fear in his voice.

"Then trust me, I got your back." Zoey then kissed him passionately, causing Oliver to spit out his drink and Wade to put his fist in the air like he just finished a marathon. "Just trust me, unwind a bit," Zoey said, pushing a drink into Daniel's face. And that was the last thing Daniel remembered.

6

Something The Boys Needed

Daniel awoke the next morning in the top bunk. Although he wasn't alone, and it wasn't his room. He woke up with Zoey next to him on his right side. Nobody else in the room was awake. As he tried to get up, he noticed he still had on all of his clothes. After lifting the blanket, he noticed Zoey was not. He quickly dropped the blanket to give her some privacy and climbed out of the bunk. After landing, however, he woke Zoey up.

"Headed out so soon?" she said in a sleepy voice as she rubbed her eyes.

"I didn't want to wake you," Daniel said, going toward her head. "I'm so sorry if I did anything to upset you last night."

She looked at him perplexedly. "You don't remember anything?" she said, even more perplexed.

"No, not at all. I'm not ordinarily a partier, so I'm so sorry if I upset you."

She smiled and said, "You had such a good time last night. You didn't do anything crazy, but you unwound that tight spring of yours."

"Well thank you, but we didn't have sex, did we?" he asked, hoping to God he didn't take advantage of a drunk woman.

"No, baby, we didn't. I wanted to, but you didn't think it was right since we were both drunk." Daniel was quite proud of himself. "You showed me such a better side of you than I was anticipating. So now, you're not getting out of my sight."

Daniel smirked. "Is that so?" he asked, giving her a kiss on the forehead.

"Although, since you didn't give me what I wanted last night, I like coffee with one sugar and half-and-half. Do with that information what you will." She smiled and pecked him on the cheek.

"You got it, I'm just going to stop into our room to be sure Wade got back okay. I'll see you later." Daniel departed from the room with a new sense of accomplishment.

He stopped by the room to see Oliver and Bill still sleeping. Wade was nowhere to be found, however. A sense of panic overcame him. He checked the bathroom, he checked the dining hall, and then the washroom. He was overwhelmed with panic. "Wade, Wade, where are you?" he shouted in each spot he checked, only to be surprised by Wade coming up behind him at the concierge desk while Daniel attempted to call the police to report a missing person.

"What are you shouting for?" he asked, putting his hand on Daniel's back. Daniel jumped from the fright at seeing his brother completely dressed and ready to walk around Amsterdam.

"Where are you going?" Daniel shouted.

Wade looked perplexed. "Danny, you said yesterday to be ready by 8:00 a.m. to go to the Van Gogh museum and do the shots over the canal.

"I did? Yes, yes I did," he said while regaining his composure. "Let me just go change and get—"

"Hold the phone," Wade said, interrupting him. "Are you not ready? Mr. Punctual isn't on time for once?" Daniel started jabbering incoherently. "You spent the night with Zoey, didn't you?" Wade asked with a big smile.

"Well, we slept in the same bed, but we didn't—"

Daniel was interrupted again by Wade picking him up and swinging him all over the place in a hug. "Danny had fun, Danny had fun!" he said in a voice reminiscent of "I know something you don't know."

"Wade, put me down or so help me." Wade let go of Daniel. "Now, I'm sorry I'm late; and yes, I had fun. I'll run upstairs and change, and we'll be on our way. After, of course, I get Zoey some coffee." Wade opened his mouth as though he was going to squeal. "Not another word about this. Control yourself, man! You're making a fool out of me."

Daniel brought coffee to Zoey, pecked her on the cheek, then got dressed. As he put on a new pair of pants and slid his phone into his pocket, it started to ring. "Fontaine here."

"You son of a bitch." It was his friend from the police department who picked up his gun from the airport.

"Dave, what're you talking about."

"You got drunk in Amsterdam, but you won't get drinks with the boys from the precinct?" Dave asked as though he was missing out on a good time.

"How did you know that?"

"Check your phone, Mr. Party Man. Let me know when you get home, and we'll tie one on," Dave laughed as he hung up. Daniel searched through his texts and saw a video sent to Dave. This was Daniel's worst nightmare come to fruition. It was a video of him in the bar screaming, hooting and hollering, and telling funny jokes. Naturally, he was humiliated. But since he couldn't do anything about it now, he moped down the stairs and met Wade outside. He told Wade about the phone call as they walked to the Van Gogh museum.

"You're not in trouble, are you?" Wade asked, genuinely concerned.

"I wish I was in trouble. Now I've lost face at the precinct. They know I'm a normal person and not this authority figure." They stopped walking for a moment. "I've ruined my reputation. Now people are going to expect me to go out with them, go to functions, be more relaxed. My career is over."

Wade handed Daniel a crepe with extra Nutella. "Danny, you're on vacation and made a dumb choice. If you want to keep face, if anyone mentions it when you go back, make an example out of them and make them do some obnoxious, meaningless task. Then they'll know not to mess with you. Be harder and more ruthless than you already are." The crepe and pep talk made Daniel feel a bit better.

"You think I'm ruthless?"

"The biggest tyrant of them all," Wade said as though he just told his son he was a good boy.

"Thanks, Wade. I needed that." They soldiered on to the museum.

They arrived at museum square and headed straight for the Van Gogh exhibit. They had limited time before the bus left for Germany, so they had to stick to their agenda. As they ascended the stairs to the exhibit, Wade said, "Okay, so before we go in there, give me a brief history of him so I don't touch any pianos."

Daniel sighed. "Wade, Van Gogh is one of the most famous and respected painters in history. He was viewed as a madman in his time due to his mental health condition. In his lifetime, he failed at just about anything he attempted except for his paintings. In fact, some accounts say he chopped off his ear in a fit of mania after fighting with a fellow painter, then gave it to his favorite prostitute at a brothel. Other accounts say it was due to learning his brother was getting married and his financial allowance would end. So he cut it off in a fit of rage and fear, then gave it to the maid of the brothel who he loved dearly." Wade became aghast when they walked in and saw the paintings, including *Starry Night*, *The Potato Eaters*, and his *Self-Portrait*.

They continued on and stopped and stared longer than usual at *Autumn Blossom*. Wade finally spoke up. "Didn't mom have this in her office?"

"Yes, she did. She had it over the couch where I'd sit and watch her work. She reminded me of myself and who I wanted to be. I just wanted to be near her, so this picture makes me think of her," Daniel said as they continued to stare.

"What were you saying about his monthly allowance again?" Wade asked, genuinely intrigued.

"His brother, Theo, was his only supporter in those days, both financially and emotionally. Some stories say that once he got married, Vincent assumed his support was over so he turned to self-mutilation." They stayed in silence for a few seconds longer.

"Does that remind you of anyone?" Wade asked, trying to remind Daniel of the years he spent giving Wade money.

"Wade, you never turned to self-mutilation."

"I know, I know," Wade continued, "but you tried to help me get my music career off the ground. Well, I tried to make a career. But Danny, you know how much your support did for me right?"

Daniel couldn't bear to look at Wade with this conversation. "Well, Wade, I did like your music and I thought others would, too. I still have it on my phone."

Wade snapped over to him. "Really?" Wade's heart melted.

"Yes, I'm still partial to "We Fall Apart." I just really like the chorus.

We were bound to break and fall apart,

We were always doomed from the start.

"I really enjoyed it." Daniel actually looked at Wade when he sang his words back to him. Wade, overcome with emotion, gave Daniel the biggest hug he'd ever given. Daniel didn't push him off. He knew he and Wade both needed it.

They walked out of the museum, went to the canal, and poured out the shots of ashes in silence. They dared not to speak and partially ruin the moment they shared in the museum. They walked back to the hostel, packed their bags, and gave each other a pat on the back, knowing they'd overcome a hurdle in their relationship. They sat next to each other on the bus and fell asleep.

7

Game Time

The bus was headed toward the Rhine Valley in Germany. The destination was meant to provide a mellow haven for rest and relaxation. The group seemed to need it since everyone on the bus fell asleep for a cat nap. About two hours later, Sean, in his first of few chipper moods on the trip, woke everyone with a horn, parading up and down the aisle like it was Reveille at a military base.

"Everyone wake up. It's time for the next game." Daniel's contempt at being woken up was displayed when he threw his book at Sean and hit him square in the face. "The mean Fontaine can't play now," he chided while holding back tears and clutching his face.

Wade jumped up quickly and said, "But Sean, he's my brother. What did you expect would happen when you wake the grouch up?"

"Fine, he can play. But I'm watching you."

Daniel retorted in a monotone voice, "Seems like you have a watery view, Sean. You may want to put the windshield wipers on."

Wade quickly jabbed Daniel on his side and mouthed, "Be nice."

Sean grabbed his iPod and the microphone for the PA system. "So today, we're going to play a trivia game. We're going to pass around a piece of paper and pencil for each team. The person next to you is your partner." Wade tapped Daniel on the shoulder in excitement, to which Daniel groaned. Wade ignored him. "We will be playing the theme songs to famous movies and TV shows. You will number them 1-20 and write the corresponding name of the movie or TV show. Does anyone want to combine teams with the people behind you?" Oliver patted the brothers on the back and Wade acknowledged it with a thumbs up. "Oliver, you really want to be with those two?" Sean said.

"Well, Bill's asleep and they're good dudes." The bus applauded to support the brothers.

"That's a very nice lie, Oliver." The bus laughed and Sean went to the playlist for the game. "Everyone ready?" Sean asked. The bus gave a collective "yes" and Sean played the first song on the list. Everyone bopped to a song that sounded reminiscent of *The Office*.

"That one was easy," Wade said.

"I've never seen an episode. I watch a lot of television, but I don't watch that," said Daniel.

Oliver fell back in his seat. "How? I want a reason why. That scene with CPR isn't funny to you?"

Daniel looked back and said, "I've done CPR. Seeing the look on people's faces who can't grasp the concept of breaking ribs to start the heart is far more hilarious than anything." Oliver laughed nervously as Wade slapped his knee in hilarity to support Daniel's black humor.

The song ended and Sean announced, "Song number 2" and started playing the theme to *Titanic*. Groans were heard from the men, and the women were all tapping each other on the shoulder, signifying the moment their hearts broke as teenagers.

"There was totally enough room on that door for him. Rose was a selfish bitch," Daniel whispered to the three of them. None of them debated him but gave a collective nod, looking straight at him.

Suddenly, there was a whimpering from Bill. "You alright, Bill?" Wade asked from over the seat.

"Jack, what a great man. I'd have let him paint me, too," he said with tears in his eyes.

"You aren't French and you have too much penis. Stop crying and get up here and help," Daniel said firmly.

Bill rose to the occasion and said, "Right, mate. Knocked out for a bit, but I'm back in action. Edibles will do that to ya."

"Tell me you have no more drugs on this bus," Daniel said.

"Nope, popped 'em all in me ass back at the hotel though. You guys want some when we get to the river?"

They all gave a collective "fuck no."

"Song number 3," Sean shouted as people were dying down with the commotion of *Titanic*. He played a song that sounded familiar, but nobody in the groups could remember.

"What is it? It sounds so familiar," Wade said. Oliver shrugged his shoulders and Daniel put his fingers to his head as though he could shake it out of his brain and fall out his ears. Bill leaned forward and took the piece of paper and pen. He jotted down the answer and slammed it down on the fold-out table. They looked at it and they uttered the same thing at once. "Dawson's Creek?"

Bill nodded his head as though it was the most serious thing in the world. "Respect Dawson," he said without a hint of hilarity in his voice.

The game consisted of 20 songs from different movies and TV shows. The different songs consisted of the themes from *Cheers, Friends, Dexter, Breaking Bad, The Simpsons,* and *Star Wars.* After the 19th song, the bus had two teams that were tied for the lead—Dan and Wade's team and Zoey's team with Zhang Wei, Chenguang, and that bitch Maria.

Maria is going to get a lot of hate throughout the story, you'll understand why later.

So, after the final tally before the tiebreaker, "Alright, everyone, we're down to two teams. Now, the winners of this game will win a free wine tasting at the Frieden Weingut. There, you will be tasting different wines, but you will try Eiswein, as well. Eiswein is a special type of wine harvested from grapes that are frozen while still on the vine."

The bus gave a collective "oh."

"The song will be answered by the raising of your hand."

The groups braced themselves as though they were getting ready for impact. Sean played the last song that confused almost everyone. Everyone except Wade. Wade stuck his hand straight up without giving it a second thought. "Yes, Wade? You know it so quickly?"

"Sean," Wade said, "if you have an infant child these days, you can't avoid this song. The song is "You've Got a Friend in Me" from *Toy Story,* sung by the beloved Randy Newman." Daniel grabbed Wade's arm in a way that signified "you better be right."

Sean looked down at the song to be sure it is what it was. "Boys, you won." The boys shot up and hugged. Zoey and the rest of their group groaned. "Now boys, the special part of this gift is you get to bring a guest; and if I may make a suggestion, I think you should ask the other group." Daniel looked at Zoey and gave her a wink. Zoey blushed and winked right back at him.

"Oi, Oliver, I'll let you have your pick at the married couple. I'm good for either," Bill said.

"I think I'll ask the sheila, Bill. If that's alright with you."

"I was hoping you'd say that," Bill said, winking at Chenguang. Chenguang looked at his wife nervously and pulled his collar as a sign of distress.

8

A Night on the Rhine

The bus drove on throughout the afternoon. Everyone took comfort in their headphones, a good book, or conversation. They pulled into the Rhine Valley at approximately 3:00 p.m. So back in New York, it was approximately 9:00 a.m. After they arrived at their hotel, they got their room assignments. It was two to a room, which meant it was Daniel and Wade alone. They brought their bags to their room and Daniel hopped in the shower while Wade tried to make sense of a German game show. As Wade finally understood the game, Sean knocked on the door.

"Hello, Wade. I know Daniel is bringing Zoey as his plus one, and the other two are trying to split up a married couple, so will you be bringing Maria as your plus one?"

Wade was confused. "Who's Maria again?" Wade asked sincerely.

"She's the other young lady in the group from the bus. She's from New Jersey, literally the only other American on this tour besides you two."

Wade looked sheepish. "I was actually hoping I could take my laptop with me. My wife is off today and is looking forward to it."

Now Sean was confused. "You're going to bring your laptop to the wine tasting? So your wife can look at you trying wine that she can't drink?"

Wade shrugged his shoulders. "She likes to hang out in any situation. Even if she can't be there, she wants to see the inside of the winery."

Sean rolled his eyes. "Alright, I'll go tell Maria."

"Hey, thanks, buddy. And hey, we're supposed to tip you right?"

Sean immediately perked up. "Yes, it is encouraged to tip your guide."

"Great, here you go." Wade tipped Sean with a Hershey chocolate bar. "Made in America. Hope you enjoy it." Wade seemed to forget that Hershey's chocolate was everywhere in the world.

Sean looked as though he could throw Wade out a window. "Thank you, you're so kind," he said as he walked away shaking his head.

Wade shut the door as Daniel came out of the shower. "Everything set then?" Daniel asked, exiting the bathroom in a towel.

"Yup, everyone has their dates."

"How'd Sean take it that you aren't bringing Maria?"

"He seemed puzzled at first; but eh, I don't blame him."

"Trust me, Wade, it is a baffling concept."

"Yeah, I can see that. But hey, Melony seems excited to see what we're doing."

"Is she even awake?"

"Yes, Danny, I sure am!"

Daniel jumped to see Melony on Wade's laptop already. "Oh, Melony, I'm so sorry I didn't see you there."

"No worries, Danny, I'm off today and little Danny is being such a good boy. Yes, he is, oh yes he is," Melony said as she kissed the baby she held on her lap.

"Danny, I'm going to go take a shower. Do me a favor and be sure the feed doesn't cut. I don't know if I'm going to lose the signal."

"Wade, the place has free wifi."

Wade turned from walking to the bathroom. "No, not us, the house. It can be a dead zone sometimes." Wade closed the bathroom door as Daniel sat at the computer on the desk.

"Sorry, Danny, I can cut the feed if you need to get dressed."

"No, no, dear. It's okay. I have my sweats on under the towel. Sorry, bad habit of the locker room at the station."

"Oh, very good then. So how is the job?" Melony asked while slightly shaking her leg to bounce the baby.

"Oh, hectic as usual. Nothing I can't handle, though. Anything new and exciting?"

"Oh, Wade and Danny are a bit of a handful, but nothing I can't handle either. I mean the baby, not you." Big Daniel giggled. "Although, with your disappearances from the planet every time you get invested at work do cause a handful with Wade, too, young man."

"Mel, you know how it is. I'm just not good with the whole communication thing."

"Yes, Danny, we know. And I know Wade can be a lot, but there's nobody more loyal and dedicated to the people he loves. He puts 150% into everything in his life. It's why I love him. So, hey, can you meet him halfway from time to time?"

"If this trip is reminding me of anything, it's how cold I can be to Wade. And I know it's not good. So I think I'll try to be in better contact after the trip. Well, a couple of weeks after the trip."

Melony smiled. "That's all I ask. Now, I have to change your mini-me, so I'll call back in a bit. If he has an aneurism, just say I'll be back."

"Will do. See you later, Mel. And see you later too, little man," Daniel said while waving his finger at the baby. Melony smiled as she cut the feed.

The group gathered in the lobby of the hotel. There was a banister overlooking the lobby that Maria glared from as they started assembling. Wade was calling Melony to start the feed-up again before they left to go across the street to the winery. "You couldn't wait until we got there?" Daniel asked.

"You never know where there's a dead zone. Then who's the one who's prepared, Danny?" Wade said without looking up from the laptop.

"Leave him alone," Zoey said, leaning over Daniel's shoulder. "He misses his wife and can't wait to see her. Kind of like how you couldn't wait to see me," she said, sitting on the arm of the chair next to Daniel stroking the back of his hair. Daniel slightly blushed at her but was quickly in a state of fear when he looked up at the balcony overlooking the lobby. Maria was scowling at him and Wade. She was furious she wasn't going on this once-in-a-lifetime experience because one person would rather bring his laptop than her. Bill nudged Wade and told him to look up at the balcony.

"Yeah, I do feel a little bit bad, but any rational person would understand a man wants to bring his wife, even if it's virtual."

"Wade, who said Maria is a rational person? We don't even know her." Wade just waved it off, speaking gibberish.

Zoey leaned in and said, "Don't be glancing at her; you're here with me," in a joking manner. Daniel laughed, but his nerves were still in a knot when Maria cracked a maniacal smile.

Sean entered the lobby and made his way to the group. "Alright everyone, we're going to the Noekerbrau Vineyard. There we will sample various wines, play a few games, and have a small dinner. Does anyone have any questions?"

Wade raised his hand. "Yes, Wade, they have wifi so your wife will be able to join us." Wade put his hand down and had a wide smile on his face. "Now the vineyard is only across the street so let's get going." Zoey tucked her arm into Daniel's, which he accepted happily. Bill put both his arms around Zhang Wei and Chenguang. Both of them looked uneasily at each other while Bill looked off into space, blissfully unaware of the amount of discomfort he was causing. They made their way into the tasting room and sat at a large table.

Wade checked his wifi and was relieved to realize he still had a good connection. He showed Melony around the room and made Daniel wave at her again. "I hope you all enjoy what you drink. I'll be here drinking a Diet Coke." Everyone waved back.

"Mrs. Fontaine, we apologize for you being unable to be here. However, you'll be happy to know everyone here will be given a sample of their favorite three wines to take home with them. And you'll have a chance to buy the Eiswein on the way out." Melony did a small dance in her seat at home from the excitement. "Now everyone, please let me introduce you to Hans Gunter, the owner of Noekerbrau Vineyards.

Hans stood at the head of the table. He was a joyful man who took great pride in his work. He spoke English but had a thick German accent. "Hello, everyone. Welcome to Noekerbrau Vineyards. We've had this establishment in our family for three generations. Not one of us is named Noekerbrau. So, I'd like to tell you all how we got our namesake. It is named after the ghost of our village." The table gave a collective "oh's and ah's" while Daniel rolled his eyes. "Legend has it that in the 1920s, Hans Noekerbrau, the local philosopher, was at the pub having a few rounds with his friends when they dared him to chase after one of the carriages carrying barrels of the local beer. He chased it down, but five barrels came off. He finished the first two, but the last three crushed him." The group laughed at his joke, including Daniel. "Which is why, late at night, when trucks pass by containing beer, you'll hear someone's clogs running at a brisk pace behind them."

Daniel rolled his eyes and said to Wade, "Or the clanging of beer cans hitting each other in a truck, but that's none of my business."

Wade kicked Daniel and whispered, "Shhh, don't ruin the fun." He sighed and drank from the water at the table.

Hans went back to the kitchen and returned with two bottles of wine and went around pouring the first bottle into everyone's glasses. After he poured the wine, he returned to the head of the table. "This first wine was the one that started it all. My great grandfather was given this wine by his grandfather as a small boy. He grew up drinking it and eventually decided to go into business for himself. This wine has been a staple of the community and is responsible for sending myself, my son, and my grandchildren to college. Since my grandson is a doctor, he brings his staff here every year for their Christmas party. So I'd recommend washing your hands after you leave." The group gave a chuckle while Daniel looked around skeptically. Hans raised a glass for a toast. "So to all who pass through here, I say to you, to your health." The group raised their glasses for a cheer and swallowed their first sip of the wine.

Everyone was startled by how smooth it was. "Good Lord, that's smooth," Daniel said astonishingly.

"Danny, I'd have this every day. Sir, please tell me there's a gift shop," Wade said across the table.

Hans laughed and said, "No, sir, we only have people come here to try the wine and send them on their way."

Wade looked down at the floor, depressed. The group laughed. Daniel leaned over to whisper, "Yes, Wade, there's a gift shop. It was a joke."

Wade looked at Daniel in confusion. "Did he just make a joke that I didn't get?"

"Yes, he did, Wade."

Wade was concerned. "Do you have a sense of humor when you're drunk?"

"Call it my superpower, I guess."

Wade raised his hand "May we buy a crate for this trip? I want to see my brother be funny." The table laughed, but Zoey traced her finger on Daniel's neck to tease him.

Hans's wife came in with two new bottles of wine. "Ladies and gentlemen, allow me to introduce to you my wife, Mila." Everyone waved and said their various "hello's." She waved back nervously and whispered something in his ear. "What?" Hans said. She continued to whisper, but she was slightly louder and sounded frustrated. Hans said something in German and Mila stamped her foot down, then walked angrily out of the room. The room seemed tense. However, Hans brushed his hands and said, "Gentlemen, never let your mother-in-law move in. Mine's stuck in the tub after she plopped in, like a pretzel getting loose from your fingers." The room laughed again.

"Anyway, the second wine we have today is an amontillado. This, everyone, has been a labor of love to my wife and a headache for me. This wine is difficult to make and even worse to maintain. This wine needs to be aged years. We only have so much of it during the year. But we keep a storage of it for events like this. Although the process is dreadful, the result is everything. Keep that in mind for life, as well." The group gave a collective head nod. He poured the wine and the group started drinking it as soon as it touched the glasses. They tasted a nutty wine that had a sherry kick to it.

"Good Lord, that's an acquired taste," Daniel said as his face changed after pounding the drink.

"Danny, I think that one's too cultured for us."

"Agreed," Daniel said, adjusting himself.

"Really? I quite like it" Zoey said, taking another sip.

"The wine is an acquired taste, you're right, sir," Hans said, returning to the head of the table. "But for those who love sherry, it is above most."

The group settled after drinking the amontillado. "Very good, everyone. For those of you who enjoyed the amontillado, I hope you enjoyed it as much as Fortunado would have." Bill chuckled so much he slapped his knee.

"Bill, you're going to have to explain that one to us," Daniel said.

Bill stopped laughing and explained. "Amontillado was used in the Edgar Allan Poe short story as a way to lure a man into a crypt to kill him by chaining him to a wall and building a new wall in front of him. All because Fortunado insulted his killer."

"And I thought you had issues, Danny."

"Keep it up, Wade. There are floorboards at the hotel. Think your heart can handle it?" Daniel said sarcastically while pointing at Bill to signify they both like Edgar Allan Poe.

Mila came out with four bottles this time, all bearing different designs. "So here, everyone, is the Eiswein. Although in Canada it is pronounced "Ice-Wine," here, it is still Eiswein," Hans said, emphasizing his German accent. "Eiswein is considered a gift in Germany. When a child is born, the parents get four bottles of Eiswein. One to drink when the child is born. It is for the parents to drink, unless you're in Ireland, then the baby gets a bit poured in its sippy cup." The group raised their eyebrows. "That's a joke, everyone." The group chuckled.

"The second bottle is opened at the child's Communion. There, the child is allowed to have a sip." Hans uncorked the first bottle. The smell alone filled the room and it smelled delightful. "The third bottle is for the child's Confirmation. He is allowed to have a glass if the parents deem him mature enough. And lastly, the fourth bottle is for the child's high school graduation. At that point, the parents give the child the bottle to signify that the child is an adult. And they get treated like an adult the next morning when they have a hangover."

Hans went around pouring the wine into the glasses. Nobody drank immediately to signify the magnitude of how precious the wine was. Hans went to the head of the table. "Welcome to Germany, everyone. Drink up." Everyone took a sip and was immediately entranced by it. Zhang Wei and Chenguang spoke fluent Chinese to discuss how magnificent it was.

Bill looked at the glass, perplexed. "Alright, mates. I'm going to have a quick wank with this," he said while getting up.

Both Daniel and Wade got up slightly with their hands up saying, "Oh, dear God, no," and "Not necessary, Bill."

"Alright, fine," he said sitting back down.

Zoey and Oliver were sitting silently. "You guys okay?" Wade asked politely.

"Oh, we have Eiswein in Australia. This is just the next level tier, so we're taking it in." The brothers nodded, looked at each other, shrugged, and clinked their glasses together. They took a swig at the same time and both relaxed in their chairs while still drinking it.

Wade looked at the glass. "You think mom and dad had this?" he asked sincerely.

"I sure hope they did. They would've missed out if they didn't."

"Gentlemen, we only have a tour like this once a month, but we keep photo albums of those who've come here. Tell me, what year did they come?"

"1979," Daniel and Wade said at the same time. Hans spoke into a walkie-talkie in German. His wife spoke back in a nasty tone, to which he yelled more in German. Wade leaned over to his computer to see Melony looking uncomfortable. "I promise, I'll never turn into that."

"Back at ya, babe," she said through the computer with a smile. "Is it as good as it sounds?" she asked.

"Honey, I'm buying several bottles. It is that good." Mel brought up the baby and made him do a small dance.

Mila returned with a photo album marked "1978/1979." They opened it up and skipped to the back. "It was in the summer, right, Wade?"

"Yeah, I think July." They flipped to the July/August page. There in the photo album were six strangers and their parents in one picture. Their mother was beaming with a smile; and their father had both his arms wrapped around her, smiling widely. Wade started crying immediately, and Daniel shed a small tear while Zoey rubbed his back.

"Look, Mom is smiling. There is photographic proof after all," Wade said.

"Your mother never smiled?" Oliver asked.

"She did around us, but she was all business while dad was a goof-ball, so that's no surprise."

The boys and the rest of the table went on through the night discussing their childhoods, funny stories, and what they were excited for on the trip to come. "Well, mate, you're parents sound swell. I'll keep that in mind if they ask any questions. Get it? Keep it in mind?" he said while jabbing Wade on the arm.

"So Daniel, why did you decide to specialize in drugs?" Oliver asked.

Wade quickly interrupted, "No no no no no, it's a bad story, Oliver."

Daniel was drunk but not as bad as in Amsterdam. "Wade, thank you, but it's okay. I can tell it."

Daniel sat upright and put his glass on the table. "I myself had a drug problem in my senior year of high school. I was addicted to coke and when my mom found out," Daniel stopped speaking remembering the sounds of his mothers threats to kick him out of the house and cut him out of the family. He composed himself and continued talking. "Well, let's just say I regretted ever trying the stuff and quit cold turkey that day. As I got older I met other people with bad habits. I saw it was destroying families and that's when I realized I needed to go into the police force and help others by stopping the drugs from coming in the first place.

Everyone felt sad for Daniel. "So, Bill, if I see any more drugs on this trip, your ass is mine and you're going in the Rhine. I don't care if we're in Venice, I'm dragging you back and throwing you in the Rhine." Daniel was laughing himself. "And if you swim in the Rhine, I'll be in it like Patton did." Everyone was rolling around with laughter. Everyone except Zoey. She turned his head lightly by his chin. They looked at each other and she pulled him in to give him a kiss.

They wrapped up and went back to the hotel. They all walked up the stairs and saw Maria asleep in a sleeping bag. "What's all this about?" Oliver asked.

"I guess she was waiting up to talk to us about the wine."

"That's a woman pissed off. Way to go, Wade," Daniel said.

"Oh boy, I guess I really should have taken her, huh?"

"How many Eiswein bottles do you have, Wade?"

"I bought four, so we can do the tradition at home."

"I think you should give her one, huh?" Daniel said, slurring his words.

"I think that's fair." Wade placed one of the bottles in her hands. Wade, Daniel, Zoey, and Oliver nodded in agreement and turned a corner. Moments later, Bill walked out of a room in his boxers.

"Chenguang, I don't know, dear. I don't think I can do another. My buzz is becoming a slight rattle." He looked down and saw the bottle left in Maria's hands. He picked it up, smiled, and walked back in. "Good news, darlin'. I found some motivation. Now, Zhang, I'm on top this time. And none of that 'find the cork' business, okay?"

"Oli, didn't you say you wanted to check out Wade's computer to book the flights home?" Zoey said to Oliver. Oliver stared at her with a "Come on, really?" look, knowing fully well she was telling Oliver to give her and Daniel some time to have fun. He exhaled and looked down.

"Yes, Wade, if it isn't too much of an inconvenience."

"Not at all! Come on, Oliver, I'll show you our room, too."

"Wade, they're all the same."

"Nope, you're wrong. Here, Zoey, I think our fridge is full. Mind chilling this for us?"

"Not at all, Wade," she said, winking at him. Wade winked back.

"Danny, do me a favor and grab Oliver's glasses for him?"

"Oli, you wear glasses?" Daniel asked, still oblivious to what they were trying to do.

Oliver squeezed the bridge of his nose in frustration. "Yup, big Harry Potter-looking ones. See you in a bit." They walked their separate ways. Daniel and Zoey to one, Wade and Oliver to the other. Daniel looked back at Wade for a moment, and he clinked the two remaining bottles together to let him know what he was going to do. Daniel blushed and Zoey lured him into the room with a beckoning finger. And yes, it happened. You can't beat a night of wine on the Rhine.

9

Munich Girl

Z oey awoke before Daniel. She looked next to her and
there he laid, sleeping with a small amount of drool
dribbling out of his mouth. She looked at the nightstand and
saw a box of tissues. She wiped his mouth then pecked him on
the head. She then got up, dressed, and walked down the hall
to see Wade and Oliver. Before entering the room, she looked
down the hall to see Maria still lying in the hallway, but the
Eisewine was no longer there. She was perplexed; but after she
walked into the room, it left her mind completely.

Wade was already up and in the bathroom taking a shower.
Oliver was in bed on his phone. "I was just about to text you.
But, I don't want to hear how your night went," he said, trying
to ignore the fact that his sister kicked him out of their room
last night to have sex.

"Oh, but it was wonderful. He was so generous," she said,
unfazed by her brother. Oliver put his earbuds in so he didn't
have to hear about it, but Zoey came over and took them out
and started telling him about how slowly and gently Daniel
undressed her. He put his fingers in his ears and started going
"la la la" so he wouldn't hear it, got up, and walked out of the

room to start his day. Zoey, however, stayed in the room and waited to talk to Wade.

Wade turned the shower off, but Zoey could hear him singing. Wade had a beautiful singing voice. It reminded her of Layne Stanley's tone but without any form of being an impression. He had his clothes in the bathroom so after he dried off, he got dressed.

"Wade, are you decent?" Zoey called. Wade jumped a little, being startled by the voice of a woman who wasn't his wife being in his room.

"Zoey, is that you?"

"Yes, dear. It is. Why didn't you tell us you had a beautiful singing voice?"

"Oh, this? It's nothing," Wade said while exiting the bathroom. "I tried to make something out of it up until I got married. Nothing really happened besides playing in a lot of pubs and pool halls."

"If there is a karaoke night, I insist you sing some of your favorites."

Wade started to blush. "Oh, no, I can't do that. I promised Danny I wouldn't."

Zoey was baffled at this. "What do you mean Danny said you can't do karaoke?"

"Well, not just karaoke, in fact, I think he'd be fine with that. But, I promised him I wouldn't perform anymore."

Zoey rose from the bed with a tone of slight anger and said, "And why is that? Don't you love it? If you enjoy it, it's not up to Danny to decide that."

"Well, it's not that simple. You see, when my wife and I were just starting our marriage, there weren't many people who wanted to hire an ex-musician in his thirties with no college and very little work experience. So when I was on my last dime, Danny pitched in and promised to pay the bills as long as I wasn't performing and was actively looking for a job." Zoey was dumbfounded. "Yeah, I was kind of a bum. A bum with a heart of gold, but I didn't try at anything else, so Danny really got us off our asses and into work mode."

"Well, that's very admirable of him."

Wade looked down at the floor in embarrassment. "It really is quite shameful to be married and have your big brother taking care of you still. But after a few weeks of pounding the pavement, he got me a job in his police department dispatching or alerting officers when there's an emergency in progress. I was pretty good at it, too. I was very kind, and all my supervisors were proud of the courtesy I was showing those over the phone. But after a while, it just got depressing. You know, hearing about all these horrible things happening to people. So after my wife went to college, got a top-paying job, and we were having a baby, we made the decision that I'd stay home and take care of the baby and be a Mr. Mom!"

Zoey giggled. "Well, that's nice, but if Daniel was kind enough to pay your bills and get you a job, I assume he went to your performances?"

"Oh, he'd go to all of them, and he'd bring his police officer buddies along."

Zoey thought even higher of Daniel. "Well, if all that is true, then why can he be so grumpy with you?"

Wade looked down at the floor again. "Well, I didn't hand in my resignation properly. I was speaking with a co-worker about how a police officer was being held accountable for

374 • SHOTS WITH MOM AND DAD

police brutality. An officer from Danny's unit was yelling about how I don't support police officers in the field and I'm 'just a dispatcher.' So I got into a verbal argument with him, and after a while, I realized I didn't need this job. So I approached my supervisor and said 'I quit,' and walked out the door. Without a two-week notice or anything."

Zoey winced at how that could be a problem in a workplace and how Daniel could interpret it.

"And Danny came to my house and berated me about how, even if I'm right in my view, there's a right way to leave a job. And I had no argument with him. So I just nodded along, saying, 'Yes Danny, you're right.' But that day, he was not having it. And he completely unloaded on me. Calling me an ungrateful brother after he supported me for years with music, paying the bills, and getting me that job. And to be honest, he was right. I was too shy and embarrassed to show him what it meant to me. So after he walked out, I've had a hard time bonding with him ever since or even talking to him unless it involved an urgent family matter."

Zoey approached Wade and gave him a hug. "Keep trying. I think this trip is unwinding him. From now on, show him how grateful you are. In fact, I don't know how much money you have on you, but take initiative from time to time to show that you appreciate what he's done for you."

Wade blushed again. "We had a great moment together in Amsterdam, and he's really kind of unwound since." Zoey and Wade stopped hugging and Wade was visibly tearing up. "I'm going to FaceTime my wife before we get on the bus, so I'll see you in a bit. Do you mind bringing him his clothes for the day?" Wade asked, hoping he wasn't asking too much of her.

"Sure, Wade, no problem." He went through Daniel's suitcase and pulled out a shirt and brought it to an iron that was a part of the wall. "I'm just going to iron his shirt, do you mind pulling out the blue suit?"

Zoey looked at him with confusion. "He is not going to wear another suit. It's a vacation, he's not at a conference."

Zoey dipped back into the suitcase and pulled out a sweater with dress pants. "I'll give these to him. Still business, but more comfortable."

Wade was elated that she was picking out his clothing for him. "Absolutely, did you guys have a fun night?" Wade asked, hoping his brother getting laid would make more progress in his attitude.

"I know I had fun. He's still sleeping. I think I wore him out," she said while playfully wiping dirt off her shoulder. Wade fell on the bed, laughing hysterically. Zoey giggled and left the room with Daniel's clothing. She walked back into her room to see him still asleep.

She went over to him and kissed him on the forehead. Daniel was so drunk that he farted in his sleep. As she held her nose and fled from the room, Wade came walking down the hall. "Did he fart in his sleep?" he asked, seeing her with a clenched nose.

"Yes, and quite putrid, in fact."

"Come on, let's get breakfast," Wade said. They went to eat while Daniel slept and talked to the rest of the group about how great the Eisewine was. This led to everyone in the group going to the vineyard after breakfast to be sure they got their own bottle. Wade went back upstairs to pack Daniel's bag. After he was finished, he walked down the hall to wake him.

Before he entered, he saw Maria giving him a nasty look. He was unhinged by it.

"Maria, is there something wrong?" he asked before entering. She said nothing but continued glaring at him. He was still shaken but walked inside and closed the door. He shook his head, trying to get the mental image of an upset Maria out of his mind.

He walked in and cleaned up the room a bit. After he was done, he cracked his knuckles, cracked his neck, and inhaled deeply. He leaned over to Daniel's ear and shouted, "Danny, wake up! The bus is gone and we have no way to get to Munich!"

Daniel immediately woke up in a panic. "Wait! What!" Daniel said in a voice that sounded half-asleep.

"The bus left! But if you get dressed, we can run after it!" Daniel, still half-asleep, lunged out of bed, stood up, and slipped and fell backward. Wade was laughing his head off. "Oh, by the way, Danny, we still have an hour. Brush your teeth and get dressed, though. We have to do the ashes before we board the bus."

Daniel stayed on the floor, exhaling and groaning that he was too hungover and telling Wade the many ways of how he hated him. Wade paid no attention to it, though, and picked him up. Daniel was still chewing Wade out as he escorted Daniel around the room to get him ready for the day. "I hate your face, long nose, big forehead-looking ass." Wade escorted Daniel to the shower where he stayed on the toilet texting his wife and making sure that Daniel didn't fall in the shower. "I hate the way you talk. All soft-voiced and even calm. Have some emotion for fuck's sake. Screaming into my ear."

After Daniel was done in the shower, Wade handed him a towel. Daniel was still talking up a storm about all the things about Wade he despised. "I hate the way you walk, too. You walk like Shaggy following the rest of the gang. And you have a positivity about it, too. It annoys me, change it." Wade still paid him no mind as he calmly wiped some lint from his clothes.

"And I hate the, uh, the way you, um," Daniel continued while buttoning his pants. Wade sat on the bed looking through his phone, not listening to a word Daniel said. Daniel zipped his fly up while still pondering things to hate about Wade.

Wade looked at his watch, then over at Daniel, and asked, "You done?"

Daniel looked up and continued for a moment to ponder things about Wade that he didn't like. "Yeah, I think so."

"Good," said Wade. "Then grab your bag and let's go. Daniel nonchalantly picked up his bag, as did Wade, and they departed from the room as if nothing had happened.

They walked to the bus and put their luggage underneath. Wade still had his carry-on, the backpack containing the Jack Daniels urn. They took it from the hotel and walked down the stairs that led directly to the Rhine River. Wade put the backpack down, took out the bottle, and poured out a small enough amount of ashes into each cup. Wade closed the bottle and put it back in his bag. They both held them up. "Did we learn anything between here and Amsterdam?" Wade asked, not sure if he had.

"I learned to reveal yourself more to people you care about. Reveal your emotions and be more open to people being able to understand you as a person. And being intimate with someone emotionally isn't the end of the world," Daniel said.

"Well put," Wade replied, and they poured out their cups. They watched the ashes dissolve into the Rhine. It was almost as though at each stop they were dissolving more of the past that had driven them apart. They boarded the bus for their next destination.

As the bus took off, each person in their seat was handed a small buzzer that was connected via Bluetooth to the front of the bus. "Ladies and Gentlemen, I hope you enjoyed the Rhine Valley of Germany. Today, we are departing for Munich," Sean said over the intercom. Everyone started to clap, including a very hungover Daniel.

Sean continued talking while Daniel rolled his head on the back of his seat to look at Wade. "Wade, my stomach is killing me. What do you have in your murse?"

"It is not a male purse, Danny. It is a backpack. Any decent parent has a bag full of–" Wade was cut off by Daniel extending out his hand while putting his sunglasses on. He put his hand out quite forcefully.

"Fix me, dammit," Daniel said in a casual voice. Wade handed him some Tylenol, Maalox, and a water bottle.

"Sip it, don't chug," Wade said, watching Daniel unscrew the water bottle.

"Thank you, Wade," Daniel said after downing the entire water bottle. "I missed breakfast. Do you have a protein snack in there or something?" Wade went back into his bag and pulled out a protein bar that Daniel barely unwrapped before stuffing what was open into his mouth.

"When you have a stomach ache and throw up today, don't blame me," Wade said.

Daniel gave a quiet burp and said, "Duly noted, Wade."

"Okay, so the reason why I gave you all buzzers is because we're going to do another trivia game!" Sean said to instant applause. "The winner of this prize is a 100 euro gift card to the beer hall we'll be attending today." The passengers gave a collective "ooh" in astonishment. Bill looked straight ahead with a serious face. Beer was on the line. This was no time for games, to Bill. "Alright, so you all need to text me your buzzer number to sign in." Everyone texted Sean their number and they were logged into Sean's phone. "Alright, so after I ask the question, you buzz in. The first one to buzz in will tell my phone, then you provide your answer. Best out of 20. Everyone understand?" The passengers nodded in agreement. "Alright, your first question is, 'Who were the founders of Apple?'" Everyone buzzed in. "Alright, the first question goes to Bill."

Bill yelled out, "Steve Jobs, Steve Wozniak, and Ronald Wayne."

"Correct, on all three answers. That's one for Bill." Bill smiled and kissed his iPhone. "Next question, 'What famous U.S. General had a picture taken of him urinating in the Rhine River?'"

Daniel buzzed in. He didn't lift his head, but said, "General," he then burped, and finished saying "Patton."

"Correct! You're disgusting but correct. One for the hungover thing that smells back there."

"Fuck," he burped again, "you, Sean."

"Next question, 'Name the Dan Brown character that was the protagonist in *Angels and Demons*, *The Da Vinci Code*, and *The Lost Symbol*.'"

Zoey buzzed in. "Robert Langdon."

"Correct! One for Zoey. And do remember to clean up your man over there, will you?"

Zoey looked straight at him. "I think he's great just the way he is," and smiled. He tilted his head over and mouthed "Thank you," and rolled it back. Zoey blushed in her chair while Sean read the next question.

The game went on with question after question. After question 17, the game was neck and neck between Zoey and Oliver. "Question 18," Sean said over the intercom. "Which member of Monty Python was a licensed doctor?" Oliver buzzer in. "Yes, Oliver?"

"Was it Terry Jones?" he asked. However, Sean frowned.

"I'm sorry, Oliver, that is incorrect."

Zoey buzzed in. "Graham Chapman!" Sean smiled.

"That is correct! One more point to Zoey." Zoey looked back at Oliver and stuck her tongue out at him. "The next question is, 'What former U.S. President was the President and Secretary of State at the same time?'"

Daniel buzzed in. "William Howard Taft."

"Correct. Second to last question, everybody. What English Monarch ruled Great Britain the longest?"

Oliver buzzed in. "Queen Victoria."

"You are correct again, Oliver. With one question left, the game is tied between Zoey and Oliver. Nobody has enough to catch up, so everyone else is disqualified." Zoey and Oliver stared at each other with a grueling intensity. "Your final question is, which of his books does Stephen King claim to have no recollection writing?"

Oliver buzzed in. "Pet Sematary?" he asked sheepishly. However, Sean frowned.

"No, I'm sorry, Oliver. That is incorrect."

Zoey buzzed in. "Cujo," she said proudly.

"Yes! Zoey, you win! You win a 100 euro gift card to our beer hall destination!"

Sean went down the aisle and handed Zoey her gift card. She looked over at Daniel and said, "I guess you're my date tonight," and gave him a wink. Daniel blushed and sank his head down. Wade rubbed his back and massaged the back of his head. Daniel did not stop him. Shortly after the game, many of the passengers took a quick nap or talked amongst themselves. Daniel and Wade stayed awake to discuss the other places they could pour out more ashes.

"Okay, so I know absolutely nothing about any of the other destinations besides Paris and Venice," Daniel said.

"Me either. Are there any rivers or anything in Venice?"

Daniel picked his head back up and turned toward him. "Say that again, Wade."

"Is there a river in Venice?" Wade said as seriously as possible.

Daniel pinched the bridge of his nose. "Wade, you were born in the '80s, and the only way you know about one of the most famous cities in the world is because you thought it was from a cartoon you saw in your 20's. I can't, I really just can't."

Wade rolled his eyes. "Danny, that's what's called a joke. You need a Pedialyte." Wade went back into his bag and pulled out the drink, then put it in a baby bottle to help Daniel with his hangover."

"I don't need a fucking Pedialyte. I need you to get your shit together and–" Wade put the bottle in Daniel's mouth mid-sentence and he started to swallow the drink. Although he was initially frustrated, he realized it was helping and laid back and let Wade feed him with a bottle.

"Good, Danny, who's a good boy? That's my good boy."

Daniel eventually came to and grabbed the bottle out of his hands forcefully. "Pain in my ass," Daniel exclaimed, taking the top off the bottle so he could drink it straight.

"Aw, now I miss little Danny."

"I can imagine, Wade, but let's stay on topic. Venice we don't have to worry about. Paris we have the Seine. What about Munich?"

Wade took out the itinerary. "Okay, so we're going out today with Matunas Motors, a bike company."

"Holy shit, we're riding motorcycles?"

"It seems it," Wade said. "But I'm looking at the bike route and it seems like we pass a system of water called the Eisbach. It's an arm of the Isar river where there's a man-made wave that surfers like to go to. I think it will be good as long as we don't hit a surfer."

"Fair enough, Wade."

"After that, we go to Austria," Wade said.

"Well, where exactly in Austria?"

"Hopfgarten in the Austrian Tyrol. I know literally nothing about that, Danny."

"Me either, Wade. Google it quick." Wade googled the area.

"The area is the largest town in the Austrian Tyrol. The Tyrol itself was where they filmed a lot of the scenes for *The Sound of Music*, and it's known for a lot of their slopes and parasailing."

Wade looked over at Daniel. "You are going parasailing, and I don't care if I have to drag you up."

"My ass I'm going parasailing."

"You're going parasailing."

"Wade, I'm not going—"

"You're going parasailing, Danny. Now shut up and look up waterways in Hopfgarten." Daniel looked up the area.

"There's absolutely nothing near the area. I'm not flushing them down a toilet again, Wade."

"Can we have them fall out in the air while we parasail?" Wade asked.

"Very funny. Maybe we can find a man-made pond in the area or something."

"Maybe a fountain, there's got to be one in like a village square or something."

"Not a bad idea either."

"And lastly, Switzerland."

"Hey Wade, did you ever think in your lifetime you would be going to Switzerland? Like that's for rich people in the U.S. and like a dream destination."

"I know, Danny. It's really crazy. Alright, so we'll be going to Jungfrau in the Bernese Oberland region of the Swiss Alps. We'll be staying in the village at one of their hostels. Now this I have an idea on."

"Go on," Daniel said, taking a swig of Pedialyte.

"When we're at the top of the mountain, there has to be snow. So how about we pour them out at the top of the mountain. It's still a form of precipitation so it counts as water, don't it?"

Daniel nodded his head while he was still drinking. "I suppose it does. That's very romantic to think of, Wade." Wade brushed his shoulders off.

They arrived at the hostel and the owner walked onto the bus. "Ladies and Gentlemen of ItourEurope, my name is Franz. I am the owner of this establishment, and I am here to neatly organize your arrival. There are four people per room. We will pick them for you so you do not. You will be brought off the bus in your groups of four, and each of you will be handed a key. They are numbered 1-4. You will hand them back to us when you leave tomorrow in numbered order with the rubber band we provide for you. We would like this rubber band back, please, so it does not go to waste. We also would like the rubber band not to have creases on them, so please be sure it is brought back smoothly." The entire bus had their mouths open in disbelief that a grown man thought he could tell an entire bus of grown adults to follow kindergarten-like directions.

He escorted the guests off four at a time and handed them their keys. Everyone walked inside and out of view to wait for who they wanted to room with. They all exchanged keys and went to their desired rooms. Immediately, Oliver took out a pen and started drawing on the rubber band. Wade and Daniel both started making origami swans out of the slits of paper that were between each of the keys numbered tags. Bill immediately started drinking everything in the minibar; but instead of putting it gently in the garbage, he'd crumple up the can of beer and spike it in the waste bin and exclaim, "Done!" After they finished their shenanigans, they got dressed to ride the motorcycles. When they all finished dressing, they went downstairs to meet Sean and get back on the bus. They loaded the bus and went off.

Once they started driving, Sean went over the loudspeaker. "Alright, so who vandalized their keys and rubber bands?" Everyone on the bus raised their hands. Sean hung his head and said, "They always do." Everyone on the bus laughed. "Anyway, today we will be going to Matunas Motors. Although they are a motorcycle company, we will be renting their bicycles to go around Munich." The crowd gave a collective groan. "Relax, people. There are a lot of people on this trip. We can't have that many people on motorcycles in the street, but we can take the bike paths. That reminds me, who rides bikes often here?" Daniel raised his hand. "How far have you ridden, Daniel?"

"I've ridden 100 miles. From Islip, New York, to Montauk, New York." The bus gave a collective gasp at how far that was.

"Great, you're going in the back of the group," Sean said.

"Wait, why me?" Daniel asked, astonished.

"Since you're the best on a bike here, you're going to make sure everyone isn't bouncing off of BMW's." The bus gave a collective laugh. Daniel rolled his eyes.

"I'm not doing it," he bellowed back.

"What's the matter, Daniel? Still not feeling great from last night?" Sean asked sarcastically.

Daniel held his gurgling stomach. "It's better than before," he said to Wade.

Wade nodded and said, "I have wet wipes if it comes to it." Daniel rolled his eyes again.

They arrived at Matunas Motors and the tour guides came on to the bus. "Hello, everyone. Welcome to our humble abode. We all are looking forward to showing you guys around town. But first, we have to know who is riding in the back behind all of us." Daniel raised his hand. "What's your name, sir?"

"Daniel," he said unenthusiastically.

"Daniel, we're going to give you a nickname right now. It's a great nickname. Your new name is 'Dan, the Ass-Man' because you're riding at the ass of the pack." The entire bus gave a roar of laughter. Daniel, however, was not pleased at all. They all filed off the bus, one by one, and were handed a bike to ride. They were instructed to ride to the end of the block and then stay there until they come and get them. Wade enthusiastically took his bike and rode down the street doing wheelies and bar spins.

Daniel was the last to get off the bus. He was handed a bike and his stomach immediately started curling. He bent over considerably enough for the tour guides to ask him. "Dan, the Ass-Man, will you be okay to ride this?"

"I don't quite know, to be honest," Daniel replied.

"Well, you're doing it anyway. So go get 'em," the tour guide said as he pushed Daniel's bike to make him start pedaling.

"Shit shit shit shit shit" he kept saying out loud as he remembered he hadn't ridden a bike since he was in high school. He gained momentum and his stomach started to settle. As he started relaxing, Chenguang started to veer off course and go toward the rear of a BMW. Daniel noticed this and hurried over to try to save her. However, the car made a left turn and Chenguang went up the curb and eventually came to a safe stop on the sidewalk. But Daniel was going too fast, and he hesitated to hit the brakes. To which his front tire hit the curb and he was launched forward into a nearby park where he landed on the grass on his stomach. "That sucked so goddamn much!" he exclaimed after he embraced the fall. Chenguang did not hear this because she took off with the rest of the group. Daniel quickly got to his feet to pursue them as they made another left turn. He was only about a block behind them when he saw Wade stop for a minute to point and laugh at him. Wade was cackling with laughter as Daniel yelled, "Get back to the group!"

Wade didn't care as he was too busy trying to catch his breath from laughing too hard. "You ate so much shit. My stomach! Holy hell, that was funny."

"I'll tell Mel you ate one of Danny's brownies on the bus if you don't move!" Wade quickly stopped laughing and started pedaling.

They stopped at different locations including Marienplatz, Nymphenburg Palace, and the English Garden. However, when they came to the Eisbach, a small channel of the Isar River where the water is particularly rough and has a continuous wave where dozens of surfers come a day to ride the wave, they all stopped to observe the various surfers. Well, except Daniel, Wade, Oliver, Zoey, and Bill. They were all laughing but also helping Daniel as he vomited from his empty stomach and several other crashes.

"How do this many people have problems riding a goddamn bike!" he said as he recovered for a moment.

"You guys don't want to watch the surfers?" Wade asked genuinely.

"Mate, we're from Australia and New Zealand. We've seen enough."

"Wade, I'm dying. Can you dump two shots for me?" Daniel asked, spitting out what was left in his mouth before he took a sip of water.

"Yeah, we've done enough foul things to these ashes, your puke is the last thing we need." Wade poured two shots of ashes into the Eisbach. The surfer riding the wave however took a full hit of mom and dad to the face and fell backward, cursing in German.

Daniel finished emptying his stomach and fell behind the pack as they took off quickly. Wade stayed close by in case Daniel fell off from exhaustion or to see him finally snap and descend into madness. The tour guide stopped in front of the Bavarian State Chancellery. Otherwise known as Bayerische Staatskanzlei. The tour stopped with him, and Daniel bumped into the rear wheel of Wade's bike while he was standing next to it. Wade was in such awe of the glass building he didn't even acknowledge Daniel. "Everyone, please take in the architectural wonder that is the Bavarian State Chancellery. Erected between 1989-1993, it is the former Bavarian Army Museum. Its primary function now is to assist the Minister-President in coordinating the activities of the Bavarian Government. The reason the building is entirely glass is quite fascinating. After the second world war, it was decreed that all government buildings were to be made entirely of glass in order to no longer hide any workings the government does from its people. The group felt a collective feeling of gratitude that the German government took its history seriously. Even Daniel felt the warmth. However, he felt moments away from death.

The group took off again and rode all the way to the Viktualienmarkt Beergarden, an outdoor restaurant serving buffet-style. Daniel rode his bike straight to the door ahead of everybody, completely ignoring his "ass-man" duties. He filled his plate and paid before Wade even got off his bike. He sat and ate bountifully, but slowly, to not upset his stomach.

"You look like you just escaped a camp," Bill said, jokingly.

"Whoa, Whoa, Whoa!" Sean said, running up on Bill.

"How you doin', mate?" Bill asked with a grin.

"Bill you cannot joke about the Holocaust here," Sean said in a panic.

"Sure you can," Bill said. "It's not polite, it's not smart, but I'm trying to make the hungry cunt laugh. Daniel did snicker at the joke."

"Bill, they throw people in jail for imitating Nazis denying the Holocaust."

"He didn't do any of that, " Zoey said, walking to the table behind them.

"I know he didn't," Sean snarled to Zoey, "but he should use his common sense and just not do it at all. Don't you think?" Sean said, looking to an approaching Wade.

"What happened now?" Wade said in a tone of exhaustion similar to Daniel's.

"Bill made a Holocaust joke and Sean's scared they'll find the family he stowed under the bus."

"Daniel!" Wade yelled. Bill doubled over in a fit of laughter.

"Daniel, goddammit the one time you make a joke in your life and it has to be that?" Sean said now in a fit of panic.

"Danny, I agree with Sean. When we get on the bus, in a room with like-minded people, or over text is one thing. But use your common sense. Do you like it when people do jokes about drug addicts? Do you like it when a rape joke comes up?

Or when I offer you donuts and ask if you had too many at work?" Wade asked calmly. Bill was rolling in the grass with laughter with zero regard to the consequences.

"No Wade, I don't. And you're right. I'll keep quiet."

The table collectively dropped their jaws. They wouldn't have believed it if they didn't see it themselves. Daniel agreed with Wade. "I'm sorry, do you have a clearer head when you're hungover?" Zoey asked in disbelief.

"No, Zoey. Wade's correct. Granted, even a drunk Bill cums twice a day, but you have to own up to when you make a mistake or do something in poor taste. You don't have to always apologize, especially when you're really not sorry. But own up to the mistake and don't do it again."

"Frankly, Danny, I can Nazi how you could think it's funny to make a joke like that. Anne-Frankly, I'm happy you've come to your senses." The table roared with laughter and Sean threw his hands in the air and walked away. Sometimes assholes were just going to go against you no matter how right you were.

They rode back to the cycle shop, and Daniel was given a special Frisby that was customized to say "Honorary Ass-Man."

"To hell with a souvenir, nothing's going to top this, Wade."

"I concur, " Wade said as they boarded the bus and went back to the hostel for a relaxing night in.

10

The People in the Bottle

Daniel and Wade spent the night with Oliver and Bill sleeping and staying in for the night. They'd had enough shenanigans over the past week and were exhausted from the partying. Wade woke up on the top bunk and swung his head down to greet his brother. Only Daniel was not there. Wade jumped down and checked the bathroom. He wasn't there either.

"Guys, any of you see Danny?" Wade asked the others.

"He went to get breakfast and then to walk off his stomach from yesterday. He said he'll be back before we have to leave," Oliver said.

"Oh, that's weird. He didn't wake me up," Wade said somberly.

"Mate, from what we know so far of Daniel, he's a loner and he's been at your hip for almost a week now. Let him have a morning to himself. If anything, call your wife back home until we leave and have your own alone time," Bill said, looking at his phone.

Wade shrugged his shoulders. "Yeah, I guess. I'll give Mel a call once I'm out of the shower.

Meanwhile, Daniel was out and about in Munich going for a jog. He admired the architecture and marveled at the kindness of people waving at him as he was jogging. He turned left down the street where the hostel was located. It was still two blocks away when Zoey, who was also jogging, cut in front of him. She looked back and blew a kiss at him as she started a sprint down to the hostel. Daniel immediately knew what she was getting at. He also took off in a sprint. They raced each other down the street. Although Daniel was gaining on her, she suddenly tripped and was about to fall face-first on the pavement, except she turned it into a forward roll and kept going as she got to her feet. Daniel was stunned. She beat him by half a block, even with her error. She stood in a bragging-like pose. He caught up with her in front of the hostel.

"I need you to teach me how to do that," he said, doubling over to catch his breath.

"I have many things to teach you; but you need to show me a few things, too," she said with a wink. "Come on, loser buys breakfast," she said, extending her hand to him. He took it and they went to the coffee shop at the corner.

Wade got out of the shower and found that Oliver and Bill were no longer in the room. He got dressed and took out his laptop to talk with his wife. She answered his FaceTime call as she was getting ready to make dinner. They were elated to talk to each other while Wade told Mel everything about what had happened in Munich.

"You guys sound like you're a crazy mob going through Europe, and I hate the fact that I'm not there with you," she said as she fed the baby.

"Yeah, Danny's out for a run and grabbing breakfast, so I figured I'll just grab something from my bag and eat when we get to a rest stop," he said, unwrapping a protein bar. "Honey," Wade asked, "do you think I have a problem with being alone?"

"Yes," she said without skipping a beat.

"Take longer to think, I beg you."

"I don't have to, dear. You can't be left alone or you get sad and overthink."

"Do you get mad when I'm sad?"

"Never, Wade. If I didn't like something about you, I'd tell you, or I wouldn't have married you."

"Well, thanks; but lately, I've been noticing if I'm not with you or the baby or Danny, I feel like I lack a purpose. I don't have this big career to talk about, so I don't feel like I have a lot to offer."

"Hi, this is your wife speaking," Mel started to add. "Your purpose is to be a phenomenal father to your son and an amazing husband to me. If you're concerned about not having a self-image besides that, we'll think of some things to do when you're home. Please don't spiral just because your brother isn't there to pull you out. You have to do some work on your own self-esteem by yourself."

———

DANIEL PAID for their breakfast with a credit card and went to get a table for the two of them. He had a German pastry with a cup of coffee, while Zoey had a green tea with honey and lemon and a donut. They sat down and Daniel instantly tried to make Zoey laugh with some of Wade's best dad jokes. Zoey cracked up at all of them. After each one, she stroked his hand and stared at Daniel adoringly. "Tell me about your parents," she said, sipping her tea. "What were they like before they were stuck in a bottle and Bill's nostrils?"

Daniel sighed with annoyance. "Don't you groan at me, you silly man," she said while slapping his hands. "I only have you for another week and a half before we never see each other again so get to it."

Daniel felt a knot in his throat at the thought of not having Zoey after a few more days, and he felt instant sadness but pushed on. "Well, mom was a business type. Very professional in everything and she never let her emotions show unless it was to dad behind closed doors."

"I see you're just like your mother," Zoey said, interrupting. Daniel raised his eyebrows as he would with Wade to show that it was a sensitive topic. She raised one hand to signify a half-apology, but she was still right. Daniel continued talking about how their mother could be distant yet loving with each of the men in her house.

"She was really hard on me, but sometimes just outright cruel to Wade," Daniel said, circling the rim of his mug with his finger.

"How so?" Zoey asked with concern.

"Well, she'd see me succeed at something in school; and since Wade was much more like dad, a good person, but not one set on accomplishing much more than being good to people, she'd look at him and ask where his accomplishments were."

Zoey gasped with a mouthful of tea. "That's horrendous!"

"Yeah, she could be. That's kind of why I always looked out for Wade. He's the best person you'll meet. Kind to all and completely non-judgemental, but no drive or ambition. Mom's constant belittling kind of killed that in him."

———

WADE WAS STARING at his computer, listening to his wife tell him all the same compliments he'd heard from people a thousand times. "You're a good person. You're so thoughtful, I wish more people were like you," but it wasn't pulling him out of his funk. Wade shook his head and looked at Mel through the computer and interrupted her.

"That's it, I know what I want to do," Wade said with a serious tone. "Mel, I want to go back to school and become a mental health counselor."

———

"WADE COMES up with all these ideas and half-brained missions for himself, but his self-esteem is so low, he never finishes anything," Daniel said, picking up his mug. "It's really sad, and I love him more than I'm willing to admit to him; but if he wants to see a rise in his self-esteem, he has to finish the things he starts."

Zoey sat back in her chair. "If you really love him, the next good idea he comes up with, you have to embrace it and tell him it's a great plan. You have to be there for him. Sure, his wife will be there to support him, but he thinks you hung the sun in the sky. He wants your approval and when he gets it, he'll follow through with it," Zoey said imploringly.

"The next good idea, sure," Daniel said, taking the tone as though he was talking to someone in an interrogation room. "It will be a cold day in hell before the next one of those pops up, but sure, the next good one."

"Talk to me like that again, Daniel Fontaine, and I'll leave you further and quicker in the dust more than on that run," Zoey said as though she was talking to one of her prisoners in interrogation.

"Yes, ma'am," he replied quickly before he sank back in his chair.

———

MEL WAS on the other side of the planet in tears with pride at her husband. "I'm so proud of you," she said. "Let's do it. When you come home, we'll look up information on programs near us."

Wade was filled with a combination of excitement and dread. "I'm nervous as to what Danny will say. You know how lovely he is when it comes to supporting people he cares about," he groaned.

"Daniel is not your mother, no matter how similar they are. And frankly, you don't need his approval in order to further yourself. You can do it yourself. I know his approval is still something that's important to you, but you have to let it go," Mel said, burping the baby, followed quickly by a face of disgust. "Speaking of letting it go, your son needs a change and you have to get ready. I love you and I'll research some programs near us," she said, waving at the camera.

"I love you, too, babe. I'll call you tomorrow or maybe the next day." The call ended and Wade packed his bag, along with setting out clothes for Daniel to change into when he got back from his jog.

11

The Tyrol

Daniel walked Zoey back to her room before returning back to his own to change. They had a kiss goodbye that lingered a little longer than they expected, resulting in the two of them wanting more before the bus ride, but they did not indulge. If they missed the bus, they would be left behind. They both needed to get control of themselves once they left each other. Daniel opened the door to find Wade laying out his clothes for the day.

"You don't do that for Mel, do you?" Daniel asked, hoping he'd say no.

"God, no," Wade said quickly. "I dare not tell my wife what to wear to work."

"Good, although you do have good taste, Wade. A turtleneck and dress pants is a nice change of pace for me," Daniel said before closing the bathroom door to shower.

Wade smiled as he saw the door close. He approached the closed door and knocked. "Hey, Danny, can I talk to you about something?" Wade asked nervously.

"Can we discuss this literally any other moment besides when I'm in the shower, Wade?" Daniel said from inside.

"Well, it's just this idea that I had."

"It's not about launching a start-up business is it?" Daniel asked.

"No, nothing like that," Wade said with a laugh.

"Good, because I have no desire to relive the 'costume for community aid' charity you tried to start.

"Well, who doesn't want Batman handing out food for the homeless?"

"Anyone who isn't under 12 years old, Wade. Now, can we talk about this when I'm done showering?"

Wade lifted his hands in the air and backed off. "You know what, I'm going to take the bags down. I'll see you on the bus."

"Now that's the idea you should have," Daniel said through a mouthful of water.

Wade waited on the sidewalk for Daniel. He finally came down, arm-in-arm with Zoey, in the outfit Wade picked out for him. Wade jumped up and down at the sight of this. He even took his phone out to take a picture of the two of them walking down the stairs, to which they both smiled.

"You two sit together to Austria, and I'll sit with Oliver." They both were taken aback but thanked Wade for the gesture. Wade boarded the bus and plopped down next to Oliver.

"Zo, you've gotten a bit more butch on this trip," Oliver said to Wade with a chuckle.

"They're sitting together on this ride, so I figured I'd crash with you!" Wade said enthusiastically.

"Not that I'm not happy to see my sister happy, but if we could not urge my sister to get with some bloke she won't see after this trip, that'd be helpful," Oliver said sarcastically, but he meant every word.

Wade seemed to overlook that unfortunate ending to the only romantic partner Daniel has had in the last few years. He had a sinking feeling that he was setting up his brother to be emotionally devastated which may possibly make him more isolated when they arrived home. "Oliver, am I a bad brother for not thinking of that?"

Oliver looked at Wade patronizingly. "Mate, you wanted to make your brother happy and open his horizons. No, you're not a bad brother. Not the best matchmaker in the world, but certainly not a bad brother. Look, Zoey's not exactly big on dating either when she's back home. She keeps to herself and focuses on work. So once she saw someone like-minded who wasn't ugly and certainly kind to her in his own way, what was I going to do? Family is tough, but even when they do something temporarily for fun, just support them. Don't tell him every scenario. They'll find out soon enough, and you'll be there when it has to end." Daniel and Zoey were laughing hysterically in their seats. What they were laughing at was anyone's guess, but the only one who cared was Wade. Hopefully, they understood what was to inevitably happen but were just enjoying each other.

The bus trip to Austria mostly consisted of reading books, listening to music, or sleeping for everyone. Everyone except Zoey and Daniel. After four destinations with the same group of people, you tend to run out of things to say. For some reason, Daniel and Zoey were engaged in conversation the whole five-hour drive. Wade would peer up and down from his book. Not out of jealousy or annoyance at the volume, but to see how happy his normally miserable brother was acting.

He couldn't have asked for anything more. He had already spent just shy of a week next to his brother, worked through some of his frustrations, and they reconnected after a feud. The trip could drive them all the way back to Long Island for all he cared.

Once they saw the Austrian Tyrol, everyone stopped talking. Its beauty and grace can hardly be overstated. The locals, however, were so accustomed to the breathtaking views that they overlooked them daily and became reluctant every time they saw a bus full of tourists roll into town. Seeing that it was the summer, not a person was skiing. However, a hang glider had flown overhead and all were amazed.

Sean came over the loudspeaker and gave the usual destination summary. "Alright, everyone, for now on we do not say hello, we say 'ha-low.' They love it when you do it in Germany, and it will carry on for all of the European Union. Let's try it." The bus gave a collective "ha-low," and everyone giggled. Actually, not one European they do this to will appreciate it, and they all will roll their eyes. Sometimes a tour guide just had to fuck with his attendees. "So we will be staying at one of ITourEurope's own hostels. The company owns it, and we can do what we want with it. There are no big plans out in Austria besides parasailing or hang gliding off the Austrian Tyrol; but most people use it to relax, do laundry, and party in the evening." Zoey and Daniel were dancing in their seats at the idea of a party with their beds just upstairs.

"Tonight is the night of convenient drinking and not getting lost. This is also where married couples end up with their 'oops babies,' so please keep in mind your finances and your fucking," Sean said, glaring at Daniel and Zoey. They both gave a middle finger to Sean without hesitation.

As they were all filing out of the bus, Wade dropped his backpack containing his laptop and the urn. "Oh no! Oh God, no!

Please tell me there's still enough in here." Wade opened his backpack and saw that only a quarter of the ashes had been spilled out with half the bottle remaining, but his laptop screen was shattered and full of mom and dad. "Oh no! How am I going to tell Mel?" he cried, looking at Daniel.

"Don't worry, you still have your phone," Daniel reminded him, trying to calm Wade down.

"Yeah, but I like seeing her on the big screen."

Daniel rolled his eyes at Wade and gestured to him that they have a drink. Daniel, Wade, Zoey, and Oliver walked into the lobby and found the bar. Bill was already on the top of the bar that was left unattended. "Mate, you're going to fall and break your neck over booze that isn't yours," Oliver said.

"Well worth it," Bill said, grasping a bottle of Jack Daniels. "Your folks sent me a message from my brain stem," Bill said, reminding the boys he still had the sniffles from when he snorted a line of their parents.

"Are you a neuroscientist?" Daniel asked Bill, genuinely curious if he was smart enough to know the conductor role of the brain stem.

"Not that brain stem, I meant the top of my cock that connects the helmet to the—" Bill began, trying to make a dick joke.

But Wade interrupted saying, "What did our dead parents say to you Bill?" clutching the brim of his nose in half a fit of laughter and disgust.

"Did they ever mention a walk through the town?" Wade and Daniel looked at each other. They both clearly remembered their parents speaking about the romantic view of the Tyrol region while walking around town, but they silently agreed not to give Bill the satisfaction.

"I don't remember, do you?" Daniel asked Wade.

"I don't remember. I was hoping you did."

Bill chuckled at them. "Lying gits. They were saying you two should take a stroll into town since everyone is happy and not snapping at each other for a day."

The boys rolled their eyes. "Fine, we'll go before dinner," Daniel said in annoyance.

"Why are you drinking Jack of all things? You can get that at any store back home, ya cunt," Oliver said.

"Mum and dad seem to like the space, so I'm just giving the people what they want," Bill said, biting off the wrapper and the bottle cap in the same maneuver. They all were stunned at this as Bill walked off with a sack he'd been carrying around as his luggage.

"Remind me never to let Bill go down on me," Wade said.

"Agreed," said Zoey, not wanting to know what his game was like.

The boys put their luggage upstairs and went for a walk through town, just the two of them. They marveled at the architecture and how it perfectly complemented the Austrian Tyrol. "So Danny, can I tell you the idea I had?"

Daniel rolled his eyes. "Sure, Wade."

Wade overlooked the eye roll. "I was thinking about, after money gets a little better, going back to school for mental health counseling." Wade expected Daniel to either berate, belittle, or make fun of his idea; however, he was pleasantly surprised.

"Wade, that's a great idea."

Wade became extremely emotional. "Really? You think so?"

"Absolutely, we need more counselors right now. Maybe before you go back to school, you should get a certification in drug counseling to see if you like it. And maybe after that, go for the degree; but I think it's a great idea." Wade hugged Daniel in the middle of the street. Daniel gave him a pat on the back instead of the full hug. A local walked past them, giving them a bizarre look; but Daniel waved and said "ha-low" as Sean instructed. The local hung his head and shook it disapprovingly.

"Wade, we have laundry to do," Daniel said, knowing Wade's parental instinct to get laundry done.

Daniel did not help with the laundry, which Wade was actually happy about. It gave him alone time, and he felt like he was at home for a moment. As Daniel walked with Bill and Oliver back to the bar that was now staffed, he got a Face-Time call from Mel. "Hey, Wade's computer broke so he only has his phone. But he's doing laundry so he may call later," Daniel said shortly so as not to hold up the other guys.

"Oh boy, tell him he doesn't have to FaceTime me at all but to call before he goes to bed," she replied. "How's Austria?" she asked inquisitively.

"Not as lively as everywhere else; but to be honest, I kind of prefer it. We've been really active the whole time, so rest is appreciated here," Daniel said.

"Did someone take all the Jack Daniels?" Daniel overheard one of the bartenders say.

"Mel, we may be in trouble. I have to go," Daniel said curtly.

"Don't be assholes," she said with a smile and wave. Daniel hung up and followed the others to the bar.

Daniel joined the camaraderie that Oliver and Bill had already started. "What's everybody laughing about?" Daniel inquired.

"Bill just drank 'The Tyrol,'" Oliver replied. "He drinks every place we go to under the table."

"No mate," Bill started. "'The Tyrol' is the house special drink."

"What's in it?"

The bartender took out the ingredients and made it in front of him. "Elderflower champagne, gin, apple juice, and simple sugar." Daniel looked confused.

"So it's a French 75 with apple juice instead of lemon?" he asked.

"Yep, but the glass is special." The bartender turned it to show Julie Andrews spinning on the Austrian Tyrol, a scene famous from the film *The Sound of Music*.

Daniel laughed and said, "I'll take that one."

Oliver grabbed his hand. "Not so fast, cunt. You have to chug the whole thing."

"Fuck that, nevermind."

"If you chug it, your drinks are free the rest of the night," the bartender interjected. "Down it goes."

Daniel took the glass, cheered his friends, and chugged the drink. After the last drop, he made a face that looked as though he had something sour. He put the glass upside down on the table to prove he finished it; and as the brim of the glass touched the bar, the Julie Andrews drawn on the glass had her skirt upside down, showing her panties.

"Now that's me, mate!" Bill said, slapping him on the back.

"A jack and coke, please," Daniel said to the bartender.

Wade finished the laundry and went back to the room. He folded both his and Daniel's clothes and laid down on the bed to take a nap. As he closed his eyes, Zoey knocked on the door and let herself in. "Wade, have you seen Dan anywhere?"

Wade didn't open his eyes. "I haven't, Zoey. I was doing laundry. Check the bar."

He fell asleep and did not wake up until about 7:00 p.m. He looked outside at the sun setting over the Tyrol. He checked his phone and saw that he had a text from Mel. He freaked out and opened the phone to see a text saying, "Working overtime, won't be home to say goodnight. I love you more than words and I'm so proud of you. Have fun tonight! Don't let Danny be the only drunk one tonight! ;)." He smiled and he felt like he could burst.

He got up and opened the door. The music was loud enough to hear in the street. After he stretched his arms, he made his way toward the stairs. While coming down, he saw Zoey talking to Chenguang and Zhang Wei. She kissed him on the cheek and yelled in his ear, "He's drunk as hell with Bill and Oli. I let him have his fun. Go join him!"

He smiled and patted her on the back. He followed the stairs down but couldn't find the crew at the bar. He went out to the patio and found Oliver and Bill laughing maniacally. They saw Wade coming and waved. "Last time we saw him, he was trying to kick Maria away from grabbing a free drink on his tab. Check the garden," Bill said.

Wade walked to the garden staring at the Austrian Tyrol at sunset. He was amazed at his situation in life. He has a wife who was proud of him, his son was his salvation, he had something in mind for a career that he had support on, and his relationship with his brother was mended. He walked a path into a garden and peered left behind a row of hedges, and his heart fell to the bottom of his chest at what he saw. Right before his eyes, was Daniel making out with Maria.

PART II

Intermission!

Witnesses
BY EOIN BURCH

As he gazed out at the panorama which presented itself before him, the actuality of his trip became clear. He had come to Maine to escape himself. Instead, he found his purpose.

The morning fog was lifting as *Miss Dot* approached the dock at Bass Harbor, Maine. The summertime getaway for so many wealthy New Yorkers and New Englanders was now the destination of William DuPont, aged twenty-seven, of Southampton.

From his position at the bow of the stern of the ship, William gazed at the surrounding archipelago of tiny, forested islands, each a tiny planet in the vastness of Frenchman Bay. The fantasy of settling on one—a log cabin with a wood stove, fish and squirrels, wood to get through winter, and the cooling sea breeze to get through summer, set his mind adrift as *Miss Dot's* skipper ordered the sails hauled in while the ship prepared to moor at the small wharf outside the village.

"Heave to. Take in the sail, Caruthers," cried the skipper at one idle sailor. His voice was loud enough to break William's trance, if even for a moment, allowing attention to be focused elsewhere.

"Excuse me, sir, are we to prepare to disembark?" the still pensive William asked of the yeoman's mate.

"Aye, tend to yah bahgs and head to stahboahd at mid-deck. The Captain will be waiting foah yah there," he barked in his New English accent.

William thanked the man and motioned toward the ship's small, musty cabin. Damp and mildewy, it was apparent that the room was seldom a place where company was entertained. As the only passenger on board, locating his brown leather bag was effortless. Swinging it over his shoulder, the bag knocked into and doused the oil lamp, which shattered upon making contact with a navigation table layered with tools, maps, and charts.

The crew had been nothing but kind to him, ferrying him from Portland to Southwest Harbor for a mere five dollars in addition to William's promise of preparing their evening supper. He was a trained cook and spent years studying Escoffier's books and art of *haute-cuisine* at one of the finest culinary schools in Paris. He had prepared for them a fine, if simplistic, bouillabaisse with a bit of their morning catch and a few supplies he obtained at a market before departure.

However, the very inner forces which caused him to leave Southampton were now convincing him to not say anything, hope not a soul heard the breaking glass, and escape into town without anyone knowing the wiser. That was until the ship bumped into the piles supporting the dock, thus causing William to lose his footing.

In a managed disarray, William spotted another lamp, mounted to a hook on a beam supporting the cabin walls. He reached for its handle and lifted it ever so slightly and caused it to fall to the floor. This time, however, he caused a commotion, and the darkness within him revealed itself.

"Jesus, Mary, and Joseph," exclaimed the skipper at the sight of the broken glass and oil about the navigation room, "What happened here?"

"When we docked, sir, it appears that these two lamps were damaged," William replied, meekly. As he searched for the words with which he formulated his response, a deep depression set over him. The sheer foolishness of his lie became apparent. Were he honest, one lamp would be broken, and he would apologize. But his penchant for deception and impulsive treachery was too strong. It was this darkness that had driven him from his life on Long Island, and it was initiating his quest for renewal in a dark way indeed. The skipper examined the lamp which had originally hung on the beam. "Damaged puts it lightly. We have *these* lamps on *these* hooks so they don't fall off," he said, gesturing toward the damaged objects. "The waves we encountered on the way here were far rougher."

He looked at William again, this time having considered the lack of confidence in William's explanation. "Son, if ye broke the lamp, you can say so. If ye don't have your sea-legs and knocked into it, all you have to do is pay us back for it. Happens to a lot-a-ya."

William looked at the skipper as if his request for money had been an insult of his personal character. As his innocent expression became a sinister glare, dark thoughts began to percolate in his mind. "How dare he ask me for money, he knows I haven't any, or else I wouldn't have bartered for the journey here."

William had internalized his own lie remarkably quickly. Having his fabricated reality questioned even slightly, hastened his proclivity to take drastic action.

———

Laurelton House was the Southampton estate of Edgar and Lilith Raleigh. They had lived here for eight years, moving to

eastern Long Island from their Manhattan townhouse after
their youngest son was deployed to the Philippines with the
Army.

Mr. Raleigh had made his fortune investing in companies that
wired America with electricity. Although he was proud of his
humble upbringing in Western Pennsylvania, the wealth he
had accumulated over the past twenty years had skewed his
worldview so much one would think he invented electricity,
not merely profited from its demand. In a true twist of irony,
Laurelton House wasn't itself powered until four years
following Raleigh's arrival.

Notwithstanding, in the spring of 1903, a stubborn Mrs.
Raleigh, while a passionate cook, admitted her age and
arthritis had finally done her in. She agreed to allow her
husband to hire a cook to run her kitchen. Their servant,
Elmira, had dutifully assisted the frugal Mrs. Raleigh in
preparing lunch and supper but was herself aging, and
incapable of running a kitchen by herself.

On the 7th of May, a young man named William DuPont
arrived to interview for the job. His resume touted five year's
experience in Paris, his specialties in seafood, desserts, and
delicate sauces, and that he would work cheap. Mrs. Raleigh
was impressed by his charm and boyish demeanor. Mr.
Raleigh was hesitant to accept William's enthusiasm and
effeminate nature. In the end, Mrs. Raleigh's will prevailed
when a perfectly prepared *eclair au chocolat* silenced her
husband.

Within months, the young DuPont had made himself a
valuable part of the Raleigh household. His roast lamb
became a family favorite. His pastries had neighbors inviting
themselves over for high tea. The mayor was so impressed by
the food at a luncheon he begged the family to permit William
to cater an award banquet for a visiting dignitary.

One morning in late-September, 1904, a smiling Mrs. Raleigh
entered the kitchen flanked by two men in overalls carrying

big wooden crates. The outer panels bore writing in Chinese, French, and English. William was at his chopping station, polishing his knives.

"William, dear, come see what Alastair sent us from his deployment in Manila," she said warmly. Pointing at one of the workmen, she said "You, open this crate, would you?" William walked over from the carving board. The laborer removed the lid from the box, revealing an interior padded with hay, and stepped away. Mrs. Raleigh quickly took his place, reached in, and removed what appeared to be a simple teacup.

"Alastair shipped us this authentic china all the way from Asia," she said, handing the teacup to William.

"It's beautifully intricate, ma'am," he said meekly after briefly examining it.

"Hold it up to the light, peer through the bottom as if it were a telescope," she said with delight.

William did so, turning to the window and holding the teacup up to the sunlight. As the cup caught a ray of light, the image of an Eastern Emperor, seated at his throne, was revealed.

"A King in his castle," he said, returning the cup to her."

"Indeed it is, William. Now, I've invited three dear friends over for tea this afternoon. I would like you to serve it on these precious dishes. Do you suppose you could put something together?"

"Absolutely, ma'am." William dutifully replied.

William spent the rest of the morning, and early afternoon, preparing a *quiche* with ham, onions, and gruyere cheese, *Madeleines* dipped in imported Swiss chocolate, and strawberries with fresh cream. He selected a black Ceylon tea for the occasion, the missus' favorite.

At three o'clock, he set a kettle on the wood stove to heat. While the water warmed, he arranged his creation on a dessert cart to wheel it into the drawing-room. He went to his carving board and retrieved a knife to cut and serve the quiche, selected one which he had polished earlier, and returned to the stove to find steam billowing out the kettle. He poured the hot water into the fancy new teapot, arranged at the center of the cart surrounded by the Imperial teacups.

"Four minutes until steeped," he said to himself as he completed the pour and gently placed the lid on the teapot. He looked to the clock above the kitchen door, scrutinizing it with his perfectionist's gaze "three minutes, ten seconds now," and proceeded to the ladies awaiting their tea.

He made his way through the richly decorated, neo-gothic corridors of Laurelton House. As he entered the foyer, the vestibule at the front of the house from which the drawing-room extended, he encountered a grandfather clock on the far wall and a carpet before him. "One minute now," he said, picking up the pace. As he did, the cart caught on the carpet, nearly tipping, "Easy does it," he said to himself, "Easy." William made his way around the table in the middle of the foyer adorned with a statue of Apollo. He approached the grandfather clock, which appeared to stand guard before the French doors leading into the drawing-room. "Thirty seconds," he said to himself, accelerating his pace.

As William crossed the threshold into the drawing-room, the four proudly dressed elderly ladies gathered for tea lauded his arrival. "There's our man," one joyously cried, anticipating the fare and ware the Chef had in tow. Overcome with pride, William neglected the room's thick carpet. As he added pageantry to his strut toward the women, the front right wheel caught on the border of the rug, causing the cart to tip forward.

William lost his footing, fell, and now, level with the catastrophe, watched as the food spilled onto the precious carpet. The thick serving platters survived the fall, but the quiche and berries with cream spilled all over the rug. At the same time, the hot pot of tea slid off the top of the cart, followed by each delicate teacup and their respective saucers.

Almost in slow motion, one by one, beginning with the teapot, each item hit the floor and shattered. Relative to their significance, the scene was rather anticlimactic.

Mrs. Raleigh was furious, "You clumsy fool!" she shouted at William, "What kind of idiot can't manage to escort a cart into a sitting room."

One of the old ladies remarked to another, "Good help is so hard to come by these days, even with the most prestigious resume." Another called out, "And to think, I skipped lunch for this."

William, looking down at the cart examining the mess before him, was overcome with grief and dissociated from the admonishment being leveled at it. He had taken such pride in each and every morsel. He had never suffered an embarrassment of this magnitude. But, as he reflected upon his mistake, a rage began simmering within him. One error was enough to earn the rage of these elderly bags.

"William!" Mrs. Raleigh called out to him, causing him to return to reality. "Don't you have anything to say?"

William was silent.

"Boy! The Lady-of-the-House asked you a question," another shouted at him, "Answer her!"

William could hear every word and remained silent. He could see the pieces on the floor. The cream on the carpet. The splash pattern of the tea. The knife.

"The knife," William thought, licking his lips, "The knife."

Without looking up, William turned to the French doors behind him and shut them. As the sound of the lock motioning into place traveled throughout the room, the ladies fell silent.

"William?" A softer-toned Mrs. Raleigh said, "William, my boy."

William DuPont turned to face the group, continuing to focus his gaze on the ground. He advanced toward them, each petrified in silence. As he rushed toward them, he kneeled ever so quickly to pick up the quiche knife. Gripped in his hand, he approached Mrs. Raleigh and stabbed her in her lower neck. She screamed as her blood erupted from the artery he had managed to puncture, and blood sprayed onto each woman seated at the table. He removed the blade and struck again. Her body went limp. He had killed her.

William, coated in blood, looked up at the other attendees, who had remained in their seats, quivering.

"Witnesses."

William assessed the physique of the skipper. The man was clearly more muscular, and taller than he, placing William at a disadvantage. However, he appeared unarmed and the Chef had a tool with him that could help.

"Alright, sir, yes, I broke the lamps. Let me see if I have any money in my bag which I could give you for the damages."

"Thank ye, son for being honest with me. Lamps are lamps, a bit expensive for a fishing crew, but we'll manage."

Very good, sir. One moment."

William, while kneeling, slung his bag off his shoulder and onto the floor. As he did, the skipper got a hand broom and dustpan and began to tend to some of the damage.

"Blazes, this oil gets everywhere," the veteran sailor said to himself.

"As a cook, I know all about oil spilling everywhere."

William unfastened his bag and found the quiche knife, still a bit bloody, wrapped in the soiled shirt he was wearing in the drawing-room of Laurelton House. He licked his lips slowly, gripped the knife in one hand, and the shirt balled up in the other. Then, he methodically turned to face the yeoman's mate, who was presented before him on all fours.

"I trust you'll get it all," William said as he placed the soiled shirt over the man's mouth and stabbed his neck. The first

blow was successful, and William moved in for another. As his
hand swung downward, the skipper jerked his back with
enough force to offset William's balance. As he did, William
inadvertently stabbed his own forearm close to his elbow. The
forward momentum caused him to push the blade forward
toward his hand.
William winced in pain as the blade entered his forearm. As
he did, he let go of the shirt. The skipper shouted "You
bastard" as he put his hand on his wound.
"I'm not a bastard," William said in distress. While the skipper
attempted to get his bearings, rapidly losing blood, William
removed the blade from his arm and stabbed at the man's
belly and groin. The skipper fell to the ground, with force.
"I am a liar," William said to the dying man. He looked to his
wound and then to his hand. William could not form a fist.
Even more distressed, he grabbed the balled-up, bloodied shirt
and wrapped it around his forearm. He threw the knife into
his bag, grabbed the straps, and exited the cabin, frantic.
Crew on deck were tying down ropes and rigging as William
dodged past them. A few tried to gesture a wave, but the
criminal paid them no mind and hurriedly moved past them
and down the rope. His parting word was to the Captain who
was negotiating with the harbormaster on the wharf. William
gave him a gruff "goodbye."
The small village faded behind him as William walked south.
The pine and birch forest lining the road guided him further
on. The wound he had sustained, nagging at him. The
occasional passerby would give him a look of concern, which
William systematically ignored. He continued on,
simultaneously awash in thought, yet with nothing on his
mind at all.
William had left Southampton to avoid the consequences of
his actions. But he couldn't.
In the distance, William could see the forest thinning and a
bright pink sky in the distance. The treed hills began to morph

into rust-colored, rocky cliffs; sunset seas crashing into the
rocks.

Growing ever weaker from blood-loss, William's pace slowed
to a shamble. Arduously, he navigated his way onto a cliff,
facing the Frenchman's Bay, staring into the setting sun.

As he gazed out at the panorama which presented itself before
him, the actuality of his trip became clear. He had come to
Maine to escape himself. Instead, he found his purpose.

Which was to die.

Part III

12

Violence in Venice

"Fucking Maria?" Wade said to himself, witnessing his brother kissing another woman. Wade stood dumbfounded looking at his brother sharing a form of intimacy with someone with whom he wasn't involved. His dumbfounded look turned to anger quickly. He did not interrupt his brother, but he did walk away huffing and puffing. He did not respond when anyone asked where he was going. Not Bill and Oliver, not Sean, and certainly not Zoey. He went back to his bed and wrestled with his thoughts all evening. He couldn't believe his brother could be so careless. Obviously, Daniel and Zoey were not going to continue dating after the trip was over; but he did think it would have been decent of him to talk it over with Zoey first. He flipped from his back to his stomach and forced his pillow to his face to cover his mouth. He inhaled and exhaled a muffled scream that nobody but him would be able to hear. "FUCKING MARIA!"

Wade thought that he would stay awake until Daniel got back so he could ream him out and possibly fight him, but he fell asleep mere minutes after he screamed into the pillow. The sun rising over the mountains shined directly into his room and awakened him. He woke up slowly and looked at Daniel's bed. He found him sleeping, naked but alone. For a few moments, he forgot what Daniel did last night and covered his bare butt that was hanging in the wind with a blanket and kissed him on the top of the head. Almost as though he was doing the same for his son Daniel back home. He pecked him on the head with a smile, but quickly recovered and stomped his feet in protest of himself. He took a bag of toiletries to the communal bathroom down the hall. He walked in his pajama bottoms and a t-shirt emblazoned with "We love you!" on the top and a picture of his wife and child.

As he was walking into the bathroom, he saw Maria walk out of Bill's room. He looked at her with anger but had no intention of approaching her. What did she care what was going on in his head about his view of his brother having a transgression with a woman he'd never see again, while he was having a vacation romance with someone he would also never see again. It would be such a pointless argument, he swallowed his anger and proceeded to the bathroom. He started brushing his teeth when there was a knock on the bathroom door. It was Maria trying to get Wade's attention.

"Like what you saw last night, Wade?" she said with a grin but also with a tone of mockery. Wade couldn't believe what he was hearing. He turned toward Maria with a mouth full of toothpaste. He quickly turned and spit the toothpaste out, wiped his face with a washcloth, and turned back to her.

"Maria, why are you having this conversation with me? Like why do you think I'd care what you do with your life?" Wade asked with genuine curiosity, but with the intention of insulting her.

"Your brother's hot, I can't help that. Maybe you should have just brought me to that winery in the Rhine Valley," she said with a whisper, as though she was telling the students of

Hogwarts to give Harry Potter over to the death caters by midnight.

Wade was so flabbergasted by her he slipped his hands off the counter. "That's why you made out with my brother?" he asked in disbelief.

"Well, we did more than that in my room, but yeah. That winery was a once-in-a-lifetime opportunity that I had to miss out on because you wanted to bring a laptop."

"Then why didn't you try to seduce me?"

"Oh, Wade, you're too married for me. Yeah, he has a vacation romance, but you're married. I'm not a monster."

"You're in desperate need of therapy, is what you are," Wade said, intending to insult her again.

"Oh? Are you going to give it to me? That's right, Daniel told me how you want to go to school to be one. But he also told me you'd be absolutely terrible at it."

Wade looked like he couldn't take another blow like that. The privacy of a conversation between him and his brother being used against him in mockery. Not to mention the insults his brother gave to someone neither of them really knew, just to get some intimacy. Wade couldn't breathe; he was so angry.

"Danny wouldn't say something like that to someone he doesn't know. He'd insult me to only close friends who'd do the same," he said as though it proved a point.

"Face it, Wade. You'll always be a loser to him," she said, leaving him in the bathroom. Wade turned and grabbed the sink and saw he was crying. He couldn't feel it, however. The emotional toll he just took was too much for his body to comprehend.

Wade went to take a shower. He turned it to hot, but he couldn't stand to take one. He only sat at the bottom of the shower and let the water hit him. He was so overcome with anger that he didn't know how to handle it. He had never really felt rage before. He'd felt sad, upset, and angry in the past, but never had it been so monumental that he was unable to stand. Is this what Daniel felt all the time at work? Is this how he motivated his life? If so, he wanted nothing to do with his brother and the trip can go fuck itself.

After Wade finished his shower, he got ready for the bus and didn't bother to wake Daniel up. *If he's going to talk about me like that to a bitch like her, he can wake himself up*, he thought to himself. He assembled his belongings and took them down to the bus. He spent the rest of the time waiting for the bus by sitting in a chair and texting his wife, even though she was fast asleep back home. He figured she could read it when she got up. He texted her the story of what transpired mere hours ago and exactly what he thought of Daniel and his intentions to never see him again after the trip.

More of the trip attendees were filing down to bring their stuff on the bus. If anyone tried to speak to Wade, he blew them off with one-word answers. It was clear to everyone that he didn't want to talk. Maria came down and smiled at him vindictively. When he saw her come down, he just stared at his phone and didn't look up at her. Ten minutes before the departure of the bus, Daniel came running down. He didn't ask Wade why he didn't wake him. Surprisingly enough, he apologized for being tardy. Wade couldn't even look at him. There were too many people around. He'd have a talk with Daniel later.

"Hey, we gotta do the ashes before we leave," Daniel said, completely forgetting the point of the trip.

"Do it yourself, I'm going on the bus," Wade said dismissively. He handed Daniel the Jack Daniels urn and two shot glasses and went on the bus to sit next to Oliver. Daniel only looked at Wade perplexedly but went over to the base of the Tyrol, which was mere feet away from them, and poured out two shot glasses on the snow of the mountain. Realizing they'd probably blow away with the wind and blind someone like every other time they did this, he tossed some snow on top of the ashes to prevent further injury. Daniel then walked onto the bus with Zoey, hand in hand, and it made Wade furious. In response, he put his headphones in and didn't speak to anyone during the whole trip to Venice, Italy. The bus ride was filled with silence, except yet again by Daniel and Zoey. They were both laughing their heads off, and Zoey punched Daniel in his arm in a form of play-fighting.

The bus did not pull into a hostel this time. Instead, they were camping in tents. Much of the tour was angered or annoyed, however Zoey and Daniel couldn't have cared less. "I've only been camping in upstate New York, so this will be one to tell the guys back at the precinct," Daniel said to Zoey.

"Let's get one together and have at least one night we can spend together," Zoey said, resting her head on Daniel's shoulders, yet looking in his eyes.

Daniel kissed her on the forehead and said he'd speak to Sean about it. As they departed the bus, he tapped Sean on the shoulder. "So, uh, Zoey and I are going to have a tent together instead of Wade and me."

"I mean, that's fine, but I need Wade's consent in order to do it," Sean replied.

"Oh, he won't care," Daniel said, blowing it off.

"I'd ask him first because he's been cranky with everyone since this morning. Go check on him and be sure he's alright with it before I make the switch."

Daniel was perplexed. He thought Wade was just cranky from being up in the morning or not having talked with Mel the night before. "Alright, I'll go ask him," Daniel replied with a tone of confusion.

Wade was setting his bunk up with Oliver when Daniel walked in. "Hey guys, I guess you got the memo about me and Zoey asking to be in each other's tent tonight," he said to the pair of them.

"Yes, Zoey told me. Not that I don't love the idea of a friend pitching his tent with my sister, but have a blast you two," Oliver said jokingly.

"Wade, you okay? You've been kind of short with everyone today," Daniel asked when Wade's back was turned to him.

"I'm fine," Wade said curtly. "I'll talk to you later." Daniel was again taken aback but walked out of the tent perplexed and not inquiring any further.

Daniel walked back to his and Zoey's assigned tent for the evening. He walked in and Zoey had just finished making one bed for the two of them. "I know it's not the Hilton, but it'll do for the night, right?" Zoey asked.

"It's with you, so I'm perfectly fine with wherever we are," he said, giving her a kiss on the lips, which she reciprocated.

"Watch where you use those, Maria may want more," Zoey said kiddingly.

"Hey, I told you getting drunk was the only way I'd be able to, and I proved that, didn't I?" he said in a humorous tone.

"I got approached by like five people asking if I was okay. I told them how I told you to, just to be sure you really only want to be with me for the trip, and we proved our point, didn't we?" Zoey asked, bouncing on the bed while sitting down.

Daniel stopped rifling through his suitcase and stood up with his eyes closed. "Do you think that's why Wade is uptight? Maybe he found out and is mad I didn't tell him?"

Zoey stopped bouncing. "That may be it. Make sure you chat with him and tell him it was a cruel joke."

I will later. Now, I need as many minutes as I can with you. We'll probably start grabbing lunch and dinners as a family again, so I'll see him plenty."

Zoey looked at Daniel with admiration in her eyes. "How does it feel to have a brother again?"

Daniel resumed rifling through his suitcase. "I have to tell you, it feels like a weight has lifted off my chest. Like I feel more peaceful."

"Maybe it's what your parents wanted to happen with this trip. Maybe they were upset at how their boys didn't get along and wanted to find a way to get the two of you back in each other's good graces."

Daniel didn't think of that. "That very well may be true. I mean, we weren't fighting; but I was so dismissive of any sign of improvement from him. Like 'oh good, you're finally catching up to the rest of us.' I'm really ashamed of how we were prior to that. I don't want it to happen anymore." Daniel found what he was looking for. Before he got too drunk with the others, he went to the Austria hostel's computer room and printed out information on different schools in New York with exemplary mental-health counselor programs. "I think getting this will show him how excited I am for him to find a career. I really think he'll be great at it." Zoey was so happy she could cry.

Hours later, the group was to gather at the ferry to be brought to Venice. When Daniel and Zoey came together, Wade moved from the back of the pack to the front to be nowhere near Daniel. Daniel noticed this and made a remark to Zoey. "Uh-oh, he really must be pissed." The avoidance continued on the ferry. Wade would find spots far away from Daniel, and Daniel would not pursue him. *There'll be plenty of time to talk the situation over later*, Daniel thought to himself. *Better not ruin the trip for more people.*

They arrived at the port for the ferries and the group was collectively in awe at the sight of Venice, Italy. As they departed the ferry, Sean took the collective to St. Mark's Square. They stood in the square and were dumbfounded at how every single one of them, like most people in the world, dream of going there at some point in their life. Sean stood there, as he had dozens of times prior. "Alright, everyone. There are no add-ons here, so everyone, please meet back here at 8:00." The pack of people dispersed and went their separate ways. However, the core group of Daniel, Wade, Zoey, Oliver, and Bill stuck together. Once the rest of the clan started dispersing, Zoey pulled everyone to walk east toward the Bridge of Sighs. It was already 3:00, so they didn't want to waste any time.

During the walk, Bill and Oliver were joking about how long Bill could go swimming in the canal before the authorities were called. "Ciao, policia, there is a naked kiwi in the canal outside my flat," Daniel joked in an Italian accent. "No it is not a peeled kiwi, I mean there is a man from New Zealand in his vestito de compleano." Daniel paused to act like the imaginary police couldn't understand him. "No, it is not his birthday! Just send a boat with a fisherman and get him out."

Bill fell on the ground in front of the Bridge of Sighs, pretending to be a fish out of water. He flopped over to an elderly woman. "Oi sheila, can you pour some whiskey on me gills? By the smell of ya, you seem to have some foul fish on ya, ay?" Everybody was holding onto a wall to control themselves from falling down with laughter, including Wade. Everybody except the old woman who hit Bill in the head with her purse. "Ow, you bloody cunt, that hurt! What do you keep in there?" Bill said in pain.

"Prendila in culo da un ciuccio imbizzarrito!" the old woman declared as she scurried away.

"If that purse has your address book in it, throw it away, your grandson's not gonna call!" Bill shouted after her.

They walked onto the bridge and everyone gave a collective "wow." Daniel grabbed hold of Wade's arm to pull him in to take a selfie. Wade smiled for the picture but went back to his frown immediately after. Daniel rolled his eyes and looked at Wade and said, "We'll talk later. Lighten up, Wade. Whatever gripe you have with me or anyone else shouldn't ruin their good time." Although he was filled with hurt and rage, he acknowledged his older brother was right. He needed to put on a smile and keep his mouth shut.

With the Bridge of Sighs being all they needed to see, the group took a collective slow walk around Venice. They marveled at the canal system, more architecture, and spoke on what they all wanted to do in Paris. Wade said very little the whole day. He chimed in when appropriate but was not his usual self. After a canal ride, they wandered the great city for hours until they found their way to the Arsenale di Venezia. It was not crowded, and it was approximately 7:00 p.m. They decided to grab a last bite to eat. They found a pizzeria open near the Arsenale and gathered in line to grab a slice. Wade tapped Oliver on the arm and mentioned how he wasn't very hungry. He then broke away from the group and found a bench near the water to stare out at. Daniel noticed this and gave Zoey his credit card to get slices for the group and whatever else they wanted. He made his way over to Wade and sat next to him.

"Hey, you want to do the ashes now that you're in a better mood?" he asked Wade.

"I'm not in a better mood, Danny. I'm still angry, but I did as you asked and put on my happy face."

"What are you mad over?" Daniel inquired. "Is it because you're homesick and miss Mel and Danny? Cuz I get that Wade, but—"

"It's not because I'm homesick. I'm just sick of you," Wade said without a tone of anger. He was stating it, as a matter of fact.

"What? Are you tired of hanging with us? Cuz that's fine. You can hang with them and I'll be—"

"Daniel, I know about Maria."

Daniel rolled his eyes back but smirked. "I knew that's what this was about. What? Are you mad nobody told you?"

Wade was dumbfounded. "What do you mean nobody told me?"

Daniel fixed his feet and put his palms together. "Wade, Zoey told me to do it because Maria kept making 'fuck me' eyes at her. And we didn't spend the night together, I just made out with her because Zoey bet me I couldn't do it while I was drunk since I couldn't bear to be drunk with her back in Amsterdam."

Wade was aghast. But he was still mad. "But what about you mentioning to her how I want to go back to school? And making fun of me saying I'd be terrible at it."

Now Daniel was getting mad. "Wade, I didn't say that."

"Then why did she come to me in the bathroom saying you did?"

"What do you mean she came to you and told you that?"

"She told me in the bathroom you were saying I'd be terrible at it and I'm just a loser," Wade shouted while getting to his feet and looking down at Daniel.

Daniel did not get up and join him. He wanted to deescalate the situation and not draw any more attention than Wade already had. Daniel spoke softly. "Wade, I didn't say that. Maria's crazy and probably wanted to get under your skin."

"Oh, bullshit, Danny. You always thought I was a loser and now you're just backpedaling because you finally started acting like someone other than yourself."

"Wade," Daniel said quietly, dropping his voice. "Calm down, you're making a scene and we can talk about this back at camp. Maria may have told you that, but it isn't true. I don't think you're a loser or would be terrible at being a counselor."

Wade was growing more excited and couldn't help but release all the frustrations he'd had with Daniel over the years. "Well, I know that's a lie. All the years you've been my brother, you always put me down or insulted me. You've always been a nasty asshole, and I'm not going to take it anymore. You're lying now, and I'm not going to keep making up excuses for you."

Daniel fixed the watch on his wrist and stood up slowly. "You've been making excuses for ME?" Daniel started speaking normally but raised his voice at the end to throw Wade off guard. It worked. "I've been making excuses for you for years! Every couple months changing what you want to do." Wade's eyes brimmed with tears. "Oh, I want to be a musician. Oh, I want to be a business owner. Oh, I want to be in real estate," Daniel said in a voice that sounded like Wade's. With each sentence, he walked closer and closer to Wade. "I've been telling people you'll find your path in time and making up excuses as to why we're so different." Daniel was now within inches of Wade. "And that's why I had to cut you out once you quit the police department and affected my reputation. I needed you out of my life and for you to quit holding me back!" Daniel said, screaming an inch away from Wade's face. Wade finally lost control and punched Daniel in the face. Daniel, being used to a punch in the face while being at work, quickly recovered, grabbed Wade, and tossed him into the canal. "You want to get physical, fine. Enjoy swimming back to the campsite. And enjoy not being near me anymore. When we get back home, we're done. You're out of my life, for good."

Wade quickly recovered after being thrown in the water. He bobbed in the water, crying hysterically. "Fine, and fuck you, too," he shouted.

Daniel went over to Wade's bag and took out the urn and the two shot glasses. "Don't worry, I'll finish the job for you the rest of the trip. Just like how I always had to clean up the messes that you started. Arrivederci, Wade," Daniel said, collecting the belongings and walking away. A crowd had slowly formed to watch Daniel and Wade have it out with each other, including their friends. Zoey was crying hysterically and went after Daniel.

Bill and Oliver went over to Wade to get him out. "Mate, I'm going to throw you a lifebuoy. Stay there!" Oliver said, trying to calm down a now-hysterical Wade. Oliver threw it out to him. Wade got to it, and Bill pulled him back to the shore and helped him back up.

"Wade, we'll help fix this. Don't think it's over, because it isn't," Bill said, reassuring him.

"I don't care if it gets fixed. I have a wife and a kid. I can't be worried about someone who doesn't care about me," Wade said, soaking wet in front of a crowd of people.

13

The Hurt Exposed

Daniel had stormed off back towards St. Mark's Square to get back to Sean and the rest of the tour. He was grabbed at the wrist by Zoey, who was crying almost as much as Wade. "You have to go back and apologize. He's your brother, and you both made so much progress in your relationship," Zoey said with tears streaming down her face. Daniel did not turn to look at her or even stop walking. He continued striding angrily through Venice with a crying woman being dragged behind him with one arm, while the other held the Jack Daniels urn and one shot glass.

"Fuck him. If he doesn't want to listen to me or think logically, who am I to tell him otherwise?" Daniel said with a matter-of-fact tone.

"But you love each other. If you two can sit down and talk it out, it can be fixed! We'll sit in between the two of you and—"

"Zoey, enough. I love my brother, but we couldn't be more different. He doesn't think I can change my attitude about him, which I did; and I showed him support. If he's so quick to think I'd never change, fine." Daniel exclaimed, continuing on with Zoey being towed of her own free will behind him. "You didn't know I was this strong did you?" he said with a smile, trying to defuse the situation.

Meanwhile, Wade was being dried with a towel from the local EMS crew and given a hot cappuccino. If his brother hadn't thrown him in the water, he'd be serenely looking out at the water of Venice, Italy, while drinking a hot cappuccino. "Wade," Bill started in on him delicately. "I'm not going to say you have to make things up with your brother or anything, because I'm not in your situation. But I am saying that maybe you should hear him out, get the facts straight, and then reevaluate your relationship with him." Wade and Oliver looked at Bill oddly.

"Of all the perverted and stupid things you've done this whole trip, now you give sage advice? What are you Sigmund-fuck-ing-Freud?" Oliver retorted back curtly.

"Hell, no. That dude has a couple of sticky skeletons I don't even want to go near."

"Guys, it's too late. I don't want to see him again after this trip. He lied about Maria—"

"No he didn't," Oliver interrupted. "Zoey told me the whole thing. Maria's just an asshole, and your brother and my sister were trying to be funny with one another. A dumb joke that was made up while they were drunk. And you can forget about him calling you a loser because I don't know many other brothers who would help the way he helped you from time to time."

"Really? 'You've been holding me back for too long and I needed you out of my life' sounds like words of encouragement to you?"

Oliver sat there puzzled. "Well, you got me there, mate. But c'mon, let's get back to the ferry and we'll figure something out in the morning. You can huff and puff all you want on the way back and to me in the tent, but we have to go back to the site and sleep." Wade rolled his eyes but conceded to Oliver's point. He refused further medical treatment from the EMT's and they took off toward the dock. Although, the ferry didn't exactly wait for them.

Zoey and Daniel boarded the ferry as the last people on. "Guys, the others know we will have to take the bus back. From there, it's a mile walk back to the campsite. We can't exactly tell the ferry to wait for them," Sean said with a look of concern.

"Oh, that's fine, Sean. But let the others get the bus. I think Wade is going to have to swim back," Daniel said with a smile on his face. Sean looked at Zoey, wondering if he should ask. Zoey rolled her eyes and pushed Daniel onto the boat. They climbed to the top deck and looked out at the water. The stars in the sky and the refreshing breeze washed any care away from them at the moment.

"Should I even bother to beg you more to talk to Wade?" Zoey asked quietly.

"No, I don't think what you'll say will make a difference, or anyone else, for that matter. But I'll tell you this. From time to time when I was a kid, I thought that my parents should just get a divorce. I'd stay with mom, Wade could stay with dad, and I'd only see Wade in small doses. Mom barely paid attention to either of us, and I was fine with it while it killed Wade inside. I'm better off on my own. Nobody to bother me, nobody to depend on every move I made. I've never really been loved by anyone except Wade and my dad. And as bad as this sounds, I didn't need either of them. I was a survivor, and I knew I'd make my way in the world. I didn't want anyone holding me back. And this just goes to show no matter what I do, solitude is my only way to live." Daniel picked the shot glass up, undid the top of the bottle, poured one portion in, and dumped it overboard. He put the second portion in and poured it out, as well. "Whatya know? Nobody got hurt when I did it alone. Destiny, isn't it?" Although Daniel displayed a small smile, Zoey was clutching her heart.

"How can you say that about them?" Zoey asked, still clutching her heart. She then socked Daniel on the arm.

"Ow! It's true, Zoey!" Daniel said in a voice that made him sound like Wade.

"Your parents loved you the best they could, and Wade worships the ground you walk on. And if you haven't noticed yet, asshole, I love you, too. Yes, this might be a holiday romance, but I do love you. And if I didn't have Oliver, my job, or my friends, I'd leave Australia and I'd find my way in America with you. You may be amazing on your own, but what if you let in the people who love you? What if the love and support you needed as a child came to you later in life and made you be better than you ever could have imagined? Did you ever think of that?" she said, hitting him in the arm again. "No, I bet you didn't. Because you're too thick-headed to see the help in front of you, and you don't reach out to ask for it." Zoey was in tears worse than before. "And I just can't bear to see you two be...be..." Zoey couldn't catch her breath, she was sobbing too hard.

Daniel quickly pulled her over to a seat, sat her down, and started hugging her; and she held him tight around the neck. They both said nothing until Zoey caught her breath and started to decompress from her anger and sadness. "I'm...fine...I'm catching...my breath," she said as she started loosening her hold around Daniel's neck.

"Do you really love me?" Daniel asked sincerely.

"Yes, I do," she replied as Daniel let go of her and looked deeply into her eyes, mere inches from her face.

"You're only the second person who told me that in my entire life," Daniel said coolly.

"That's not true," Zoey said, shaking her head while tears streamed down her cheeks.

"Before this, Wade was the only one. Our parents never said it to us."

Zoey clutched her heart again. "Have you ever said it to anyone?" Zoey asked, hoping she wasn't going into cardiac arrest.

"Only to Wade when we were kids so we'd hear it from someone."

"Well, do you love me?"

"I lo– I, I think I love you. I'm not sure. I feel something really strong about you, really. But I'm not sure I even know what love is. It wasn't a word we said much around the house. Sure, there was affection. Plenty of that, but never anything that made me understand what love really is." Daniel looked down at the floor. Zoey clutched her arms back around him. She knew he loved her but didn't want to push him further into an emotional hole. He had been through enough in the last hour. She didn't need him unraveling and descending further into pain.

14

Switzerland Shock

Daniel and Zoey awoke in their tent early in the morning. After quick morning sex, they washed up at the campsite's showers. On the way back, they grabbed coffee and cereal and walked over to Wade and Oliver's tent to be sure they got back okay. "You peer your head in and see if they're still asleep," Daniel said to Zoey.

"I don't take orders from you, so you do it," Zoey sharply retorted.

"And I don't take orders from you!"

"You're the one who's supposed to make up with his brother. You do it."

"I'm not going to be the one who apologizes for something I didn't do. And you still like your brother. So I insist, as your superior officer, to check and be sure my brother didn't get eaten by sharks in the Venice waters and got back okay." Zoey gave Daniel a withering look that caused him to second guess what he had just said. "We peek in together?" Daniel asked in a voice that pleaded with Zoey not to kick his ass with the three days they had left with each other.

"Can you two shut up before you wake Wade up?" Oliver said, peering his head out. Daniel and Zoey jumped, but Oliver giggled. He came out of the tent and gave both of them a hug.

"So, how'd you guys get back?" Daniel asked.

"Well after the ferry left, we contemplated taking the bus; but Bill treated us to a water taxi. It was actually pretty awesome," Oliver replied.

"How is Wade after everything that happened?" Zoey asked.

"Probably about the same as the javelin tosser here. Doesn't want to speak to Daniel again; and after this trip, he doesn't want anything to do with him."

"Well, that settles it. Told you he'd be like that," Daniel said, throwing his hands in the air.

"Lighten up, mate. It's not over, and you know that. Listen, do you think Zoey and I get along all the time? Hell no. Zoey and I can be at each other's throats one minute; but after we talk shit out, we go out for a pint and push it aside. Every family has melodrama. No family doesn't have a form of hatred for one another at one time or another. I'm not saying to make up right now, but give each other some space. Maybe after today or even after the trip, you'll find a reason to talk to one another," Oliver said in a matter-of-fact tone.

Daniel rolled his eyes and bit his lip. "We'll see, Oliver. Just make sure he doesn't do anything stupid for the rest of the trip."

Zoey snapped her head at Daniel. "Since when is my brother a babysitter?"

"Zoey, it's fine. Bill and I already told him he's our guy and we got his back. But Dan, let me ask you something." Daniel put his hands on his hips showing how little patience he had left. "You guys didn't talk to each other for a while before this trip. I know you'll say it was pure bliss being on your own, but was it really? Did you really enjoy not having someone who loves you as a constant part of your life? Did being cold and hollow really make you feel good about yourself? Cuz if I'm being honest, I think you're full of shit. After having Zoey around, do you think you can go back to that?"

Daniel looked flustered. Nobody at work or in his personal life had ever called him out on his behavior. And now that he thought about it, he loved his time with Wade on the trip; and solitude wasn't looking too promising. "Just tell Wade we checked in on him," Daniel said, tapping Zoey on the back to turn and walk away.

An hour later Wade woke up. "Hey, did Bill wake up yet?" Wade asked, rubbing his eyes.

"I haven't checked. But you know who did check up on you?" Oliver asked, sounding like a guidance counselor. Wade shook his head. He didn't even think that Daniel would acknowledge he was still at the campsite. "Dan and Zoey."

Wade swung his legs over and got out of bed. "I'm guessing Zoey dragged him here kicking and screaming?"

"No, actually. Daniel asked how you got back last night and was making sure you're okay."

"That's funny, he didn't seem to care how I got out of the water, did he?" Wade said bluntly.

"Jesus, the two of you are so melodramatic. Fucking Americans thinking you're the only ones with a dysfunctional family. I'm going to tell you the same thing I told him. Zoey and I can be at each other's throats; but in the end, we're still family and I'd kill for her."

"Did you ever throw Zoey into water?"

"No, but I did try to put her in a kangaroo's pouch when she was a baby. Mom will still call her 'Joey' when she's being a bitch." Wade laughed so hard putting on his shirt that he put it on backward. "But listen, you don't have to make up in the next few days or even immediately after the trip is over. But end your bullshit between each other. Get it all out in the open and figure out a way to function within each other's boundaries."

"Are you a therapist back home?" Wade asked seriously.

"No, I'm in retail. Now fix your shirt, and let's get our stuff on the bus." Wade conceded and got ready. They had a quick bite for breakfast and put their bags on the bus. Daniel and Zoey sat at the back of the bus while Wade, Oliver, and Bill sat in the front.

Hours later, they approached the border into Switzerland. During the entire drive, they had imagined how welcoming the Swiss would be to them as they crossed the border. They had received no border checks since Amsterdam, and they anticipated the reputation the Swiss had for kindness to be what they encountered. "Think they'll offer us the country if we're nice enough?" Wade asked Bill.

"I bet we could probably buy Geneva at a steal with a bit of charm by a dashing Kiwi like myself."

However, at the border, the Swiss guards stopped the bus and ran a mirror under the carriage to check for drugs. The driver was pulled out and questioned if anyone was bringing illicit substances into the country, and he mentioned that Bill was a bit of a partier. With that being said, Bill was pulled off the bus and brought to a small building to have a strip search. Anyone in their right mind would feel violated and scared, but Bill trotted across the parkway. He was more eager than Eoin Burch meeting Kevin Smith in a cupcake store.

Bill, however, was not happy when he returned. He got back on the bus almost shaking. "Bill, are you okay? Were they rough with you?" Oliver asked.

"Blimey gits. Told me it would be an invasive strip search. Barely cupped the side of my leg. Didn't even go near my arse." The entire bus erupted into laughter. "Shame, really. The agent was a handsome bloke. I think he might have stolen my last roach from Amsterdam. I don't think he knew what it was, though."

"Would you split a roach with him?" Oliver replied.

"He could eat my roach and I'd dip him in chocolate," he retorted as the bus took off.

Sean stood up and turned on his microphone. "Bill I'd like to thank you for reminding me to tell you guys about Switzerland. Yes, the Swiss are beyond kind and humble. Yes, they will show you endearing hospitality and the chocolate is to die for, but they are some of the most war-fearing people on Earth." The bus started to laugh.

"What a crock of shit, Sean," Daniel said from the back.

"Dan, shut up," Sean replied. Daniel gave him a menacing look while Wade put one leg over the other and put his arms behind his head.

"Continue, Sean," he said with a wide smile.

"Since Switzerland is a landlocked country and because of their suspicious dealings with the Germans during World War II, they fear retribution. The amount of gold and cash they have amassed from the Nazi's and the goods and finances of Jews who hid their assets from countries occupied by German forces, not to mention all the receipts of services magically vanished by the Nazi's and the majority of people who lost their receipts, is staggering. And they refuse to give back anything. Therefore, they mandate all citizens serve four years in the military after high school; and they have every bridge, tunnel, and road entering or exiting the country wired to explode.

The passengers were dumbfounded and showed their disbelief with their jaws almost scraping the floor of the bus. "Now you're fucking with us," Wade replied.

"Oh, yeah?" Sean said accusingly. "Driver, stop at the middle of the tunnel." The driver stopped the bus, and Sean pointed to the right side of the tunnel. There, clear as day, was a wired explosive. The group was stunned. "So can you all shut up and listen to me about a country I've been to ten times a year and none of you have ever visited?" The bus collectively nodded their heads.

They continued along the parkway and were in awe of the landscape that was Switzerland. They had never seen water so blue and clean. The Alps stood taller than anything the group could possibly imagine. The bus arrived at another hostel owned by the tour company near Mount Jungfrau in the village of Grindelwald. Before they departed the bus to walk around the village, Sean made an announcement. "Alright, tonight we have another party scheduled. Unless everyone votes to relax, we'll continue as planned. Who wants to party tonight?" Maria was the only one who raised her hand. "Who wants to relax and explore the village at their leisure?" The rest of the bus raised their hands. "Phenomenal, get your bags off, pick your roommate, and tomorrow we'll be ascending Mt. Jungfrau via the train in the village." Maria didn't depart the bus. Instead, she sulked on the bus until everyone got off, but nobody cared; fuck Maria.

Daniel was checking his bag to be sure the urn was intact and safe when Wade approached him. "Give me the urn. You did it in Venice, I want to do it here," he said sternly.

"You're going to have to ask me nicely," Daniel replied, not looking up from his bag.

"I'm serious, give me it now."

"Now you want to take charge? Good job, Wade. There's a first for everything."

"That's right. And you better give it to me before I lose what patience I've gained for you in a night." Oliver, Zoey, and Bill closed in quickly to break up the argument.

"I'll tell you what, Wade. I'll give it to you if you promise not to get it wet. What happened in Venice can happen again if you're not careful," Daniel said, getting to his feet and shoving Wade. Wade charged back at him but he was caught by Sean.

"Alright, both of you. Calm down before I kick you off the tour. You know who you want to room with. So Daniel, give Wade the bottle and register at the desk."

Daniel exhaled sarcastically. "Bill, ask mom and dad what they want since they're still knocking around in your head."

"Bro, stop. Just give it to Wade and walk away," Bill replied shortly. Daniel looked back at Zoey and she gave him a stern look.

"Fine. But don't fuck it up," Daniel said, pushing the bottle to Wade's chest.

"Don't worry, I can take care of things other than myself," Wade replied sarcastically as Daniel and Zoey walked away.

Chenguang and Zhang Wei, who had been on their own and avoiding the dysfunction of the Fontaine brothers, approached

Wade. "Wade, we want to thank you and Daniel for all you've done on the trip." Wade was very confused. "We see now what happens when a family doesn't cooperate, and we don't like it. So going forward, we made a promise to each other that our kids will never be like the two of you," they took turns saying. This would have made Daniel irate, but Wade just frowned. He put the bottle in his bag and climbed on a nearby rock.

"Ladies and Gentlemen of the ITourEurope trip," he said to the group. "I'd like to apologize on behalf of myself and my brother if we have added any stress or annoyance to your excursion in Europe. This was not on any of your or our itineraries. I swear we'll try to figure out how to cooperate for the rest of the trip. I'm sorry, and I'm sure he is, or would be, if he realized how much trouble we're causing." The group applauded Wade while Sean told him to go inside and check in before he kicked them off the tour before dinner.

That evening was easygoing. Most members of the group kept to their rooms until Bill opened up his, Oliver's, and Wade's room for people to come in and drink. They had a balcony overlooking Jungfrau, and it was almost illegal for any site to be that beautiful. Everyone either stopped at the bar or brought their own liquor to the room. Everyone was laughing heartily, drinking, and overall having a good time.

Daniel and Zoey decided that before they went over to the room, they'd take a walk through the village and stop by the waterfall that was a half-mile walk from the hostel. "Well, at least Wade spoke to me before I made it worse," Daniel said.

"Yes, yes, he did. And yes, yes, you did," Zoey replied.

"Why did I have to goad him? I could have just given it to him and we'd probably have made up tonight."

"It's not too late, you know. We're going to their room after we walk."

"Eh, I think I'll just say hi to the guys, then go to bed. I'm a little embarrassed at myself."

"If that's what you think is right, then do it. I'm not going to tell you what to do anymore. You don't listen anyway," Zoey said, egging on Daniel's anger at himself.

"Zoey, I'm already mad at myself. I don't need you mad, too."

"I'm not mad at you. I'm just making sure you realize what you're doing. You're not listening to Wade, you're just being snarky back at him. You've been doing that a lot on this trip."

"Name one other time," Daniel asked, putting his hand under the waterfall.

She rattled off a list. "You told me you gave the TSA a hard time back home. The Amsterdam border when you were rude to the security guard about what was in your bag. When Wade was being angry in Venice and instead of listening to him and talking to him calmly, you told him he was holding you back and you made it worse."

"Well, at least you listen," Daniel said, trying to make a joke. Zoey shot him another look and he straightened up. "Okay, I'll apologize for before and tell him we have to cooperate with each other when we get back."

"Good boy," she said, tapping his nose and giving him a kiss.

The party in the room was getting rambunctious. Bill was playing spin the bottle with himself, Oliver was telling a group of girls he could get them a discount on the online shopping for his store, and Wade was having a drink while pondering what he'd tell Mel about Venice and how the progress he and Daniel had made had been thrown out the window. He looked over the balcony and saw Daniel and Zoey walking back from the waterfall holding each other's hands and talking. Wade kicked his feet up on the banister and sat back to contemplate what it would take for him to get over how angry he was at Daniel. He debated with himself if the conversation with Maria really mattered and if Daniel had spoken out of anger because Wade had upset him so much by not even considering that Maria could be lying. He also mulled over if he could get over being thrown in the water in Venice. As he was pondering these issues, there was a commotion at the door.

"Nope, no home-wrecking sheila's in this room. Get out before we alert the front desk," Bill yelled drunkenly.

"You don't own the room," the female voice retorted. Wade heard the annoying voice and obnoxious tone of Maria.

"And you aren't invited to this two-day rental, so you can fuck off and all," Bill yelled back at her while slamming the door in her face.

"Bill, was that really necessary?" Oliver asked.

"Probably not, but she's a drama-starting bitch and we don't need her," Bill said as he walked out to the balcony to join Wade. "Oi, Wade. You hear the—"

"The verbal ass-kicking you just gave Maria? Yup, and well-done, Bill," Wade said while he held his glass up to give Bill cheers.

"Mate, you and your brother may be fighting like two blokes over the last whore at a brothel, but I'd shag you both. You're alright fellas," Bill said, not even looking at Wade. Bill was just speaking from what he called his heart while staring out at the mountains.

"I think that's the nicest thing a man has ever said to me," Wade said with a nervous giggle.

"No worries, mate. Don't worry, I won't look at you while you sleep like I did in Amsterdam," Bill said, walking back into the party. Wade could only sit in his chair and shiver at the thought of Bill staring at him while he slept.

A few minutes later, Wade heard the sound of Zoey coming in and giving everyone a hug and a peck on the cheek. Daniel walked in right behind her and went straight out to Wade on the balcony. Daniel stood looking out at the Alps and was quiet for the first few moments. "You know," Daniel started. "When you were born, I wasn't one of those kids that was jealous that a new kid was born and brought into the house. But I wasn't obsessed with the idea of showing you how life goes on and teaching you my ways." Wade only looked up at him. He had no hatred or animosity. He just looked at him objectively and was hearing him out. "I was just okay with it and did my own routine, as usual. Once we got older and things started to come to light that our parents weren't experts on raising kids, I started thinking I should take more interest in you. I liked your music, got you jobs, paid for your mortgage for a few months, but I couldn't handle the idea that you would back out on me and reject something I gave you. I guess what I'm trying to say is, I understand that I have some anger and I could have been a better brother to someone who hung on my every word. You were right, Wade. At times I thought you were a loser. But you're nowhere near the loser I am for not being as good as I could have been." Wade sat in his chair taking it all in. Daniel didn't look at him the whole time. He just looked out at the Alps and had a slight grin on his face. "So I hope this makes up for it in some small way." Daniel took several folded pages out of his pocket. He unfolded them and rolled them on the railing of the balcony to smooth them out. He turned around and handed them to Wade.

The pages were the information on a New York college's licensed mental health counselor program. He handed them to Wade who took them with his non-beer-holding hand.

Daniel started to walk back in when Wade got to his feet. "Danny, I uh," Wade said, startled by the pages Daniel handed him. Daniel turned around slowly. "I'm over the Maria nonsense, and I understand you don't think I'm the biggest loser in the world. But I'm still mad at how angry you get, how you speak to me, and you throwing me in the water. I told Sean we'll get along for the trip, but I think we should try to find a way to fix things before we get home. I think mom and dad would like that, and I think it's something we need." Daniel stood stoically as he noticed Wade's hands shaking. He was clearly nervous to voice his discontent in a way that wasn't yelling.

"I agree, Wade. We'll figure it out."

"Not tomorrow, though. I have plans with the guys to go up to Jungfrau tomorrow early in the morning and I think it'll take all day."

Daniel shrugged his shoulders. "No biggie. Zoey and I are sleeping in tomorrow anyway and doing the mountain around noon. Maybe in Paris, it can be just the two of us."

"I'd like that," Wade said coolly, as they joined the party.

"Well, wait a tick there, Wade. You told me we'd be kissing at the top of the Eiffel Tower in Paris," Bill said sarcastically. Everyone in the room laughed.

The boys didn't even say goodbye to each other. They just raised their hands in a gesture of "see you later," and Daniel and Zoey went to their room to sleep as the party continued. Wade sat back down, chugged his beer, and raised his fist in the air like he had accomplished something he had been meaning to do all his life.

15

Joints on Jungfrau

The next morning, Bill farted himself awake. He awoke in a fright, thinking someone had joined him in bed without him knowing. He looked around but nobody was in the room besides Oliver and Wade sleeping in their respective bunks. He laid back down and looked at his phone. It was seven in the morning and Bill remembered Wade saying the train to the top of Jungfrau was at eight. He hopped out of bed and shook both Oliver and Wade awake.

"Morning lads, Jungfrau is waiting for us." The Jungfrau, nestled among sister peaks called the Eiger and Mönch, dominated the Berner Oberland region of Switzerland. The hostel was located just a half-mile from the train; and the boys wanted to eat, shower, and shit before they took off.

"Bill, if you wake me up with your dick hanging out again, I'm going Lorena Bobbitt on you," Wade said with a tone of exhaustion. "My stomach is in knots, what did I drink last night?" he asked.

"Two beers, that's more than you had the whole trip," Oliver said, rubbing his eyes to start the day.

"Never thought I'd see the day when a man could go all around Europe without having a drop of a pint," Bill said, putting on underwear.

"Yeah, well, alcohol doesn't sit well with me," Wade said, stretching before he got out of his bunk.

The boys all did their daily beauty rituals, had a hearty breakfast, then set off on the walk to the train station. "You think there's any security on the top of the mountain, gents?" Bill asked.

"I can't imagine anyone trying to bomb a mountain except for Lex Luthor, so no. Why?" Wade asked, hoping Bill wasn't going to do something stupid.

"Well, I brought along the last roach from Amsterdam. Figured it'd be a hell of a spot to blaze up," Bill said, taking out the roach. However, this was no roach. This was a pre-rolled joint that was four inches long.

"Dude, you said it was a roach!" Wade said, flabbergasted by Bill's joint.

"Compared to what I have back home, it is!" Bill said matter of factly.

"Well, I'm game. What say you, cunt?" Oliver said to Wade.

"Guys, I haven't smoked a joint since Danny caught me in my room when I was a senior in high school."

"What did he do when he caught you?" Bill asked.

"He was a trainee in the police department, so he acted like he was arresting me and brought me to a holding cell for four hours. He never made a report or anything, but it scared me enough to swear off it."

Bill and Oliver were laughing at him as Bill put the joint in his mouth and took his lighter out. "Dude! You can't do it here, ya cunt," Wade said.

"Whoa, whoa, whoa," Oliver and Bill started saying.

"What? You guys call me it all the time!"

"Yeah," Oliver started. "But it's different when you do it. It just doesn't feel right coming from an American. Stick to your own language like douche bag, ninny, and poppy-cock." Wade shook his head and took the joint from Bill. Before we leave, I need to teach you guys some American curse words.

Wade put the newly-lit joint to his lips and inhaled. Immediately his eyes widened. He hadn't had marijuana this strong. It was beyond anything he was used to. "Whoa, is this a strong strain?"

"I don't know, mate. The bloke in Amsterdam didn't exactly give me brand recognition," Bill snarked. Wade was now coughing uncontrollably and Oliver was patting him on the back while taking a deep drag.

"Don't worry, junior. Uncle Oli and Willy will take care of you," he said as he passed the joint to Bill. The three finished it before the train arrived. They were the only ones on the platform so they were as free to be as stupid as possible. The train ride up was steep but it was also gorgeous as they climbed the mountain, watching the town disappear the higher they went up. The boys were amazed at how quickly the temperature dropped and how snow appeared out of nowhere.

"Wait, there's snow up here?" Oliver asked Wade.

"Bro, you're climbing a mountain. Yes, there's snow up here," Wade said, sounding like Daniel.

"I've never seen snow before, have you?" Oliver turned to ask Bill.

"Nope, first-timer here," Bill said, staring out at the landscape.

"Oh, guys, this is going to be cold," Wade said, zipping up his jacket.

"I'm sure we'll be fine," Bill said, rubbing his arms for friction and heat.

The boys reached their destination—the ice cavern that was situated at the top of Jungfrau along with the visitor center. Wade stepped out with his hands in his jacket. He was chilly but comfortable enough for the excursion. Oliver and Bill, however, were shivering uncontrollably. A tour guide was situated at the entrance willing to take anyone into the ice cavern.

"Hello, my name is Leon; and I'm one of the employees in the ice cavern. Would you like a tour around and see the top of the summit?" he asked with a heavy Swiss accent.

"That would be lovely," Wade said.

"Mate, how far until we reach the gift shop?" Oliver asked with his teeth chattering.

"I'm sorry, sir. But the gift shop is an hour's walk away, even with the tour. If you'd like a hand warmer we have a box for—" Oliver and Bill didn't need telling twice. They dived into the box and grabbed two hand warmers each. "That'll be five franks, each," Leon said.

Wade paid for them, and that would have been the end of it if Bill had been satisfied with putting them in his pockets like Oliver. Leon went under his desk and pulled out some duct tape for Bill to tape the hand warmers to his chest and back. "What the hell are you doing that for?" Oliver asked him.

"I know I'll drop them!" Bill said, thinking he was being logi-
cal. He'd regret it later. They started the tour of the ice
cavern. None of the ice was man-made. They were at the
highest point in Europe, so they were walking on a floor of
sheer ice. It didn't take long for them to realize they'd need to
hold onto the handrails the entire time. Even so, Wade and
Oliver slipped and fell a few times, as everyone did. Bill,
however, took to sliding on the ice with his hands behind his
back looking like Bug Bunny. "Yah dah-dee, yah da-dah," he
sang out loud, going up and down a pathway.

They reached the summit and stepped outside to enjoy the
vista. Although it was cloudy and the snow was blocking their
view of the town below, they were still in awe at the rock
formations and how high in the sky they were. Oliver and Bill
were looking over the edge, taking it all in, when Wade pelted
both of them with snowballs. "Learn to make them quick,
mother fuckers, or you'll be getting pelted all day," Wade said,
giggling. Although Bill and Oliver didn't need to be told twice
about throwing snowballs, Wade was rolling in the snow with
laughter at their pathetic attempts to pack snow.

"How the fuck does it stay!" Oliver said, trying to pack sludge
together.

Bill was so high that he was trying to pack snow on the railing.
"I'm coming, you cunt," he yelled after them. Wade was just
packing and throwing snowballs left and right.

After the snowball fight and staring out from the summit, the
boys continued their tour and visited the gift shop to get
proper jackets. "You guys know you're only going to wear
those for about an hour, right?" Wade asked.

"Don't care, Wade. I'm cold and I could use a souvenir."
Oliver picked out a sleek black winter coat. Bill picked out a
woman's poncho, thinking that was sufficient. "You want to

tell him or should I?" Oliver asked Wade as they watched Bill put on his new pink poncho.

"Nope, let's let him walk into town with it," Wade replied.

The boys boarded the train back down to the village. They had been gone for five hours. As they were descending, they noticed that Zoey and Daniel were on the opposite side of the tracks, ascending. The train moved very slowly so they were able to shout hello across the tracks. Daniel even shouted to Wade, "How cold is it?"

"You're fine, although your jacket would be good for Zoey!" Zoey gave Daniel a playful punch in the arm for not giving her a heavy jacket since she was in a short-sleeve shirt and shorts. This levity in their complicated situation filled both brothers with a sense of warmth. Things weren't better, but they were getting there. The trio went back to the hostel and immediately got back in bed to heat up. The hand warmers were good for ten hours so Oliver and Bill held onto them while they napped.

At about five o clock, Daniel came into the room and shook Wade awake. "What? I'm napping," he said through gritted teeth.

"We have to do the ashes. Come on, let's go," Daniel said patiently.

Wade sat up to see Oliver and Bill still napping. "Alright, where do we go?"

"Let's go to the waterfall. Zoey and I went there yesterday." Wade nodded in agreement, put on his jacket over his pajamas, and they went for the walk toward the waterfall. "How'd you guys like the mountain?" Wade asked.

"It was stunning. Zoey kept punching me every time she slipped on the ice since she didn't have a jacket."

Wade looked at him puzzled. "She understood that a jacket wouldn't help her from slipping, right?"

"I think it was because her bare back kept hitting the ice when she slipped," Daniel said, giggling. Wade laughed and the two of them stayed silent until they reached the waterfall.

"Alright, so before we do the shots, let's establish where we are," Daniel said, unscrewing the bottle.

"Alright, well, to be honest, I was thinking about it on the mountain and I think I'm over everything," Wade said honestly. "But, I'd like to talk about how we go forward," he continued.

"I think I am, too," Daniel replied. "And I think Paris is still the place for that. Let's just enjoy being here in Switzerland while we can." Wade agreed. "Well, that wasn't so hard. Was it?" Daniel asked, pouring the ashes into two shot glasses.

"Can I say something before we pour?" Wade asked.

"Sure," Daniel said with a smile.

Wade took a deep breath. "Mom, dad, we're sorry about the one slight hitch in the trip. Shit happens, but your boys are okay. Although things are better than ever, there's still work to be done. So I think tomorrow may either be a laugh-filled day or fists being thrown. Regardless, we'll probably cry, too."

"I concur," Daniel said as they dispensed the second to last ashes they would ever pour. They stood looking at the waterfall and stayed silent.

"Can I kick you into the waterfall?" Wade asked jokingly.

"Not in your life, sport," Daniel replied.

"Oh, come on, it's only fair."

"It's a fair way to die, too, Wade."

"Don't worry, I'll get you back for Venice."

"I'm sure you will." They stood silently for a few more minutes.

"Want to go rip the taped hand warmers off Bill's chest and back?"

"Now that, I'll do," Daniel chuckled while replying.

They were on their way back when they heard a roar of pain. "FUCKING CUNT," the voice screamed. It came from the hostel.

"Oh, man, Oliver beat us to it," Wade said.

"Don't worry, we can figure out someone else to cause pain to."

16

The French Don't Hate Us That Much, Right?

D aniel was up early. He looked out the hostel window to admire, for the last time this trip, the precious Alpine pastures and dramatic mountain peaks. He was followed shortly by Wade, with whom he exchanged a brief gaze expressing their recent reconciliation. As he nearly opened his mouth to express some touching words, Bill farted himself awake once more.

"Christ, all this cabbage and meat! Someone sink a well in me so we solve the energy crisis and retire."

Daniel looked at the gassy fellow from down under. "You know, I'll finally say it. You kiwis are disgusting."

"And you Americans are violent materialists who are too proud and too ashamed of themselves at the same time. I'll fart before I make war any time."

Wade chimed in, agreeing, "He may have a point." Shortly after, the rest of the troupe awoke and, groggy as hell, assembled their bags and made their way toward the bus. The last leg of their trip was upon them—Paris.

On the bus, Daniel was lucky to get a window seat. While Bill, Oliver, and Wade boarded, he had hoped that a passing glance at Wade would hint to his brother, "Sit next to me, fucker. I have something to say."

Instead, Oliver caught the look, "Sure, I'll sit here with ya." Wade and Bill sat behind them, and Zoey got the window seat in front of Daniel. The approximately five-hour drive was more boring than uncomfortable. The French autoroutes, after crossing the border from Switzerland, took them through mostly farmland, interspersed by the occasional village and TGV train darting along its track. In time, things became more urban and industrial—charming medieval townscapes became large apartment towers and traffic. They had entered Paris' *Île-de-France*.

Wade tapped Daniel on the shoulder. "Hey, so I was wondering. Paris is in a part of France called the *Île-de-France*. *Île* means island. We're not on the coast. This isn't an island. Where the hell are these cheese-eating surrender-monkeys thinking of these names?"

"Perhaps they thought if people believed there was a moat or something around Paris, they wouldn't be invaded and thus not surrender so frequently."

Zoey chimed in, "Actually, I read the French have the most successful military record in all history."

To which Daniel replied, "See, there it is, Wade. No wonder they hate Americans. We are so good at war, we beat them at their own game."

The bus shortly arrived at the massive *Gare du Nord*, a train station in the north of Paris at 12:15 p.m. The group attendant on the bus announced to the group, "Alright guys, welcome to Paris! Just a reminder to be back at the bus at 8:30

p.m. so we can get to Charles de Gaulle Airport. The flight to Australia departs at 11:15 p.m. and to the U.S. at midnight!"

Wade nudged Bill, "And you remember to get to the airport at 7:00 tonight so you can gas up all the planes, won't you, son?" Bill gave Wade a wryly devilish grin. Daniel, Wade, Zoey, Oliver, and Bill stepped off the bus and made their way toward the metro, sparing no time to mock the French taste for cheese, sex, and cigarettes.

"Combined with their infrequent bathing, it's starting to make sense why they excel in making perfumes," remarked Oliver.

As they gazed at the map of the city's many sights and destinations, light bickering broke out. "I will not leave here before visiting Sacre Coeur!" Zoey protested. Oliver spoke of his desire to see the Moulin Rouge.

Wade hinted at his love of the Arc de Triomphe, to which Daniel replied, "Ahh, the Napoleon complex revealed."

Bill sighed. "Mates, I will be real with you. I've heard stories of the *Bois de Boulogne*, this fuckin' huge park that people just cruise and fuck in. I fancy headin' there and taking in the City of Lights myself...buried in some twinky *monsieur* who I'm going to convince that I am a Hemsworth."

"But aren't the Hemsworths Aus–" Daniel began to say before Bill kissed him with a peck on the mouth.

The group laughed as Bill said, "I'm gonna miss ye, cunt. If you're ever in the need of the company of a kiwi...look me up in New Zealand, as I will never, ever visit America." Bill looked at Wade, gave him a wink, and said "It's nothing personal, love. I can't do brothers."

"I assure you, neglect is the most sincere form of flattery. I'll see you around, Bill."

Oliver and Zoey looked at each other, then at the group. "Perhaps this is a good time for us to go, too," Zoey said. She grabbed Wade and Daniel with each hand. "You both take care of each other, won't you?"

"Don't worry, Zoey, I think we'll manage," Wade said.

"And if we don't, you'll read all about it online, 'American kills brother in Paris' is a perfect scoop," Daniel said, as deadpan as could be. She smiled at the boys and looked at Oliver.

"Safe back to New York, guys. It was nice meeting you both."

"Same to you, man," Daniel said.

"It has been the pleasure of a lifetime to be in the company of Oliver and Company," Wade chimed in. The group moved in for a big hug before Bill farted again.

"Sorry gang. We left Switzerland, but my innards refuse to remain neutral."

Daniel looked Bill dead in the eyes, "Whatever you do, man, please do not bottom today." The group laughed and parted ways.

Wade put his hand on Daniel's back, "Where to now."

"You're right, that was stupid. We looked at that map for like half an hour and never decided where to go."

"Then let's just wander."

Daniel and Wade left the *Gare du Nord*, and the streets of Paris opened themselves up to the brothers. They made their way down the Boulevard de Magenta, popping into back alleyways and small roads. They passed an old church-like building, now the *Musée des Arts et Metiers*, and the almost bizarre *Centre Pompidou* at Les Halles.

"You know, Zola wrote a book about the market which used to be here—*The Belly of Paris*," Daniel said to Wade, distracted by the ambiance of the city alive with police siren echoes, church bells, and the din of the public.

"How'd you learn that?"

"Google, circa just now" Daniel replied, "Which reminds me, I'm starving." Wade and Daniel found a medium-quality café with a perfect view of the *Tour Saint-Jacques*. They enjoyed cider and Croque-madames and discussed their trip. As Daniel studied the map, he remarked "Wade, we're really close to the *Arc*!"

"Awesome—and we're running short on time, too. Let's get out of here."

The brothers departed the café and made their way out onto the streets to the royal *Rue de Rivoli*. They passed the Louvre Museum, the legendary *Jardins des Tuileries*, and, soon enough, arrived at the *Place de la Concorde*. As they sat on a bench to marvel at the fountain in the center, Wade decided to speak up.

"So that wasn't too long of a goodbye with Zoey, was it?"

Daniel didn't look in his direction; he continued to marvel at the fountain. "Yeah, we said our goodbyes last night. We cried a bit, exchanged information, and promised to keep in contact. But I'm not delusional, Wade. I know we're never going to get together, but it's nice knowing someone is out there who cares," he revealed with a tone that was somber, yet grateful. "I know you care, but we're brothers. This is someone who doesn't have to care, yet she does."

"I hear ya, Danny. I don't know what I'd do without Mel. She keeps me together and is the soul of our family." The two brothers stared at the fountain a little longer before they looked at their watches. "So what time is the flight?" Wade asked.

"Midnight. What time is it now?" Daniel replied.

"Five o'clock. How about we stop by the Eiffel Tower before we get the bus to the airport?"

"Sounds like a plan, Wade."

The brothers made their way to the Eiffel Tower in silence. They didn't want to talk about their future with each other. They thought it'd be best to save it for the last minute. They took the thirty-minute walk to the Eiffel Tower and they both said the same thing. "Way bigger than the one in Vegas."

They took a walk over to the ticket booth to see the price before they committed to climbing it. "Twenty-five euros? Fuck that, half of it is shopping and restaurants, anyway," Daniel said.

"Yeah, let's walk," Wade confirmed. The brothers took a stroll around the streets of Paris. They would've loved to stay, but Wade needed to get back to see his family and Daniel needed to get back to work.

"Alright, so let's have this talk," Wade said.

"You know what, I need a drink before," Daniel replied. He took a look around the street for a bar, but none were in immediate sight.

"Wait, you know what'd be good for this?" Wade said.

"What?"

"Let's use the Eiswein from Germany."

"Wade, that's brilliant!" Daniel ran into a convenience store and got two empty coffee cups and a bag of ice. Wade walked down the block and saw a nearby park with a fountain.

"Danny, down here, we can do the ashes, too," Wade yelled from down the block. This talk may be unpleasant, but it was necessary, so why not make it a little practical and pseudo-luxurious?

The boys opened the bottle, dropped in an ice cube each, and poured the wine. They were gawked at by people passing by with disapproving looks, but they didn't care. "Alright, I'll start," Wade said. Daniel sat up with his cup and took a sip as Wade began. "You're my brother, and I'll always love you, but I'm tired of your uptight attitude that creates a toxic environment for everyone. Learn to control it a little bit, and I'll be fine."

Daniel swished his cup around. "Wait, what? I didn't know this was a business transaction," Daniel snorted at Wade.

"Will you take this seriously, please?" Wade implored, raising his voice.

"Then let's not establish terms for going forward. Let's get the shit out. We're not lords negotiating the terms of land usage."

"Well, then, you start. I'm sure you'd love to be in charge, like usual," Wade said, putting one leg over the other and crossing his arms.

"Well, I'll start with this. Although I'm willing to admit I can be a bastard, I will not let you forget I kind of have a lot of shit going on," Daniel said, raising his hands in the air. Wade quickly shooed his hands away as a sign to get on with it.

"Look," Daniel stated. "I'm never going to change who I am; and frankly, you aren't either. People don't change, they repress different aspects of their personality and find coping mechanisms in order to deal with them. Look at that, I just gave you your first lesson in counseling."

"Well what do we do, Sigmund Freud?" Wade bellowed in frustration.

"I say we tell each other what we absolutely disdain about the other and find ways to not do them around the other while we accept each other for who we are. And if the one slips and displays such behavior in front of the other, they can be called out by one and work on it," Daniel said.

"So shame each other into being better people?"

"Yup, what do you say?"

Wade shook his head. "I don't know, Danny."

"Well, then, it seems we're at an impasse, aren't we?" Daniel said, finishing the rest of his cup and immediately refilling it.

"Look, is it too much to ask my brother to not be such an asshole to me constantly? I don't care where else you do it, just be respectful to me and my family and come over every once a while."

Daniel took a sip. "I don't suppose that's too much to ask of me," he said, looking back at his cup.

"Exactly, and while we're at it, I've already decided to go back to school; and now that I have your support, it's given me more drive and ambition to prove myself. So I guess you were probably going to rant and rave to me how I never take anything seriously and I have no drive or ambition?"

"It might have sounded like that, except sounding like a man and not a pu–"

"Exactly, if anything, let's just accept the past; and now that we know what the one wants from the other, let's just do it and stick to it. So when one slips up, they can shame the other if it comes to that," Wade said, now moving his hands frantically from talking.

"I think you're right for that program, Wade," Daniel said with a smile.

"Alright, I think that just about settles it. Let's get the bottle." Wade pulled out the container from his carry-on.

"I think we ought to just take turns pouring out the rest of the bottle. Those ashes were a major detriment to all of Europe. Between London, hitting someone in the face, Bill snorting them, hitting someone in the face in Munich, let's end it here," Daniel said with a chuckle. Wade was laughing along with him. He poured out half of what was remaining, and Daniel poured out the other half. Their mission was complete. Both missions, actually.

"Fuck, you know what I just remembered?" Daniel said.

"What?"

"We didn't get a single souvenir the entire time we've been here besides an Eiswein bottle that we're going to kill before we get to the airport."

"You know what, we'll rinse out the Jack bottle at the airport and keep both," Wade replied.

"That sounds good to me, Wade." The brothers started walking. "Oh, one last condition going forward," Wade said.

"Fuck, what."

"We have to go on another trip once in a while," Wade said with a smile.

"We just went on a week and a half vacation, no. I have work to do," Daniel said, rolling his eyes.

"Not saying now," Wade said, sounding exasperated. "But ya know, maybe near the end of the year. Like a weekend thing!"

"We'll see, Wade."

The brothers said barely anything on their way to the airport. They said barely anything waiting for the plane. Not much was said besides, "Going to the bathroom," or "I'm grabbing food, do you want anything?" In fact, even the flight back was met with silence. Silence and sleep the whole way home. What else was there to say? Once the plane landed and they were back in the United States, it took them past exiting the plane, grabbing their luggage, and going to the curb for one person to speak. "I don't think it'll be hard Danny," Wade said. "I mean, it's really all about keeping to our word and being accountable for our actions. It shouldn't be so bad, right?"

Daniel looked up at Wade. "Since when have we been held accountable in our personal lives, Wade? Our parents taught us our toxic behavior. It may take some time. I'm not saying I'm not going to do it, but don't get your hopes up all the way. Maybe just be cautiously optimistic. That's really the best we can do when the odds are stacked against us, right? It's not magic, it's work." Daniel's car service pulled up to the curb. He stepped to the door and opened it. He looked back at Wade who was getting visibly upset. "Look, I'm not saying I'm not going to keep my word, but don't expect every "T" to be crossed. I love you, and I'll see you later."

Wade grabbed the door. "Hey," Daniel was caught off guard by this. Wade just stared at his brother, and said "I love you, too," and gave him a hug.

17

Going Forward

The brothers went on vacation in July. We now find them in Maine at the beginning of September of the following year. Both brothers have, so far, kept their word. Daniel comes over every other week for dinner on Sunday nights and has not been his rude self to his family in a long time, although, his staff is considering a coup. Wade has also enrolled in school. Unfortunately, it made the family's financial situation a bit tight, but Daniel is happy to help when he can in non-financial ways. The last year has not all been rosy, though. They have gotten into a few minor verbal arguments but nothing taking a break from each other for a day and then talking it out couldn't fix. Although we find them a year later doing better, we also find them on a four-day excursion to Maine.

Wade is just waking up and getting dressed in his tent. Daniel is already outside making a quick breakfast over the fire. "You slept in," Daniel said, not taking his eyes off the eggs.

"I had a hard time falling asleep. Were you wrestling someone in your sleep? Or do I need to go to therapy from hearing you whacking it on an air mattress?"

"If you would put your headphones in, you wouldn't hear me," Daniel said, looking up at his peeping-tom brother.

"How the hell do you even have service?"

"The place has wifi, and Zoey worked the night shift so we were about to fall asleep at similar times."

"Will you leave that poor girl alone?"

"Hey man, she messaged me first. Don't be shaming her," Daniel said, pouring his eggs onto two plates. "Now hurry up and eat. We have some fish to catch." Wade hopped over while he buttoned his pants.

They ate quickly and drove over to the dock where they were to go fishing. They both set up their chairs, and Daniel sat down with their poles as Wade went to the car to retrieve the bait from the back seat. He closed the door and sauntered over to a pole that had a sign on it signifying the history of their location. The sign told the story of William DuPont and his suicide.

"Yo, Dan did you hear about the guy who–"

"Yes, Wade. I saw the sign. Now c'mon, man, we only have until tomorrow, so let's fish."

"Keep your badge on, I'm coming." The brothers sat in silence for about an hour.

"I think dad would've liked it here," Daniel said.

"I was thinking the same thing," Wade replied. They both looked at each other and said "Not mom, though."

An instant after they stopped talking, Daniel's line started pulling away. A fish had caught his line. "Oh shit!" Daniel stood up and started reeling in.

Wade saw an opportunity and thought it was too good to pass up. "Hey, you remember how cold the water was in Venice?" Wade asked.

"No, I never swam in it, Wade," Daniel said, not taking his eyes off the water.

"Oh, yeah, right," Wade said coolly. "Well how's the water in Maine?" he shouted as he pushed his brother off the dock. Daniel hit the water, completely caught off guard. After a dramatic splash, he immediately composed himself. He was livid.

Wade, however, was cackling with laughter. "Payback's a mother fucker, ain't it?" Wade said, red in the face from almost crying.

"Alright," Daniel said while hitting the water. "We're even."

Wade stopped laughing eventually as Daniel struggled to pull himself out of the water. He reached his hand out and his brother met it. "Just remember, dude," Wade said affectionately. "I may be your little brother, but I can still kick your ass."

About the Author

JD Dipalma is an author, musician, podcaster from Babylon, New York.

Spotify/Apple Music: Dipalma
Instagram: @Dipalmaproductionsofficial
Tiktok: Dipalmaproductionsofficial
Website: www.Dipalmamusic.com

www.ingramcontent.com/pod-product-compliance
Lightning Source LLC
Chambersburg PA
CBHW021209090426
42740CB00006B/167